INFANT EDUCATION;

OR,

PRACTICAL REMARKS

ON THE

IMPORTANCE OF EDUCATING

THE

INFANT POOR,

FROM THE AGE OF EIGHTEEN MONTHS
TO SEVEN YEARS;

CONTAINING

HINTS FOR DEVELOPING THE MORAL AND
INTELLECTUAL POWERS OF

Children of all Classes.

BY S. WILDERSPIN.

FOURTH EDITION,
CAREFULLY REVISED, WITH CONSIDERABLE ADDITIONS.

⁓⁓⁓⁓⁓

" Whoso shall receive one such little child in my name receiveth me."
Matt. xviii. 5.
" Take heed that ye despise not one of these little ones." Matt. xviii. 10.

LONDON:

PUBLISHED BY W. SIMPKIN AND R. MARSHALL,
Stationers' Hall Court, Ludgate Street.

SOLD ALSO BY OLIVER AND BOYD, EDINBURGH; COLLINS,
AND OGLE, GLASGOW; WILLIAM CURRIE, JUN. AND CO.;
AND WESTLEY AND TYRREL, DUBLIN.

1829.

INFANT SCHOOL DEPÔT.

—————

$\Big\{$ *Alpha House, Alstone, Cheltenham,*
18 .

Mr. S. Wilderspin begs to inform his Friends, that he has opened a Depôt in Cheltenham, from whence he purposes to supply all necessary articles for the use of Infant Schools.

Mr. Wilderspin has just published a new and complete set of Reading, Spelling, and Interrogatory Lessons, accompanied by sets of Prints on Scripture, Natural History, and other subjects, the whole of which are founded on the strong basis of his own experience, attained by a personal attendance on Infant Schools, in various parts of England, Scotland, and Ireland.

He intends to dedicate himself, and the profits on the sale of Lessons and Apparatus, to the promotion of Infant Schools, in any country he can gain access to. He purposes, with the assistance of his daughter, and suitable agents, *taught by him*, and of known experience, to visit the various counties of the united kingdom, to Lecture on the System, to give Private Lessons, to organize Infant Schools of any class, and impart such information as will be necessary for their proper management, and ultimate success. He has laboured nine years in this cause, without one School having failed, when properly begun ; had many thousand babes under his tuition ; and undertakes to reduce two hundred Infants to complete order in four weeks, so as to exhibit them to any audience in any town in the kingdom. Whoever doubts this, may send for him, and give him the trial.

Every information may be had of Mr. W. respecting Infant Schools. Address, (post paid) Alpha House, Alstone, Cheltenham.

A Case for a School of one hundred Infants, containing every requisite, properly mounted, fit for immediate use, from £8. to £10. for two hundred Infants, from £10. to £15. A Case for a nursery, from £5. to £10.

The Fourth Edition of Mr. W.'s Work (the Whole re-written, with Additions) is now published, price 4s. 6d. and may be had at the depôt, and of all Booksellers.

—————

Griffith and Co. Chronicle Office, Pittville Street.

J. S. Hodson, Printer, 15, Cross Street, Hatton Garden.

TO

JOSEPH WILSON, Esq.

OF CLAPHAM COMMON;

JOHN SMITH, Esq. M.P.;

AND THE

NOBLEMEN AND GENTLEMEN

OF THE COMMITTEE OF

THE LONDON INFANT SCHOOL SOCIETY;

𝕿𝖍𝖎𝖘 𝖁𝖔𝖑𝖚𝖒𝖊

IS RESPECTFULLY INSCRIBED

BY THEIR OBLIGED AND DEVOTED SERVANT,

THE AUTHOR.

THE FOLLOWING EXTRACTS

*From the different Reviews, are inserted as testimonials
in favour of the former Editions of this Work.*

" We have no space to enter upon the subject of
early juvenile delinquency, to the consideration of
which, **Mr. Wilderspin's** book naturally invites us,
and for the prevention of which, Infant schools seem
to present a more hopeful remedy, than most other
plans which have been suggested. Our author shall
relate, in his own way, one of his adventures, in
his benevolent rambles, which will furnish a good
commentary on all that has been stated both in and
out of parliament, on this great moral and national
question."

Christian Observer, May, 1823.

" We cordially approve of the plan, particularly as
due care seems to be taken for the exercise, amusement, and health of the little pupils; and we hope a
cheap edition of this book will be printed, for circulation through the country, whereby it may prove a
national benefit."

Evangelical Magazine, April, 1823.

" We found it impossible to lay the book down
until we had read the whole, and were, in consequence,
induced to take the earliest opportunity of visiting the
School, a visit which afforded the highest gratification."

Christian Guardian, April, 1823.

A 3

" We cannot conclude our remarks without return-ing thanks to Mr. W. for this interesting and useful, though plain and unadorned volume, and we sincerely recommend all our readers to procure it for their own use, and should they be heads of families, we may add, that there are, throughout, many valuable hints, founded on experience, which deserve the serious attention of every parent."

Teachers' Magazine, February, 1823.

" We have read this little book with uncommon pleasure.—Infant Schools, under religious and judi-cious management, would be an inestimable blessing, in every considerable town and village of the kingdom.

" All who feel it a duty to preserve their genera-tion, are, we think, bound in conscience to encourage and extend this new and most important scheme for the prevention of juvenile delinquency, and for the promotion of the best interests of Society."

Wesleyan Methodists' Magazine, for April, 1823.

" We clearly gather, from the information which Mr. W. gives us, that similar schools must be of essential service to the labouring classes in every part of the kingdom; and that, as is well observed by Mr. Lloyd, who writes the preface, they are particu-larly needed in manufacturing districts."

Inquirer, April, 1823, *p.* 345.

" We take this occasion, in announcing the second edition of this interesting volume, to join others of the critical corps, in thanking the worthy author for a most valuable performance; and from the perusal of which many parents and teachers may derive much practical instruction, in the right management of children from the early dawn of reason. Many pleasing anecdotes are interspersed through the vo-lume, that cannot fail of interesting the reader."

PREFACE.

THE three former editions of this work being out of print, I have availed myself of the assistance of a friend in re-arranging, and in part re-writing its contents; and I hope that it will be found in this fourth edition to have been not only considerably altered, but considerably improved likewise.

The first part of the Volume now presents a treatise on juvenile delinquency; in which its prevalence and lamentable extension are shewn by a variety of instances, adduced partly from the public journals, and partly from personal observation. Some of the information that will be found I obtained with great difficulty and hazard, by mixing with persons of the lowest description; and although this method must be considered as very disagreeable, and a sacrifice of time is likewise attendant upon it, yet, in some instances, it is expedient to resort to it, inasmuch as the information needed can be obtained from no other source, and by no other method. I have in the next place shewn that the origin of the evil is to be found in the neglect of the Infant Poor, and that its only remedy is, the establishment of Infant

Schools for their protection and instruction. It will perhaps be thought by some, that in the portion of the work devoted to the consideration and refutation of the objections which have been advanced against the education of the poor, I have used more pains than was needed; but from the experience which 1 have had, in various parts of the three kingdoms, I can assure my readers, that the old and certainly dying prejudice against universal education, is not yet defunct; many well-disposed persons have a sort of nervous apprehension of some indefinite evil likely to result therefrom. For the satisfaction of such, 1 deemed it proper to consider the matter somewhat at large.

There is one point on which I feel it imperative, before concluding, to say a few words; and that is, as to the origin of the system developed in the pages of this volume, and practised in the Infant Schools established throughout the kingdom. It has been ascribed to Pestalozzi. That he might long ago have practised a similar system I should not have denied had it been asserted, but after having put forth the former editions of this work without any acknowledgment to that individual, or to any one else, it becomes me to state the simple facts of the case. The first edition of this work was written before I had read a single work on the subject of Infant Education by that individual or any other; and the plan described in it was that which Necessity, the long-reputed mother of invention, taught me, during my labours as master of the Spitalfields Infant School. It is a matter of no consequence, who shall be accounted its inventor; but having received much encouragement in my progress to extend the system, and likewise much praise on account of its utility, I could not in justice to myself suppress the above brief statement; having on no occasion, as would have become a pupil, referred either the public or individuals, to my master or instructor.

With respect to the volume itself, it is my hope that it contains information which may be generally useful. The greater part of it I have derived from practice. This, I really think, surpasses all theoretical views; for experience must ever be considered as the test of truth. I have endeavoured to establish and enforce the compatibility of sound religious impressions with the rudimental education of the infant heart; and this, I hope, upon mature deliberation and reflection, will ever be found desirable. Many circumstances mentioned in the following pages, evidently shew the utility of an early education, and particularly that of an affectionate kind. The improvement of the labouring classes of society has been, and will most assuredly be effected. How many parents have had to lament that their children were not properly instructed during their infancy; stubbornness of disposition has often been the result of such neglect. But in addition to this, the low desires that children of a very early age manifest, as stated in this work, are sufficient to create in any feeling breast, a desire to rescue them from the power and influence of false affections; and surely no way can prove more effectual to accomplish so desirable an end than the system which this work advocates and recommends. I have endeavoured to steer clear of the various theological opinions professed by Christians of different denominations, conceiving that institutions of this kind ought to receive the support of all. What sort of religious doctrine and faith, therefore, the children ought to be taught, I have not ventured to declare, as I consider it must be the wish and desire of *all* the disciples of Christ, that children should be instructed in the leading and fundamental truths, as made known in that source of eternal light, the everlasting Gospel. With these remarks, I humbly submit the following work to the perusal of the Christian reader, hoping that those who approve of it will use their endeavours to extend its circulation ; and trusting that He who is Life itself, will prosper this endeavour to extend His kingdom among men.

CONTENTS.

APPENDIX.

ON

INFANT EDUCATION.

CHAPTER I.

JUVENILE DELINQUENCY.

" This is a beaten track :—ne'er beat enough,
Till enough learnt the truths it should inspire."

YOUNG.

It has long been a subject of regret as well as astonishment to the reflecting and benevolent, that notwithstanding the numerous institutions, for the education and improvement of the poor, which exist in this country, and in defiance of the endeavours of our police establishment and the vigilance of our magistracy, crime should rather increase than diminish. Many persons from this fact have been induced to infer that our Sunday Schools, Parochial Schools, and National Schools, as well as our Bible Societies, and institutions of a similar nature, are of no use whatever; that the country would be just as well without any of them. Absurd as the inference is, I have known more than one or two persons make it; not reflecting, that although these means may not

B

be sufficient to counteract the cause of crime, or to prevent its evil effects, yet, nevertheless, they must certainly check its progress, and oppose its farther extension; and that, if there be many offenders in spite of these institutions, there would, doubtless, be many more if they were not in existence;—to revile or neglect them, therefore, is little worthy of good sense or good feeling. It is not my purpose in the present Chapter to dwell on the existence of crime generally, but of that of juvenile delinquency in particular; neither shall I here stop to point out, or to expatiate on, the remedy for the evil, which it is the purpose of the succeeding chapters to propose and explain. I will, previously to doing so, bring before the eyes of the public a collection of facts, some of which were obtained at considerable personal hazard and inconvenience, shewing the alarming nature and extent of juvenile delinquency.

It is said by Dr. Pole, in his Observations on Infant Schools (p. 17), that in the year 1819, in London alone, the number of boys who procured a considerable part of their subsistence by pocket-picking, and thieving in every possible form, was estimated to be from eleven to fifteen hundred. One man whom he mentions, living in Wentworth Street, near Spitalfields, had forty boys in training to steal and pick pockets, who were paid for their exertions with a part of the plunder; fortunately, however, for the public, this notable tutor of thieves was himself convicted of theft and transported. This system of tutorage is by no means uncommon, nor is it confined to the male sex. I remember reading some time back in the Police Reports, of a woman who had entrapped eight or ten children from their parents; had trained them up, and sent them out thieving; nor was it until one of these infantile depredators was taken in the act of stealing, that the affair was made known, and the children restored to their homes. In this case, we see, owing probably to the negligence of their fathers or mothers, eight or ten children, enticed away no doubt by the promise of a few cakes, or other trifling reward, were in a fair way of becoming confirmed thieves, had not a providential discovery of their situation taken place; and we know not how many children may have been won to evil practices in like manner.

Facts of this nature, if no other arguments could be adduced, would be sufficient to shew the utility, indeed I may say, the necessity, of providing some means, more efficient than those at present in existence, for the protection and improvement of the infant poor; that they may not thus, from the negligence of their parents, fall into the hands of those evil and designing wretches who make a living by encouraging the children of the poor to commit crimes, of the produce of which they themselves take the greatest part.

The younger the children are, the better they suit the purpose of these vile miscreants; because, if such children are detected in any dishonest act, they know well, that few persons would do more than give the child or children a tap on the head, and send them about their business. The tenth part of the crimes committed by juvenile offenders never come under public view, because should any person be robbed by a child, and detect him in the act, he is silenced by the by-standers, with this remark,—" Oh! he is but a child, let him go this time, perhaps the poor thing has done it from necessity, being in want of bread."

Thus the child is almost sure to escape, and in‑ stead of being punished, is not unfrequently re‑ warded for the adventure, as was the case in the following instance. Having had occasion to walk through Shoreditch, some time since, I saw a number of persons collected together round a little boy, who, it appeared, had stolen a brass weight from the shop of a grocer. The account the shopman gave was as follows : He stated, that three boys came into the shop for half-an-ounce of candied horehound, and that while he was get‑ ting down the glass which contained it, one of the boys contrived to purloin the weight in ques‑ tion. Having some suspicion of the boys, from the circumstance of having recently lost a number of brass weights, he kept his eyes upon them, when he saw one of them put his hand into a box that was on the counter, take out the largest weight, and then run out of the shop, followed by the other two boys. The boy who stole it, slipped the weight into the hand of one of the others; but the shopman, having observed this manœuvre, fol‑ lowed the boy who had the weight, who, being the youngest of the three, could not run very fast; he, finding himself closely pursued, threw away the weight into the road, and when he was taken, de‑ clared it was not he who took it. The man wished to take the child back to the shop, in order that his master might do with him as he thought proper, but the by-standers, with a charitable *zeal* which evinced little *knowledge*, prevented him; one man in particular seemed to interest himself much in the boy's behalf, stating that he knew the child very well, and that he had neither father nor mo‑ ther. The child immediately took up the plea, that he had no father or mother, adding to it that he had had no victuals all day. The individual before-mentioned then gave him one penny, and his example was followed by many more, till I think the boy obtained nearly a shilling. I put several questions to the child, but was checked by this fellow, who told me, that as I had given the child nothing, I had no right to ask so many questions; and, after a great deal of abuse, ended by telling me, that if I did not " take myself off," he would " give me something for myself." Feeling a great desire to sift further into this mystery, I feigned to withdraw, but kept my eye upon the boy, and followed him for nearly two hours, until I saw him join two other boys, one of whom I had not seen before, and who had a bag with something very heavy in it, which, I have every reason to believe, were weights, or something which they had obtained in a similar manner. Wishing to ascertain the fact, I approached the boys, but they no sooner perceived me, than the little fellow who had been principal actor in the affair, called out, " *Nose, Nose,*"—a signal-word, no doubt, agreed upon amongst them,—when they all ran down some obscure alleys. I followed, but was knocked down, as if by accident, by two ill-looking fellows, who continued to detain me with apologies till the boys had got safely away. I have little doubt that this was an instance of that organized system of depredation of which I have before spoken, and that the man who took so active a part at the first was at the bottom of the business,—was, in fact, the tutor and employer of the predacious urchins. His activity in preventing the boy from being taken back to the shop—his anxiety to promote a subscription for the boy,—and lastly, his threat of

personal violence if I interfered in the matter, by
questioning the child,—all these circumstances
confirm me in this opinion.

It is only by the knowledge of this fact—the
association of infant offenders with those of maturer and hardened habits—that we can account
for such strange cases as the following. On the
17th of July, 1823, a child only seven years old,
was brought before the magistrate at Lambeth-
street office, charged with frequently robbing his
mother, and was ordered to be locked up all night
in the gaol-room. In the evening, however, when
his mother returned, he forced his way out of the
room, and behaved with such violence that they
were obliged to iron both his hands and legs!
There can be no doubt that this child had been
for a long time under the instruction and evil
influence of some old and hardened offender;
he must have undergone much training before he
could have arrived at such a pitch of hardihood,
as to make it necessary to handcuff and fetter a
child of so tender an age; and to enable him to
hold even the magistrates, officers, and his own
parent, in defiance.

The two following cases afford further proof of
the same lamentable truth; the first is extracted
from a morning paper of the 20th of September,
1824. "A little boy, not more than *six years
of age*, was brought before the Lord Mayor at
the Mansion House, on Saturday, the 18th instant,
having been found in a warehouse, where he had
secreted himself for the purpose of thieving. At
a late hour on Friday night a watchman was
going his round, when, on trying a warehouse in
which there was much valuable property, to see
whether it was safe, he heard the little prisoner

cry. The persons who had the care of the warehouse were roused, and the prisoner was taken out. In his fright he acknowledged that a man had taken him from his mother, and induced him, upon a promise of reward, to steal into the warehouse; upon a concerted signal, he was to act as directed by the fellow on the outside; but becoming terrified at being confined so long in the dark, he had cried out and discovered himself. His mother came forward, and received a good character as the wife of a hard-working man. The Lord Mayor gave her son up to her, with an injunction to act carefully and strictly with him. There was reason to believe that several considerable robberies had been recently committed by means of children like the prisoner, who stole in and remained concealed until midnight, when they gave admission to the robbers. The police should have their eyes upon him."

"William Hart, an urchin *seven years of age*, was indicted for stealing twenty-two shillings in money, numbered, from the person of Mary Conner. The prosecutrix stated, that on the day named in the indictment, she took twenty-five shillings to get something out of pledge, but as there was a crowd in Mary-le-bone, assembled to witness a fight, she was induced to join the mob. While standing there she felt something move in her pocket, and putting her hand outside her clothes, she laid hold of what proved to be the hand of the prisoner, which she held until she had given him a slap on the face, and then she let him go; but on feeling in her pocket she discovered, that the theft had actually been committed—that only three shillings were left. A constable took the urchin into custody, and ac-

cused him of robbing her of twenty-two shillings.
The prisoner said, 'I have twenty-two shillings
in my pocket, but it is my mother's money; she
gets so drunk she gives me her money to take
care of.' The officer stated to the same effect as
the prosecutrix, and added, that in a secret pocket
in his jacket he found fourteen shillings and six-
pence. *It was the practice of gangs of pick-
pockets to have a child like this to commit the robbery, and hand the plunder to them.* Witness went
to his parents, who said he had been absent seven
weeks, and they would have nothing to do with
him. Mr. Baron Garrow, in feeling terms, la-
mented that a child of such tender years should
be so depraved. He added, 'I suppose, gentlemen, I need only ask you to deliver your verdict.'
His lordship then observed, that he would consult
with his learned brother as to the best manner of
disposing of the prisoner. They at length decided, that although it might seem harsh, the Court
would record against him fourteen years' trans-
portation; and, no doubt, government would
place him in some school; if he behaved well
there, the sentence might not be carried into full
effect."

I remember a query being once put to me by
a person who visited the Spitalfields Infant School
at the time I had it under my management: " How
can you account for the fact," said he, " that notwithstanding there are so many old and experienced thieves detected, convicted, and sent out
of the country every session, we cannot perceive
any diminution of the numbers of such characters; but that others seem always to supply their
places?" The foregoing instances of the systematized instruction of young delinquents by old

depts in the art of pilfering affords, I think, a satisfactory answer to the interrogatory.

The dexterity and aptness of experienced thieves, shews that no small degree of care and attention is bestowed on their tuition. The first task of the novitiate, I have been informed, is to go in companies of threes or fours, through the respectable streets and squares of the metropolis, and with an old knife, or similar instrument, wrench off the brass-work usually placed over the key-holes of the area gates, &c. which they sell at the marine store shops; and they are said sometimes to realize three or four shillings a day, by this means. Wishing to be satisfied whether this was actually the case, I have walked round many of the squares in town, and in more than a solitary instance, have found that not one gate in ten had any brass-work over the key-hole; it had evidently been wrenched off; a small piece of the brass still remaining on many of the gates. Having practised this branch of the profession a considerable time, and become adepts in its execution, the next step, I have been informed, is to take the handles and brass knockers from doors, which is done by taking out the screw with a small screw-driver: these are disposed of in the same manner as the former, till the young pilferers are progressively qualified for stealing brass weights, &c. and, at length, become expert thieves.*

* The following fact will shew what extensive depredations young children are capable of committing. I have inserted the whole, as it appeared in the public papers:—" *Union Hall; Shop Lifting.*—Yesterday, two little girls, sisters, very neatly dressed, one nine, and the other seven years of age, were put to the bar, charged by Mr. Cornell, linen-draper, of High-street, Newington, with having stolen a piece of printed calico, from the counter of his shop.

Another very cruel practice of these young delinquents, is to go into some chandler's shop,

---

"Mr. Cornell stated, the children came to his shop, yesterday morning; that while he was engaged with his customers at the further end of the shop, he happened to cast his eyes where the prisoners were, and observed the eldest roll up a large piece of printed calico, and put it into a basket, which her little sister carried: the witness immediately advanced to her, and asked if she had taken any thing from off the counter; but she positively asserted that she had not. However, on searching her basket, the calico was found; together with a piece of muslin, which Mr. Cornell identified as belonging to him, and to have been taken in the above way. Mr. Allen questioned the eldest girl about the robbery, but she positively denied any knowledge as to how, or in what manner the calico and muslin had got into her basket, frequently appealing to her little sister to confirm the truth of what she declared. When asked if she had ever been charged with any offence, 'O yes, sir, some time back, I was accused of stealing a watch from a house, but I did not do it.' The Magistrate observed, that the father should be made acquainted with the circumstance, and in the mean time, gave the gaoler instructions that the two little delinquents should be taken care of.

"Hall, the officer, stated that he had information that there was a quantity of goods, which had been stolen by the prisoners, concealed in a certain desk in the house of the father; and that a great deal of stolen property would, in all probability, be found there, if a search-warrant were granted, as the two unfortunate children were believed to be most extensive depredators.

"Mr. Allen immediately granted the warrant; and Hall, accompanied by Mr. Cornell, proceeded to the residence of the father of the children, who is an auctioneer and appraiser, at 12, Lyon-street, Newington.

"Hall returned in half an hour with the father in his custody, and produced a great quantity of black silk handkerchiefs, which he had found on the premises; but the desk which had been spoken of by his informers as containing stolen property, he had found quite empty. The father, when questioned by the witness as to whether he had any duplicates of property in his possession, positively denied ns sly as possible, and take an opportunity of stealing the till with its contents, there being

hat fact. At the office he was searched, and about fifty uplicates found in his pockets, most of which were for silk andkerchiefs and shawls. There were also a few rings, for he possession of which the prisoner could not satisfactorily ccount. He was asked why he had assured the officer he ad no duplicates? He replied, that he had not said so; but Mr. Cornell, who was present during the search, averred hat the prisoner had most positively declared that he had ot a pawnbroker's duplicate in his possession.

" Mr. Watt, a Linen-draper, of Harper-street, Kent-road, tated, that he attended in consequence of seeing the police eports in the newspapers, describing the two children; he mmediately recognized the two little girls as having fre-quently called at his shop for trifling articles; and added, that ie had been robbed of a variety of silk handkerchiefs and hawls, and he had no doubt but that the prisoners were he thieves. It was their practice he said, to go into a shop, nd call for a quarter of a yard of muslin, and while the shop-keeper was engaged, the eldest would very dexterously slip whatever article was nearest to her to the little sister, who was trained to the business, and would thrust the stolen pro-perty into a basket which she always carried for that purpose. Mr. Watt identified the silk handkerchiefs as his property, nd said that they had been stolen in the above manner by he prisoners.

"The father was asked where he had got the handker-hiefs? He replied, that he had bought them from a pedlar or half-a-crown a piece at his door. However, his eldest aughter contradicted him by acknowledging that her sister ad stolen them from the shop of Mr. Watt. He became readfully agitated, and then said — ' What could I say? Surely I was not to criminate my own children !'

" Mr. Allen observed, that there was a clear case against he two children, but after consulting with the other Magis-rates, he was of opinion that the youngest child should be given up into the charge of the parish officers of Newington, is she was too young to go into a prison; and desired that he other girl should be remanded, in order to have some of he pledged goods produced. The father was committed in default of bail, for receiving stolen goods. The child has

always some older thief ready to take charge of it,
as soon as the child brings it out of the shop.*
Many a poor woman has had to lament the loss
of her till, with its contents, taken by a child,
perhaps, scarcely six years of age.   There is
always a plan laid down for the child to act
upon.   Should he be unable to obtain possession
of the till himself, he is instructed to pretend
that he has missed his way, and to inquire the
way to some street near the spot;   or, he will
address her with " Please, ma'am, can you tell
me what it is o'clock."   The unsuspecting wo·
man, with the greatest kindness possible, shows the
child the street he inquires for, or leaves the shop
to ascertain the hour for the artful inquirant, and
for her kindness she is sure to find herself robbed,
when she returns, by some of the child's com·
panions.   Should he be detected in actual pos·
session of the property, he is instructed to act his
part in the most artful manner, by pretending that
some man sent him into the shop to take it, who
told him that he would give him sixpence to buy
cakes.

It is not uncommon for these young offenders

---

since been found guilty. The prosecutor stated that the
family consisted of five children, *not one of whom could read
or write!"*

* So complete is the science of pilfering rendered by its
perpetrators, that they have even a peculiar vocabulary of
their own, rendering their conversation to those who may
chance to overhear them, as mysterious and incomprehen·
sible as though they were conversing in a foreign tongue;
for instance, the scutcheons they steal from the key-holes are
called *porcupines;* brass weights, *lueys;* while the theft of
which we have spoken above, purloining the contents of a
till, is called *taking the ding.*   In short, they have a peculiar
name for almost every thing.

to stop children, whom they may meet in the street, unprotected, and either by artifice or violence, take from them their hats, necklaces, &c.; thus initiating themselves, as it were into the desperate crime of assault and highway robbery.

Young as the subjects of the foregoing narrations mostly were, I have little doubt their pupillage commenced at a much earlier age; they could not otherwise have attained to such proficiency in the practice of crime, and hardihood on detection. However possible it may be thought to reclaim children of so tender an age, I am convinced that thieves of more advanced years, become so thoroughly perverted in their wills and understandings, as to be incapable of perceiving the disgrace of their conduct, or the enormity of the offence. I was once told by an old thief that thieving was his profession, and he had therefore a right to follow it; and I could plainly discover from further conversation which I held with him, that he had confirmed in himself an opinion that thieving was no harm, provided he used no violence to the person; he seemed to have no idea of the rights of property, other than that expressed as the maxim of a celebrated Scottish outlaw— that,

> " They should take who have the power,
> And they should keep who can."

When this lamentable state is attained to, it is to be feared, all modes of punishment, as correctives, are useless; and the only thing left is to prevent their further depredations by banishment.

The incorrigible state to which a child may attain, who has once associated with thieves at an early age, may be learnt from the following case.

c

" Richard Leworthy, aged fourteen, was indicted for stealing five sovereigns, the property of
William Newling, his master. The prosecutor
stated, that he resided in the Commercial-road,
and is by business a taylor; the prisoner had
been his apprentice for four months, up to the
28th of August, when he committed the robbery.
On that day he gave him five pounds to take to
Mr. Wells, of Bishopsgate Street, to discharge a
bill; he never went, nor did he return home; he
did not hear of him for three weeks, when he
found him at Windsor, and apprehended him.
The prisoner admitted having applied the money
to his own use. He was found at a public house;
and said he had spent all his money except one
shilling and six-pence. A shopman in the service of Mr. Wells, stated that in August last, the
witness owed his master a sum of money; he
knew the prisoner; he did not bring money to
their shop, either on or since the 28th of August.
The prisoner made no defence, but called his
master, who said he received him from the Refuge
for the Destitute, and had a good character with
him. He would not take him back again. Mr.
Wontner stated, that he had received two com-
munications from the Rev. Mr. Crosby, the Chap-
lain of the Institution, stating they would not
interfere on his behalf. The Jury returned a
verdict of *Guilty*. Mr. Justice Park observed,
that the best course would be to send him out of
the country."

Here we see, that notwithstanding the discipline
he had undergone, and the instructions he had
received during his confinement in the establishment of the Refuge for the Destitute; he had not
been four months from that place before he fell

into his old habits. It is moreover to be remarked, that such had been his conduct during his confinement, that the directors of the establishment thought themselves warranted in giving a good character with him. They were probably little surprised on hearing of this relapse on the part of the boy — experience had doubtless taught them it was no uncommon thing, and we plainly see it had taught them to consider all further attempts at reclaiming him as useless.

Having collected the foregoing instances of juvenile delinquency, and presented them to the public, I cannot refrain from adducing a few other cases which came under my observation, evincing it would almost seem, an inherent principle of dishonesty in some children. Various, indeed, are the opinions of the wise on these matters; some have boldly asserted that they *are* inherent principles, and are the result of a peculiarity of cerebral conformation; but as my wish is rather to diminish evil, than ascertain its origin or nature, I will leave the philosophers to settle these doubtful points amongst themselves. I know it exists,—it is the purpose of my present chapter to shew, by examples, to what an alarming extent it exists — in the rising generation of the poor classes; it will be my next object to point out one cause of its existence, quite distinct from any about which the learned have disputed,—a cause which is in fact indisputable: namely, the neglect, bad habits, and examples of parents amongst the working class; and I shall then explain that which I think alone offers a remedy for the evil—the protection and education of the infant poor.

Whilst conducting the Spitalfield's Infant School, several instances of dishonesty in the children came under my notice. On one occasion the mother herself came to complain of her little boy, not more than four years old, on the following grounds. She stated, that being obliged to be out at work all day, as well as her husband, she was under the necessity of leaving the children by themselves. She had three children besides the little boy of whom she was complaining. Having to pay her rent, she put eighteen-pence for that purpose in a cup at the top of the cupboard. On stepping home to give the children their dinners, she found the boy at the cupboard, mounted on a chair, which again was placed on the top of a table. On looking for the money she found fourpence already gone; one penny of this she found in his pocket, the rest he had divided amongst the other children, that they might not tell of him.

After this relation I kept a strict eye upon this child, and three or four days afterwards the children detected him opening my desk and taking halfpence out of it. The children informed me that he had been at the desk, and while they were bringing him up to me the halfpence dropped out of his hand; I detected him in many other very bad actions, but have reason to hope, that by suitable discipline and instruction he was effectually cured of this sad propensity.

About the same time I observed two little children, very near the school-house, in close conversation, and from their frequently looking at a fruit stall that was near, I felt inclined to watch them having previously heard from some of the children in the school, that they had frequently seen children in the neighbourhood steal oysters, and other things. I accordingly placed myself in a convenient situation, and had not long to wait, fo the moment they saw there was no one passing, they went up to the stall, the eldest walking alongside the other, apparently to prevent his being seen, whilst the little one snatched an orange, and conveyed it under his pinafore, with all the dexterity of an experienced thief. The youngest of these children was not four years old, and the eldest, apparently, not above five; there was reason to believe this was not the first time these children had been guilty of stealing, though perhaps unknown to their parents, as I have found to be the case in other instances.

Another little boy in the school, a very fine child, whose mother kept a little shop, frequently brought money with him, as much as threepence at a time. On questioning the child how he came by it, he always said that his mother gave it to him, and I thought there was no reason to doubt the child's word, for there was something so prepossessing in his appearance, that, at that time, I could not doubt the truth of his story. But finding that the child spent a great deal of money in fruit, cakes, &c. and still had some remaining, I found it advisable to see the mother, and to my astonishment found it all a fiction, for she had not given him any, and we were both at a loss to conceive how he obtained it. The child told *me*, his mother gave it him; and he told his *mother* that it was given to him at school; but when he was confronted with us both, not a word would he say. It was evident therefore that he had obtained it by some unfair means, and we both determined to suspend our judgment, and to keep a strict eye on him in future. Nothing, however, transpired for some time; I followed him home several times, but saw nothing amiss. At length

I received notice from the mother, that she had detected him in taking money out of the till in her little shop.   It then came out that there was some boy in the neighbourhood who acted as banker to him, and for every twopence which he received from the child, he was allowed one penny for taking care of it.   It seems that the child was afraid to bring any more money to school, on account of being so closely questioned as to where he obtained it, and this, probably, induced him to give more to the boy than he otherwise would have done.   Suffice it, however, to say, that both children at length were found out, and the mother declared that the child conducted her to some old boards in the wash-house, and underneath them there was upwards of a shilling, which he had pilfered at various times.

It would have been easy to multiply cases of juvenile delinquency, both those which have been brought under the cognizance of the law, and those which have come to my own knowledge, but I think enough have been related to show how early children may and do become depraved. I have purposely given most of them with as few remarks of my own as possible, that they may plead their own cause with the reader, and excite a desire in his bosom to enter with me in the next chapter into an enquiry as to the causes of such early depravity.

CHAPTER II.

REMARKS ON THE CAUSES OF JUVENILE DELINQUENCY.

" Why thus surpris'd to see the infant race
Treading the paths of vice? Their eyes can trace
Their parents' footsteps in the way they go:
What shame, what fear, then, can their young hearts know?"

ANON.

GREAT as the *effects* of juvenile delinquency are, I think we may discover a principal *cause* for them in the present condition and habits of the adult part of the labouring classes. We shall find very frequently, that it is only the natural perpetuation of evil, by the infallible mode of precept and example. I do not mean to make the illiberal assertion, that many parents amongst the poor classes actually encourage their children in the commission of theft; we may indeed fear, that even this is sometimes the fact; as in the instance of the two little girls detected in shop-lifting, whose case we detailed in the preceding chapter; but still, I should hope that such cases are not frequent. If, however, they do not give them positive encouragement in dishonesty, the example they set is often calculated to deprave the heart of the child, and to induce dishonesty, amongst other evil consequences; whilst

in other cases we find, that from peculiar circum
stances the child is deprived, during the whol
day, of the controlling presence of a parent, an
is exposed to all the poisonous contamination
both of precept and example, which the street
of large cities afford; and there cannot be a
more obvious cause of the evil, than the wron
associations which children form, when, at a
early age, they are suffered to pass their tim
in the streets, without any one to protect o
control them. It is in this sphere they come i
contact with maturer vice, and are won by it
influence from the paths of innocence; we hav
shewn many instances, in our preceding pages
which will confirm and illustrate this fact. Wha
resistance can the infant make to the insidiou
serpents, which thus, as it were, steal into it
cradle, and infuse their poison into its soul
The guardians of its helplessness are heedless o
unconscious of its danger, and, alas! it has no
the fabled strength of the infant Hercules, to
crush its venomous assailants. Surely such a
view of the frequent origin of crime must awaken
our commiseration for its miserable victims, and
excite in us a desire to become the protectors o
the unprotected.

It will, however, be inquired by some, "Where
are the natural guardians of the child? Where
are its parents? Are we to encourage their
neglect of duty, by becoming their substitutes?
It is their business to look after their children,
and not ours." Frequently have I heard such
sentiments put forth, and sometimes by persons
in whom I knew it was rather a want of reflection
than of philanthropy. But, a want of thought, or
of feeling, one or the other, it must certainly be;

ecause, on no principle of reason or humanity
an we make the unnatural conduct of the fathers
nd mothers, a plea for withholding our pro-
ction and assistance from the helpless victims
f their cruelty and neglect. If we do so, we not
nly neglect our duty toward such children, but
re permitting the growth and extension of the
vil. We must recollect that these children will
ot merely play their own wicked parts during
heir lives, but will likewise become the models
o the next generation.

It should be remembered here, that I am treat-
ng of an evil which extends its bad consequences
o all classes of society; I am appealing to the
rudence of men, that they will, for their own
akes, investigate the cause of that evil; I shall
ereafter appeal to them as philanthropists, and,
till higher, as Christians, that they will examine
he merits of the remedy I shall propose.

The culpability of many parents is beyond dis-
ute. They not only omit to set their children
ood examples, and give them good advice, but,
n the contrary, instil into their minds the first
udiments of wickedness, and lead them into the
aths of vice. Their homes present scenes which
uman nature shudders at, and which it is impos-
ible truly to describe. There are parents who,
working at home, have every opportunity of train-
ng up their children "in the way they should go,"
f they were inclined so to do. Instead of this, we
often find, in the case of the fathers, they are so
lost to every principle of humanity, that as soon as
they receive their wages, they leave their homes,
and hasten with eager steps to the public-house ;
nor do they re-pass its accursed threshold, till the
vice-fattening landlord has received the greater

part of the money which should support thei
half-fed, half-clothed, wives and children; til
they have qualified themselves, by intoxicatio
to play the part of brutes, on their return home
in ill-usage toward the victims of their crime—
cursing, swearing, and frequently beating bot
wives and children.   To men of this descriptio
it matters not whether or no their children ar
proving themselves skilful imitators of their evi
example,—they may curse and swear, lie an
steal,—so long as they can enjoy the society o
their pot-companions, it is to them a matter o
total indifference.

During my superintendance of the Spitalfield'
school, I had a painful facility of examining int
these matters.   Frequently, when I have inquire
the cause of the wretched plight in which some o
the children were sent to the school,—perhap
with scarcely a shoe to their feet, sometimes totall
without,—I have heard from their mothers th
most heart-rending recitals of the husband's misconduct.   One family in particular I remember
consisting of seven children, two of whom wer
in the school; four of them were supported entirely by the exertions of the mother, who declared to me, that she did not receive a shilling
from their father for a month together; all the
money he got he kept to spend at the public-
house; and his family, for what he cared, migh
go naked, or starve.   He was not only a grea
drunkard, but a reprobate into the bargain; beating and abusing the poor woman, who thus endeavoured to support his children by her labour.

The evil does not always stop here.   Drive
to the extreme of wretchedness by her husband's
conduct, the woman sometimes takes to drinking

kewise, and the poor babes are ten thousand mes more pitiable than orphans. I have witessed the revolting sight of a child leading home th father and mother from the public-house, a disgusting state of intoxication. With tears d entreaties I have seen the poor infant vainly deavouring to restrain them from increasing eir drunkenness, by going into the houses on eir way home ; they have shook off the clingg child, who, in the greatest anxiety, awaited thout to resume its painful task ; knowing all e time, perhaps, that whilst its parents were us throwing away their money, there was not much as a crust of bread to appease its hunger home. Let it not be thought that this is an ercharged picture of facts; it is but a faint, a ry faint and imperfect sketch of a reality which fies exaggeration. Cases of such depravity, the part of mothers, I with much pleasure nfess to be comparatively rare. Maternal affecon is the preventitive. But what, let me ask, n be hoped of the children of such parents? hat are their characters likely to become under ch tuition ? With such examples before their es, need they leave their homes to seek conmination, or to learn to do evil?

And here I must say, if I were asked to point t, in the metropolis or any large city, the eatest nuisance, the worst bane of society, the ost successful promoter of vice,—I should, without a moment's hesitation, point to the first publicuse or spirit-dealer's that met my view. Nor an I, in speaking of the causes of juvenile denquency, omit to say, I think these houses, directly, a very great cause of it. Why I think , my readers will readily conceive from what I

have said above. I am sure that Satan has n
temple in which he is so devoutly worshipped, s
highly honoured, as in the ale-house,—no prie
so devoted as its landlord,—no followers so zea
ous in his behalf as its frequenters.

Let any one in the evening visit the homes
the labouring class, in a poor neighbourhood
he will find, in many cases, a barely-furnishe
room, a numerous family of small children,
these, perhaps, may have forgot the pangs
hunger in the obliviousness of sleep,—a wif
with care-worn features, sitting in solitary wretc
edness, ruminating on wants which she kno
not how to supply—namely, clothes and food f
her children on the morrow,—on debts, perhap
which she has no means of discharging. B
where is he who should be sharing her car
bidding her be of good cheer, and devising wi
her some means of alleviating their mutual d
tress? Where is the father of the sleeping bab
the husband of the watchful wife? Go to t
public-house; you will see him there with a h
of his companions, of like character and circu
stances, smoking, drinking, singing, blasphemi
gambling—ruining his health, spending his m
ney; as jovial as though he had no wretch
wife, no starving babes at home; and as lavi
of money which should procure them food, as t
man who is thriving on his excesses could wi
him to be.

I never look upon a public-house, without co
sidering it as the abode of the evil genius o
neighbourhood; the despoiler of industry,
destroyer of domestic comfort: and heartily
I wish, that some means could be devised
abolishing these resorts of wickedness; that so

egislative enactment may render it unlawful for
iny one to keep such places. It is at present, with
espect to a peculiar sort of beverage, declared to
ie illegal to afford its purchasers accommodation
or drinking it on the premises. Why not extend
t to other liquors? I know this would be pro-
iounced an infringement on English liberty! The
vorst of men would raise this outcry against the
neasure. But surely it should rather be called
preventitive of English licentiousness. All good
nen would consider it as such. I would not rob
ne labourer of his daily allowance of a beverage
vhich is believed by many to be of essential ser-
ice, when taken in moderation — but I would
ave him enjoy it at home, that his wife and chil-
ren may participate in his enjoyment. Perhaps,
will be said, a man closely confined to labour
ll day, needs some relaxation from domestic
ires—that this can only be found in change of
sene, and in social company. I will concede
iis. The plea of health, though often speciously
dvanced, cannot be denied. But is it necessary
ir his health, that this change of scene should be
to a close tap-room, within a few yards of his
ome, where he drinks to a ruinous excess till a
te hour,—breathing all the while a hot atmo-
ihere of tobacco-smoke? Were it not possible to
itain the change of scene, the relaxation of social
nverse, by mutual interchange of visits amongst
iends similarly situated,—by a ramble to the
iburbs,—or, in cases where the daily occupation
fords too little opportunity for exercise, are there
it places established for gymnastic exercises,—
d might not others be formed for the like pur-
ises? Certain I am that the abolishment of
iblic-houses, in large cities, as places of daily

D

resort for the adult labouring poor, would be
attended with the most salutary consequences.   I
know of nothing that must so certainly tend to
their improvement both in character and circumstances.   Another measure should then be adopted,
—destroy the facility of spirit-drinking, by laying
on a heavy duty.   It is in vain that interested
sophistry would plead its benefits in particular
cases—such, for instance, as the ludicrous plea of
the needfulness of drams for market-women on
wet and frosty mornings.   Set these specious benefits against the dreadful results to men's health
and pockets, of the present low price of spirits,
and their consequent enormous consumption; and
then let common sense and honesty deliver its
judgment.

I have spoken thus candidly and at length
upon the subject in the present chapter, though
somewhat out of place, because my feelings denied me to be less plain or more brief, or to
postpone the matter to " a more convenient season."   Perhaps in talking of legislative alterations
I have been wandering upon forbidden ground;
if so, in returning to my proper path, I will
comfort myself with this thought.   The progress
of improvement, however slow, is sure, and it is
certainly advancing in this country;   I require no
other assurance of its progress than the establishment of Infant Schools and Mechanic's Institutions; it *will* advance, and what the legislature
may never be able to accomplish, the spirit of
improvement eventually will.

But having considered those cases, in which
wilful neglect and positive bad example may be
charged upon the parents, we should not forget
to tell those who object to our interference in the

duty of the child's natural protectors, that it is not, in every instance, *wilful* neglect on the part of the parents, that their children are left unprotected in the streets. The circumstances of the labouring classes are such, in many cases, that they are compelled to leave their children either wholly unprotected, or in the charge of some one who frequently becomes a betrayer instead of a protector. The father, perhaps, goes to his daily labour in the morning, before the children are out of bed, and does not return till they are in bed again at night. The mother goes out, in like manner, the earnings of the husband being insufficient for the maintenance of the family, and the children are intrusted throughout the day to the care of some girl, whose parents are as poor as themselves, and are glad to let her earn something towards her support. Numbers of little girls go out in this capacity, before they are twelve years old, and they teach the little children all they know —all they have learnt themselves, to be deceitful, and not unfrequently dishonest. The parents, careless or unsuspecting, only make enquiry when they return home if the children have been good and quiet, and of course receive an answer in the affirmative. In the course of a few years the evil consequences begin to shew themselves, and then the good folks wonder how or when the seeds of such depravity could have been sown. Many I know will be inclined to smile at the insignificancy of the cause pointed out. I can only say, it is from such insignificant springs the great stream of vice is supplied; and, what we laugh at now, in its origin, for its insignificance, will hereafter, in its maturity, laugh at us for our impotence, in vainly endeavouring to overcome it.

What are parents to do with their children, situated, as those of whom we have just spoken?
And very many are so situated. Is it possible
for them to perform their duty, as protectors of
their children? It requires all their time to labour
for their support, and they therefore leave them,
unavoidably, either in such hands as we have
described, or to take care of themselves; to range
the streets, and form such associations as may
there happen to fall in their way. They get into
company with older delinquents, and become first
their instruments, and then their associates; till at
length they find their way into a gaol.

This is no theoretical mode of accounting for
the matter, adopted from reasoning on the subject;
it is one which experience and observation have
taught and established. I have traced the progress
of delinquency in actual life, from its earliest
stages, from the little trembling pilferer of the
apple-stall, not more than four or five years old,
—to the confirmed thief of nine or ten years—
who had been in gaol three or four times, and
was as proud of his dexterity in thieving, and
hardihood under punishment, as he could have
been of the most virtuous accomplishment, or the
most becoming fortitude. The infant thief, with a
consciousness of shame, and trembling with fear,
will tell you on detection, that "Tommy" or
"Billy," some older associate, set him to do it;
you let him go: he joins his companions, who
laugh at the story he tells, ridicule him for his
fears, praise him for his dexterity, and rejoice in
his escape. It will be very easy to imagine how,
under a course of such treatment, the young offender so soon dismisses both shame and fear.

and learns to forget everything but the gain and the glory of his crimes.

It is no small matter of credit with older thieves, —(by older thieves I still mean, in the present instance, boys of nine or ten years old)—to have under their tuition two or three pupils. I have seen in my walks, as many as seven or eight sallying forth from the allies in the neighbourhood of Spitalfields, under the command, as it were, of a leader, a boy perhaps not more than nine or ten years old. I have watched their plans; and have noticed that it was usual to send first the youngest boy to attempt the theft—perhaps the object to be attained was only a bun from the open window of a pastry-cook's shop—if he failed, another was sent, whilst the rest were lurking at the corner of some court, ready to start in case their companion was detected;—and I have sometimes witnessed, that after all the rest had failed, either from the want of dexterity, or from the too great vigilance of the shopkeeper, the boy who acted as leader has started out, and by a display of superior dexterity, would have carried off the object, had it not happened that some one was thus purposely watching his conduct. When detected, if an old offender, he will either look you in the face with the greatest effrontery and an expression of defiance, or he will feign to cry, and tell you he was hungry, has no father nor mother, &c.; though frequently on further enquiry I have found the whole story to be false.

The two grand causes of juvenile delinquency we have seen, then, to be—the evil example of parents themselves; and the bad associations which children form at any early age, when, through neglect, they are suffered to be in the streets. In the first instance, the parents of the children are wholly without excuse; in the second, though in some cases we may blame them, in others we cannot justly do so; but must admit, as an exculpation, the unfortunate circumstances of their condition in life.

It would be easy to produce a multitude of instances, to shew the evil effects produced on children of a tender age, by street associations. But I think enough has been said to convince every reflecting mind that it is highly necessary that we should interfere on the behalf of children so situated; and I shall conclude the present chapter by some remarks on various habits and practices of the poor classes, which have at least an injurious tendency on the character of the rising generation.

As children are such imitative beings, I cannot help making a few observations on the tricks which are usually introduced into our pantomimes. It is well known that the tricks of the clown form a principal part of the entertainment. It is also equally well known, that pantomimes are particularly suited to amuse children, for which reason they are generally introduced during Christmas holidays. If pantomimes were first intended to amuse children, they who introduced them have gained their object; but what kind of *instruction* children have received from them, I shall here attempt to shew. I do not recollect to have seen a pantomime myself without pilfering being introduced under every possible form and contrivance, such as shop-lifting, picking pockets, &c. Can it be for a moment supposed improbable that children, after having witnessed these exhibitions, should endeavour to put the thing into practice, whenever an opportunity offers, and try whether they cannot take a handkerchief from a gentleman's pocket with the same ease and dexterity as the clown in the play did; or, if unsuccessful in this part of the business, they might likely try their prowess in carrying off a shoulder of mutton from a butcher's shop, a loaf from a baker, or lighter articles from the pastry cook, fruiterer, or linen draper. For, having seen the dexterity of the clown, in these cases, they will not be at a loss for methods to accomplish, by sleight of hand, their several purposes. It is my humble opinion, that children cannot go to a better place for instruction in these matters, or to a place more calculated to teach them the art of pilfering to perfection, than to a theatre, when pantomimes are performed. To say that the persons who write and introduce these pieces are in want of sense, may not be true; but I must charge them with want of sufficient thought, in not calculating upon the baneful effects of its tendency on the rising generation, for whose amusement it appears they were chiefly produced. Many unfortunate persons, who have heard the sentence of death passed upon them, or who are now suffering under the law, in various ways, have had to lament that the first seeds of vice were sown in their minds while viewing the pilfering tricks of clowns in pantomime. Little do we calculate on the direful effects of this species of amusement on the future character of the rising generation; we first permit their minds to be poisoned, by offering them the draught, and then punish them by law for taking it. Does not the wide world afford variety of materials sufficient for virtuous imitations, without descending to that which is vicious? It is much easier to make a pail of pure water foul, than it is to make a pail of foul water pure. It must not be supposed that I wish to sweep off every kind of amusement from the juvenile part of society, but I do wish to sweep off all that part which has a pernicious tendency. The limits which I have prescribed to myself will not allow me to enter more at large into this subject; otherwise I could produce a number of facts which would prove, most unquestionably, the propriety of discontinuing these exhibitions.

A conversation which I once heard between some boys who were playing at what they call *pitch-in-the-hole*, will prove the truth of my assertions.—Bill, said one of the boys to the other, when did you go to the play last? On Monday night, was the reply. Did you see the new pantomime?—Yes. Well, did you see any fun? —Yes, I believe I did too. I saw the clown *bone* a whole *hank* of sausages, and put them into his pocket, and then pour the gravy in after them. You would have split your sides with laughing, had you been there. A. B. C. and D. were with me, and they laughed as much as I did. What do you think A. B. did the next night?—How should I know. Why, replied the other, he and C. D. *boned* about two pounds of sausages from a pork shop and we had them for supper.—This conversation I heard from a window, which looked into a ruinous place where the boys assemble to toss up for money, or pitch at the hole. This fact alone, without recording any more, is sufficient to shew the evil of which I have been speaking. And I do most sincerely hope that those persons who have any influence over the stage,

will use their utmost endeavours speedily to ex-
punge every thing thus calculated to promote evil
inclinations in the souls of children, and vicious
habits in the lives of men.

As I have had much experience from being
brought up in London, I am perfectly aware of
the evil impressions and dangerous temptations
that the children of the poor are liable to fall into;
and therefore must solemnly affirm, that nothing
in my view would give so much happiness to the
community at large, as the taking care of the
affections of the infant children of the poor.

There is a practice, very prevalent among the
poor, which does more mischief than people are
generally aware of, and that is, sending their
children to the pawnbrokers. It is well known
that many persons send children, scarcely seven
years of age, to these places, with pledges of
various sorts, a thing that cannot be too severely
condemned. I know an instance of a little boy
finding a shawl in the street; being in the habit
of going to the pawnbroker's for his mother,
instead of taking the shawl home to his parents,
he actually pawned it, and spent all the money,
which might never have been known by his
parents, had not the mother found the duplicate
in his pocket. It is evident, then, that many
parents have no one but themselves to blame, for
the misconduct of their children; for had this
child not been accustomed to go to such a place
for his parents, he would never have thought of
going there for himself; and the shawl most likely
would have been carried home to them. Indeed,
there is no knowing where such a system will
end, for if children are suffered to go to such
places, they may in time pledge that which does

not belong to them; and this is such an easy way of turning any article into money, that we find most young thieves, of both sexes, when apprehended, have a few duplicates about them. Those persons, therefore, who take pledges of children (contrary to the act of parliament whether they know it or not,) ought to be severely reprimanded; for I am persuaded, that such conduct is productive of very great mischief indeed.

Taking children to fairs, is another thing which is also productive of much harm. The first year the Spitalfields' school was opened, when there was any fair near London, seventy or eighty children were frequently absent; but the parents were afterwards cured of this, and we seldom had above twenty absentees at fair-time; several of the children have told me that their parents wished to take them, but they requested to be permitted to come to school instead. Indeed the parents, finding that they can enjoy themselves better without their children, will be very willing to leave them at school.

It is a difficult matter to persuade grown persons of the impropriety of attending fairs, who have been accustomed to it when children; but children are easily persuaded from it; for if they are properly entertained at school, they will not have the least desire to attend fairs.

I cannot quit this subject without relating one or two more very bad habits to which children are addicted, and which are perhaps fit subjects for the consideration of the *Mendicity Society*. As it is the object of that society to clear the streets of beggars, it would be well if they would put a stop to those juvenile beggars, many of whom are children of respectable parents, who assemble together to build what they call a GROTTO; to the great annoyance of all passengers in the streets, begging for money. However desirous persons may be of encouraging ingenuity in children, I think it is doing them much harm to give them money when they ask for it in this way. Indeed it would appear, that some of the children have learned the art of begging so well, that they are able to vie with the most experienced mendicant. Ladies in particular are very much annoyed by children getting before them and asking for money; nor will they take the answer given them, but put their hats up to the ladies' faces, saying, "Please, ma'am, remember the grotto;" and when told by the parties that they have no money to give, will still continue to follow, and be as importunate as any common beggar. However innocent and trifling this may appear to some, I am inclined to believe that such practices tend to evil, for they teach children to be mean, and may cause some of them to choose begging rather than work : I think that the best way to stop this species of begging is, never to give them any thing. A fact which came under my own observation will shew that the practice may be productive of mischief. A foreign gentleman walking up Old-street-road, was surrounded by three or four boys, saying, "Please, sir, remember the grotto."—"Go away, I will give you none." "Do, pray sir, remember the grotto." "No, I tell you I will give you nothing." "Do, sir, only once a-year." At length, I believe, he put something into one of their hats, and thus got rid of them; but he had scarcely gone two hundred yards, before he came to another grotto, and out sallied three more boys, with the same importunate request: he replied, " I will give you nothing; plague have you and your grotto." The boys still persevered, till the gentleman, having lost all patience, gave one of them a gentle tap to get out of the way, but the boy being on the side of the foot-path fell into the mud, which had been scraped off the road, and in this pickle followed the gentleman, bellowing out, " That man knocked me down in the mud, and I had done nothing to him." In consequence a number of persons soon collected, who insulted the gentleman very much, and he would certainly have been roughly handled, had he not given the boy something as a recompence; he then called a coach, declaring he could not walk the streets of London in safety.

Those who know what mischief has arisen from very trifling causes, will, of course, perceive the necessity of checking this growing evil; for this man went away with very unfavourable impressions concerning our country, and would, no doubt, prejudice his countrymen against us, and make them suppose we are worse than we are.

Nearly allied to this is, " Pray remember poor Guy Faux;" which not only teaches children the art of begging, but is frequently the means of their becoming dishonest, for I have known children break down fences, and water-spouts, and, in short, any thing that they could lay their hands upon, in order to make a bonfire, to the great danger of the inhabitants near it, without producing one good effect; yet how easily might this practice be put down. The ill effects of it are so self-evident, that there can be no need for enlarging upon it.

I also disapprove of children going about beg-

ging at Christmas; this practice is calculated to
instil into the children's minds a principle of
meanness not becoming the English character,
and the money they get, seldom, if ever, does
them any good. If persons choose to give children any thing at this time of the year, there can
be no objection to it, but I dislike children going
about to ask for money like common beggars;
it cannot be proper, and should be generally dis-
countenanced. All these things, to many men,
may appear trifling, but to me they are of consequence; for if we mean to improve the general
character of the labouring population, there is
nothing like beginning in time; and we should,
amongst other things, get rid of these mean and
improper customs.

E

CHAPTER III.

THE REMEDY PROPOSED — EDUCATION OF
THE POOR.

" Prevention is better than cure."

An Old Adage.

HAVING brought the nature and prevalency of
juvenile delinquency immediately before the eyes
of my readers, by various examples, in the first
chapter, and in the second exhibited a few of the
causes of its prevalency, I shall now proceed to
point out what in my humble opinion appears
to be the only efficient remedy, namely, the education of the infant poor. It may not be amiss,
however, to glance at the means which have heretofore been resorted to, and found, if not altogether useless, at least inefficient for the end sought
to be attained.

As a preventitive, I may notice the numerous
National and Sunday Schools, Tract Societies,
&c. established throughout the kingdom. These
have doubtless much good effect, and deserve the
zealous support of every one who has at heart
the welfare of society in general, and the improvement of the labouring classes in particular. Many

have been plucked, " as brands from the burning," by these institutions, and have blessed on their dying beds the happy hour when they first entered the portals of a Sunday School; they are a blessing to the objects of their benevolence and a honor to their conductors and supporters. That they are not wholly efficient, in conjunction with other institutions, to effect the purpose desired, is to be attributed in one case, to the small portion of time in which their salutary influence is exerted; and, in the other, to their not admitting children at a sufficiently early age. At the period usually assigned for their admission into these schools, they have not only acquired many evil habits, but their affections have become so thoroughly perverted, as to offer insuperable obstacles to the corrective efforts of their teachers. Each child brings into the school some portion of acquired evil, making, when united, a formidable aggregate, and affording every facility for mutual contamination ; add to this, in the case of Sunday Schools, the counteracting effect which the bad examples they meet with in the course of six days, must have upon the good they hear on the seventh. I do not say this to dishearten those who are engaged in this labour of love, or to abate the zeal of its promoters. At the same time that their experience confirms the truth of my observations—and I know they would candidly confess that it does so—they must have many gratifying instances of a contrary nature, in children, who from evil habits have been won to a love of goodness and of religion, shewn not merely in a punctual attendance to their school, but in that goodwill toward their fellow-scholars, and grateful love to their teachers, which are the only infallible signs of a change in the affections. These things encourage them, in spite of many difficulties and mortifications, to persevere in well doing; and may the God of love bless their labours with an increase of fruitfulness! It is only my purpose here to state, that the most likely human means to produce such an increase, is the establishment of Infant Schools;—schools designed, particularly, for the cultivation of the affections,—for preparing the heart to receive that wisdom whose ultimate is to worship God in spirit and in truth, and to love our neighbour as ourselves. With respect to the system of instruction pursued in Sunday Schools, as well as other free schools, it is, indeed, my opinion, that some alteration for the better might be made in it, but as I intend to speak of this matter in a future place, I shall say no more on the subject at present, but pass on to the notice of prison discipline—which is, I fear, entitled to any term but that of a *remedy*.

That the end of punishment should be the prevention of future crime, rather than the gratification of vindictive feelings,—whether those of states or of injured individuals — a few will venture to deny; yet how little calculated is the punishment usually inflicted on young offenders in this country, to answer that end! They are shut up in a prison, in company with other thieves, perhaps older and more experienced than themselves, and all that was wanting to complete their education in dishonesty is here attained. Previously to their confinement within the walls of one of these places, in spite of the assertions of their hardened associates, that it was nothing to fear, it is probable, a sort of dread or apprehension hung over their minds; the last vestige of shame had not been banished from their minds by a public appearance as criminals—and this dread, this shame, properly taken advantage of, might have made their reformation possible! But, having encountered the object of their fears, and endured the shame of a trial—shame and fear are alike gone for ever; and when once they find their way into those sinks of iniquity, there is very little hope of amendment. From that period a prison has not the least terror to them. Being a place of idleness, it calls forth the evil inclinations of its inmates, and as they have opportunities of indulging those inclinations, it loses all its utility. I heard a boy who had been confined in Newgate, say, that he did not care any thing about it; that his companions supplied him with plenty of victuals, that there was some good fun to be seen there, and that most likely he should soon be there again; which proved too true, for he was shortly after taken up again for stealing two pieces of printed calico, and transported. This will shew that there are few who do not become more depraved, and leave that place worse than when they entered it. A gentleman who visited Newgate told me that he had been very much surprised at finding so many children there; some of whom were ironed; and on his inquiring the cause of so much severity towards children so young, he was told by one of the turnkeys, that it might appear severe, but he could assure the gentleman that he had much more trouble with them than he had with old offenders. This is by no means improbable, for the impressions which had been made upon those children had formed, as it were, a part of their very lives, and being probably the first were the strongest, and sooner than

part with them, they would almost part with life
itself.

To the bad habits of a prison and the association with guilt, must be added the deplorable,
unprovided state, in which, at the termination of
the period of imprisonment, they are again turned
out into society. What friends have they but
their former companions? What habitations, but
their former resorts of iniquity? What means of
procuring a livelihood, but their former evil practices? We accordingly find, that it is not unfrequently the case, with these young offenders,
that scarcely a day elapses after their liberation,
before they find themselves again in custody, and
within the walls of a prison. One cannot indeed
view the exertions made by the Society for the
improvement of prison discipline in this respect,
without feelings of gratitude to those who take
an active part in it*; neither should we forget to

* I will make a short extract from one of the reports of
this society, to shew that the chief end they have in view, is
the prevention of crime. They state, that " in the course
of their visits to the gaols in the metropolis, the Committee
very frequently meet with destitute boys, who, on their discharge from confinement, literally know not where to lay
their heads. To assist such friendless outcasts has been the
practice of the society; and to render this relief more effi-
cacious, a temporary refuge has been established for such as
are disposed to abandon their vicious courses. This asylum
has been instrumental in affording assistance to a considerable
number of distressed youths, who, but for this seasonable
aid, must have resorted to criminal practices for support.
On admission into this establishment, the boys are instructed
in moral and religious duty, subjected to habits of order and
industry, and after a time are placed in situations which
afford a reasonable prospect of their becoming honest and
useful members of society. To extend these objects, and to
render its exertions more widely beneficial, the society so-
licits the aid of public benevolence. Its expenses are una-

return thanks to the Author of all good, that he should have strengthened the hearts of persons to venture even their lives, to improve the condition of the prisoners in Newgate and elsewhere;—that even females are found, who, conquering the timidity, and foregoing the diffidence of their sex, have visited these abodes of vice and misery, for the purpose of ameliorating the miseries of their inhabitants. There have been men, claiming to be considered wise men, who have ridiculed the exertions of these daughters of philanthropy, and have made them a subject for " the fool-born jest;" but, happily, the votaries of benevolence are impervious to the shafts of folly; are as heedless of the unjust censures, as they are undesirous of the applause of man. Their aim is, the good of their fellow-creatures,—their reward, the pleasure of doing good, and the approbation of Him who is goodness itself. That their well-meant and praiseworthy exertions are not more successful can only be accounted for by the depravation of affections which habitual vice produces; when every principle of action, which should be subservient to virtue becomes actively employed in the cause of wickedness; for, whatever may be the impulse which first induces offenders to do wrong, in course of time they become so totally lost to all sense of right as to " glory in their shame." Whether it may be possible to devise any plan of prison discipline sufficient to remedy the evil, I cannot

---

voidably serious, and its funds are at present very low; but it is trusted that pecuniary support will not be withheld, when it is considered, that on the liberality with which this appeal is answered, depends in a great measure the success of the society's objects—the reformation of the vicious, and the prevention of crime."

pretend to say; and I shall only repeat the burthen of my song—*educate and protect the infant poor;* and it will be found that *to prevent* is not only better, but easier, than *to cure.*

That this remedy is effectual, experience has taught me and many others; and experience is a guide on whom we may safely rely. It has shewn me that by taking children at an early age out of the reach of contamination in the streets, and removing them in a great measure from the no less baneful influence of evil example at home, we may lay such a foundation of virtue, as can never be shaken. Nor do I think it difficult to shew the reason of this. It is confessed on all hands that our first impressions are the most powerful ones, both as to their immediate effects and future influence; that they not only form the character of our childhood but of our maturer years. As the mind of a child expands, it searches for new objects or employment to gratify that mind; and this is the time when they fall an easy prey to those who make a business of entrapping them into the paths of dishonesty, and from that to crimes of a deeper die. What, then, but a most salutary result can ensue from placing a child in a situation, where its first impressions will be those of the beauty of goodness,—where its first feelings of happiness will consist in the receiving and imparting kindness to its little neighbours. In after years, and in schools for children of maturer age, it is reckoned an unavoidable evil, that they should be congregated together in numbers; not so in the infant school; it is there made use of as a medium for developing those kindly feelings, to one and all, which must conduce to individual and general comfort, not only in an infant school, but in society in general. It is not merely by instructing them in *maxims* of honest principles, that we seek to provide against the evil; but by the surer way of exciting that feeling of love toward each other—towards every one —which, when found in activity, must not only prevent dishonesty, but every other species of selfishness.

Consider the difference of the cases. In the one case we behold a child associated, in happy communion, with a society,—a little world—of its own age and feelings,—continually proving the possibility of giving and imparting happiness by receiving and exercising kindness to its companions —secured from every danger—supplied with a continual variety of amusement, which is at the same time instruction; and all this under the care of a master or mistress, acting the part, not of a petulant school-dame, or a stern pedagogue, but of a kind and judicious parent.

In the case of the child not thus befriended, we see it, either exposed to the dangerous associations of the street, or to the bad examples of its parents; to their unkindness and severity, or misguided indulgence; and presented, moreover, with every facility as well as every temptation to do wrong. Now, is there any wonder that, in the former case, kind, obedient, honest characters should be the result; and in the latter, such as we have, in our preceding examples, exhibited? — Reason tells us such a consequence is likely, and experience has shewn us that it really happens. I could enumerate a thousand cases of honest principle in the infants who have been under my care. I will notice but one or two circumstances illustrative of the matter. In many schools, there are fruit-trees planted in the play-ground, to which the children will not do the least injury, nor will they touch the fruit. Flowers in pots, such as geraniums, auriculas, and other plants, are placed in the middle of the play-ground, without the least danger of being injured; such is their respect to private property.

Another instance always particularly excited my notice amongst the children of the Quaker-street school. The children are permitted to bring their dinners with them, and there are boxes in the school to put them in. Every child in the school has access to these boxes, for they are never locked, and yet I never knew a child to lose his dinner, or any part thereof, notwith-standing many of the children, to my knowledge, had been kept extremely short of food. I have known an instance of a slice of bread and butter being left in the box for several weeks, by some child that could not eat it, but none of the other children would dare to touch it. I have found in the boxes two or three pieces of bread, as hard as possible, and as a proof that many were hungry, and that it did not remain there, because they could not eat it, but out of pure honesty, I have offered it to some of the children, and they have eaten it in that state. Cold potatoes, pieces of fat, &c. were not unacceptable to them when given; but sooner than take any thing without leave, they have actually let it spoil. These are facts which shew, that notwithstanding all the disadvantages to which poor children are ex-posed, their character may be so far formed as to produce the effects above described. " Would you take a piece of bread out of this box that did not belong to you?" said I to the children one day. "No, sir," replied a little girl of four years old.—"Why not?" "Because," said the child, "it would be thieving." "Well, but suppose no one saw you." Before I could speak another word, a number of the children answered, "God can see every thing that we do." "Yes," added another little boy, "if you steal a cherry, or a piece of pencil, it is wicked." "To be sure," added another, "it is wicked to steal any thing."

I cannot do better than introduce in this place the opinion of Mr. Serjeant Bosanquet, on the subject of the education of the infant poor. Some valuable hints, likewise, will be found in his remarks on prison discipline. It is an extract from a charge to the jury delivered at the Gloucester assizes for April, 1823. "Gentlemen, I have reason to believe that the offences for trial on this occasion are rather less than usual at this season, and, to whatever the diminution of crime may be ascribed, I cannot forbear earnestly to press upon your attention, a constant perseverance in two things, *which, above all others, are calculated to diminish crime*—the first, is an unremitted attention to the education of the children of the poor, and of all classes of society, in the principles of true morality and sound religion—the next is the constant and regular employment of such persons as may be sentenced to imprisonment, in such labour as may be adapted to their respective ages and conditions. I believe that these observations may be considered as quite superfluous in this county, and therefore I have taken the liberty of using the word perseverance, because I believe your attention is already strongly drawn to that subject, and it requires no exhortation of mine to induce your attention to it. I am not quite sure whether in the gaol for this city the same means are provided for the employment of those persons sentenced to terms of imprisonment, which are provided in the gaol for the county. The magistrates for the city are equally desirous of promoting the education of all the poor under their care, I have no doubt; and I do hope and trust, if the means of labour have not been provided in their gaol, that no time will be lost in providing those means by which imprisonment may be made a real punishment, by which offenders may be reformed during their imprisonment, and by which the idle and dissolute may be prevented from any inclination to return there."

I have hitherto only been considering the *prudential* motives which should induce us to promote the education of the poor. I have shewn, that it will be for the benefit of society, inasmuch as it is likely to decrease the number of those who transgress its laws—that it will prove a greater security to our persons and property than laws or prisons afford. But, there are other motives, which, if these selfish ones were wholly wanting, might be sufficient to advocate, in every humane heart, the same course of conduct. If the duty of promoting honesty amongst the labouring classes did not exist, that of increasing happiness and piety amongst them would not be the less imperative. That there is much room for an increase of both, few, I think, will be inclined to deny; the less so as they have had the greater opportunity of ascertaining their condition. Let us only for a few moments reflect how great a blessing an Infant School is, even

when considered as a mere asylum, to take care
of the child's bodily welfare.

I have mentioned before, that the poor are
unable to take that care of their children which
their tender age requires, on account of their
occupations, and have shewn, that it is almost
certain, that the children of such persons will
learn every species of vice. But there are other
kinds of dangers which more immediately affect
the body, and are the cause of more accidents
than people in general imagine. I shall here notice some of the most prominent, and hope to be
able to convince the unprejudiced mind, that it
would be a charity to take charge of the infant
poor, and thus preserve them from falling into
those dangers, even leaving the idea of their
learning any thing good at school entirely out of
the question; and surely those persons, who disapprove of educating the poor at all, will see the
propriety of keeping, if possible, their children
safe from those casualties, and saving the lives of
many little ones, who would otherwise be lost to
their country by the many accidents that are likely
to occur.

It is well known that many poor people are
obliged to live in garrets, three or four stories
high, with a family of six or seven children; and
it will not appear improbable that when the children are left by themselves, they should frequently meet with accidents by tumbling down
stairs; some breaking their backs, others their
legs or arms; and to this cause alone, perhaps,
may be traced a vast number of the cripples that
daily appear as mendicants in our streets. When
the poor parents return from their daily labour,

F

they sometimes have the mortification of finding
that one, or probably two, of their children, are
gone to an hospital; which of course makes them
unhappy, and unfits them for going through their
daily labour. This dead weight, which is continually on the minds of the parents, is frequently the cause of their being unable to please
their employers, and the consequence sometimes
is, they are thrown out of work altogether;
whereas, if they were certain that their children
were taken care of, they would proceed with their
daily labour cheerfully, and be enabled to give
more satisfaction to their employers than they
otherwise can do.

Other parents I have known, who, when obliged
to go out, have locked their children in a room
to prevent them from getting into the street, or
falling down stairs, and who have taken every
precaution, as they imagined, to protect their
children; but the little creatures, perhaps, after
fretting and crying for hours at being thus confined, have ventured to get up to the window,
in order to see what was passing in the streets,
and to gratify their little minds, when one, over-
reaching itself, has fallen into the street, and
been killed on the spot. Numerous cases of this
kind are to be found in the public papers, and
hundreds of such accidents occur which are not
noticed in the papers at all. Many children,
again, are burnt to death or run over for want
of proper care; whilst others strolling into the
fields, fall into ponds and ditches and are
drowned. In short, so many are the dangers
which surround the infant poor, that it becomes
a public concern, and speaks to the hearts of the
pious and humane, and calls loudly on them to

unite their efforts to rescue this hitherto neglected part of the rising generation from the perils
to which they are exposed.

It is much to be regretted that those persons
who most need employ, should be the last to
procure it, but such is the fact, for there are so
many obstacles thrown in the way of married
persons, and especially those with a family, that
many are tempted to deny that they have any
children, for fear they should lose their situation,
though it is certainly an additional stimulus to a
servant to behave orderly, when he knows that he
has a family to look to him for support.

I cannot but admire the noble method which
has been adopted by that eminent philanthropist,
Mr. Owen*, who, instead of throwing obstacles
in the way of *his people*, does all he can to make
them happy; he not only finds employment for
the parents, but likewise persons to take care of
their children, for which purpose suitable buildings have been erected, and all other conveniences
supplied for their improvement, thus training
them to become useful members of society.

Shall I close this appeal for the necessity of
educating the infant poor by another and weightier
plea? They are immortal and responsible beings.
It may be thought that I should have given this
plea the precedence of every other. I did not,
because, I felt more anxious to make good my
cause with the prudent and the philanthropic—to

* Whatever may be thought of the theoretical and religious opinions of this gentleman—and I must here candidly
express my dissent from them—no one can do otherwise
than admire his practical benevolence; it is to be wished
that every one, according to his means, would " go and do
likewise."

shew them that self-interest and humanity demand our exertions in this cause. I knew that when I came to urge my cause upon the attention of the Christian I could not possibly fail. No one who is a sincere follower of Him who said " Suffer little children to come unto me, and forbid them not, for of such is the kingdom ;" no one who professes to abide by the maxims of Him whose commandment was, " Love thy neighbour as thyself," can turn a deaf ear to the entreaties of humanity. Thousands there are among those of whom we have been speaking, who are brought up in as great ignorance of God and religion, as though they had been born in a country where the light of Revelation had never shone—where the glad tidings of salvation had never been pro-claimed. With continual examples of evil before their eyes, both at home and abroad, we see and hear its consequences daily, in the wickedness with which our streets abound, and in the lisped blasphemy and profanity of those who learn to curse and swear before they can well walk.

Any person who has been accustomed to walk the streets of London, must have heard how con-tinually children take the name of the Almighty in vain; seldom or ever mentioning his most holy name, but to confirm some oath. I have seen boys playing at marbles, tops, and other games, who on a dispute arising about some frivolous thing, call upon the Supreme Being to strike them deaf, dumb, or blind, nay even dead, if what they said were not true, when nevertheless I have been satisfied from having seen the origin of their dispute, that the party using the expres-sions has been telling a falsehood; indeed so com-mon is this kind of language in the streets, that

few persons notice it. I am inclined to think,
that children accustomed to use such expressions
on every trifling occasion, will, when they grow
to riper years, pay very little respect to the sanc-
tity of an oath. It is, perhaps, one of the reasons
why we hear of so much perjury in the present
day. At all events, little children cannot avoid
hearing such expressions, not only from those who
are rather older than themselves, but, I am sorry
to say, even from their parents. I have known
repeated instances of this kind. Many little children, when they first come to our schools, make
use of dreadful expressions, and when told that it
is wrong, will say that they did not know it was
any harm; others, with the greatest simplicity,
have told me, that they had heard their fathers or
mothers say the same words. I have had much
difficulty in persuading some children that it was
wrong, for they very naturally thought, that if
their parents made use of such expressions, they
might do the same. Hence the necessity of good
example; and did parents generally consider how
apt children are to receive impressions, and to
copy them, both in their words and actions, they
would be more cautious than they are. There are
many parents who make use of very bad expressions themselves, that would correct their
children for using the same; as a proof of this,
I will mention one circumstance, out of many
others, that took place in the Quaker-Street
school. We had a little girl in the school, five
years old, who was so fond of the school, that
she frequently stopped after school-hours to play
with my children, and some others who chose to
stay in the play-ground; many of them would
stop till eight or nine o'clock at night, to which

I had no objection, provided their parents approved of it, and they did not get into mischief, it being desirable to keep them out of the streets as much as possible. It happened that some of the children, one day offended this child, and she called them by dreadful names, such as I cannot repeat here; of course, the other children were terrified at the expressions, and told me of them immediately. I was soon satisfied, that the child was ignorant of the meaning of what she said, for, as an excuse for her conduct, she told me that she heard her father and mother say the same words. I told the child, that notwithstanding her parents might have made use of such words, it was wrong and very wicked, and that I could not let her stay another time to play, if she ever again made use of them. Having sent for the mother, I informed her of the expressions the child had used, but did not tell her what she had mentioned relative to her parents, for if I had, she would have beaten the child most unmercifully. The mother, after having heard me relate the circumstance, immediately flew into a violent passion with the child, and declared, that she would " skin her alive," (this was her expression,) and I had much difficulty to restrain her from correcting the child in the school. Having pacified her a little, I inquired where the child could have heard such wicked expressions. She said she could not tell. I then told her, I hoped the child did not learn them of her, or her father. To this she made no answer, but I could perceive that she stood self-convicted, and having said what I conceived necessary upon the occasion, I dismissed her, observing that it was useless for ladies and gentlemen to establish

schools for the education of the infant poor, if
the parents did not assist by setting them a good
example.

I am happy to state, that the advice I gave her
was not thrown away, as I have never known the
child guilty of saying a bad word since; and the
mother soon brought me another child, of two
years and a half old, and said she should be very
glad if I would take it in the school, and that
she wished a blessing might always attend the
gentlemen who supported the institution. She
also requested me to take an opportunity of
speaking a word or two to her husband, for she
was thankful for what had been said to her.
And here I would observe, that although it is
most undoubtedly true, that the good children
are taught in our Infant Schools, is greatly
counteracted by the conduct and discourse they
witness on their return home, yet we occasionally
see, that these little children, by the blessing of
God, are made the means of reforming their own
parents. What a gratifying fact it is, to think
of the adult and hardened sinner, turned from
his evil ways—from death unto life—by an infant's example.

Nor is it only in profane expressions that we
see the effect of evil examples. Some children I
have known, in the same neighbourhood, who
even beat their parents. There was a poor
widow, very near the school, who was frequently
to be seen with her face dreadfully bruised by
blows from her own son; he had been taken
before a magistrate, and imprisoned for three
months, but it did him no good, for he afterwards beat his mother as much as ever, and the
poor woman had it in contemplation to get the

miscreant sent out of the country. One Sunday, I remember to have seen a boy, under twelve years of age, take up a large stone to throw at his mother; the boy had done something wrong in the house, and the mother followed him into the street with a small cane, to correct him for it, but he told his mother, that if she dared to approach him, he would knock her down. The mother retired, and the boy went where he pleased. These, and many such scenes, I have frequently witnessed, and I am afraid, that many such characters have been so completely formed, as to be past reformation. So essential is it, to embrace the first opportunity of impressing on the infant mind, the principles of duty and virtue.

I am aware that many excellent institutions are in existence for the spread of the gospel amongst the ignorant and depraved, at home as well as abroad, but I must here again advert to the readier reception of religious truths in infancy, than by the confirmed adult sinner. I would not say to those who are engaged in the painful task—painful because so often profitless —forego your labours; but I would call upon all who have at heart the everlasting welfare of human souls, to exert themselves, that the rising generation may not likewise grow up into that state of perverseness—that they may not in future years prove themselves to be a generation, which " like the adder, turneth a deaf ear to the charmer, charm he ever so wisely." I am satisfied, from the experience I have had, that if the seeds of piety and virtue are sown early in the infant mind, they will mature and ripen, and finally triumph over vice and immorality.

It was a Christian-like wish expressed by his

late majesty, that every one in his dominions should be able to read the bible; and from the increased facility of gratuitous education, the number of those who cannot is much less than formerly; but in many cases the necessitous circumstances of the parents prevent them from allowing their children, except during their infant years, the advantage of instruction, even though it cost nothing. The time for the children of the poor to receive instruction, is between the ages of two and eight; after that period many are sent out to work, or detained at home, for they then become useful to their parents, and cannot be sent to school. There are many little girls who, having left the infant school, go out to work for a shilling a week, and the mothers have declared to me, when I have endeavoured to persuade them to send them to the National School, for at least one year, that they could not do it, for they were so poor, that every shilling was a great help; they have, however, promised me that they would send them to a Sunday School. This may account, in some measure, for there being so many more boys than girls, in almost every school in London, and shews the great good that has been done by Sunday Schools.*

* It is to be observed here, that the children do not come to our school on Sundays, but many of them between five and six years old, who have brothers or sisters in the National School, go with them to church, and others of the same age go to a Sunday School in the neighbourhood. In short, I may venture to say, that almost all the children that are able go either to a Sunday School, or to church; but to take them all in a body, at the early age that they are admitted into an Infant School, to any place of worship, and to keep them there for two or three hours, so as to profit them, and not to disturb the congregation, is, according to my view, impracticable.

Many of my readers, who have been in the habit of noticing and pitying the poor, may think the detail into which I have entered superfluous, but I can assure them the want of information on the subject is but too general, and is sufficient to account for the indifference which has so long been exhibited on the subject. So far, indeed, are the views I have taken from being universal, that I think it necessary before closing the present chapter, to notice a few of the objections which have been advanced against the education of the offspring of the labouring classes.

The objection, that education is altogether improper for poor people is not quite obsolete. There are not wanting persons who still entertain the most dreadful apprehensions of the " *march of intellect*," as it has been termed; who see no alternative but that it must overturn every thing that is established, and subvert the whole order of society. I would willingly impart comfort to the minds of those who are afflicted with such nervous tremours, but I fear, if the demonstration of experience has not quieted them, the voice of reason never will. It cannot fail to remind us of the apprehensions of the popish clergy in former times, who decried the art of printing, then recently introduced, as a branch of the *black art*, which, if encouraged, must eventually demolish the social fabric, and introduce civil wars and discord into every country. Time, that test of truth, has shewn us how groundless their apprehensions were. Instead of injuring that fabric, it has strengthened its foundation, so that it cannot be shaken and has surrounded it with defences, which bid defiance to assault. It is possible, how-

ever, that in the case of our monkish progenitors,
their pretended fears for the safety of society,
were really fears for the safety of superstition; in
short it was, I suspect, in their case, fear arising
from foresight. Education and enlightenment in
any and every form, are certainly inimical to
error of all kinds; and if there be any thing which
can only flourish in the shades of ignorance, we
need not be long at a loss to guess its character.
But surely, such is not the state of things in our
day, and in our country. Those who suppose
that insubordination,—a dissatisfaction with every
thing short of universal equality,—will be the result
of imparting knowledge to the working classes,
form, in my humble opinion, very strange and
erroneous notions of the origin and foundation of
the social compact; which, according to my view
of the subject, is to be found in the wise decree of
Providence, that we should be mutually dependent
for comfort on each other. Ignorant men may
not be able to see it in this light—may wonder
why stations of servitude should fall to the lot of
one man, and rank and ease to another — and
seeing no need for it, may repine, and murmur,
and rebel against such a state of things,—but
this better-informed man will see why these things
are,—he will see that he is not precluded from
emulation, and from striving to ascend in the
grade of society ; more than this, he will learn
that *happiness* is of no particular rank or station;
that the real comforts of life are more equally
distributed than the ignorant suppose; and if, in
his acquirements, his faculties have been directed
rightly, he will have felt the possibility, " having
food and raiment," to " be therewith content."

Education is thus as productive of benefit to the
rich as of comfort to the poor.*

I have heard persons assert that since the establishment of so many schools in the country,
they could not keep a servant; that many servants

* The following excellent observations on this subject
appeared in the Morning Chronicle the day after the meeting
at Freemasons' Hall, for the establishment of the Infant
School Society, an account of which will be found in the next
chapter. " We lately enjoyed the pleasure of seeing the
Infant School established by Mr. Wilson, in Quaker Street,
Spitalfields, at which nearly two hundred children were
attended to, all of them happy and contented.

" It was truly observed by many of the speakers at the
meeting, that in this great metropolis there is a large class of
the population unable to attend to their children, so that the
Infant Schools do not withdraw children from the care of
their parents, but withdraw them from the streets of this
crowded metropolis, where they are exposed to every vice,
and where they become a prey to veterans in iniquity.

" A conviction seems to be fast gaining ground in this
country, that the well-being of the labouring classes is
essential to the security of the rich. We trust this is a
subject on which there will soon be little diversity of opinion.
To those who think that the ignorance and wretchedness of
the poor is a desirable state of things, we would say—read
the accounts we this day give from Spain, and look to Ireland.
Read the evidence of Mr. Blacke, and the other magistrates
examined by the select committee on the districts of Ireland
under the Insurrection act :

" ' Some gentlemen's houses are dark almost all day ; all
the houses were barricadoed in some part of the house ; the
barricadoes being necessarily of a heavy description, it is
inconvenient to move them ; in some houses they had but
one sitting-room in the house, where the light was admissible
at all in the day time, and not all the windows even of that
room ; the barricadoes, which were bullet proof, were of
course of a considerable thickness.'

" Such are the fruits of ignorance and oppression. It is
wisely ordained that we are all interested in the well-being of
each other."

idled away their time, in reading novels, instead
of attending to their business, and have become so
high-minded, that they can scarcely be spoken to,
in consequence they condemn the system of educating the lower orders on this account. But it
appears to me that a man might as well condemn
eating and drinking, because there are persons to
be found who abuse the former by making glut-
tons of themselves, and the latter by getting in-
toxicated. Besides, the principle in itself is such
a selfish one, that it surprises me how any person
should encourage it for a moment. Is it just, that
because a person is poor, he should be deprived
of all the means of obtaining knowledge? If, indeed, talent were confined exclusively to those in
a high sphere of life, there might be some reason
for advocating the cause of ignorance : but it
must be admitted that many persons of the meanest
extraction, and in different countries, have become
men of eminence, by having an opportunity given
them for the developement of their talents and
abilities, which otherwise would have been lost to
themselves and their country. But it still remains
to be proved that ignorant servants are the best;
and until that is done, I trust there will always
be found persons, who will advocate the cause of
the uneducated poor.

A child cannot gain too much experimental
knowledge in the first eight or ten years of its
life, to render it unfit for a state of servitude. If
the Christian spirit be generated in an influential
manner during the early period of existence, it is
impossible that the knowledge therewith acquired
can indispose the mind to a subjection to authority,
or create an unwillingness toward useful labour.
One of the first duties of Christianity, is to do our
duty in that state of life to which it has pleased

God to call us. It is the ignorance or disbelief of this dispensation of providence which is the source of so many evils in the social system. A thorough impression of its truth, will restore order where it has been violated. The poor, as we have before said, will become more satisfied with their condition, because it is of God's appointment, and because they perceive something beyond the mere gratification of their animal nature to take delight in, and the rich, being excited to greater mental exertion, will rise in the scale of morality in the same proportion. Thus will mutual good feeling, which is the bond of union in society, subsist among all ranks—each rendering to each that respect which is due to their station in life.

So far are our trans-atlantic friends from thinking education detrimental to the well-being of society, that, I am informed, in some of the states of America there is a law to compel parents to send their children to schools, which are accordingly provided by the government, and that this is considered as no hardship by the inhabitants, but rather as a blessing.* This law, however, does not take effect until the children are eight years of age; how far such a law would be advisable in this country, I will not pretend to say; but if crimes in the two countries be compared together, it will be found that it is three to one against us.

Much good must result from the establishment of Infant Schools in Ireland; ignorance and idle-

* I was informed by the same gentleman, who is an inhabitant of one of the States, that this plan answers so well, and the people so generally approve of it, that the schools have become very rich, by persons leaving them property, and that they had more money than they knew what to do with in that channel; it is to be hoped that when they hear of infant schools being approved of in this country, they will soon find another channel for the overplus money.

ness are frequently found together, and are the promoters of every sort of evil. It is well known that the lower classes of the Irish people have been much neglected in their education, and I think we may in this manner account for many peculiarities of their character and conduct. If individual or local observation were insufficient to convince us of the futility of all that is advanced against education, we could not do better than refer to those two great national instances of the respective effects of neglecting the poor and in-structing them—Ireland and Scotland. At a meet-ing of a society for promoting education in the latter country, held a few years since, it was ob-served by a gentleman, that the effects of educa-tion were to be plainly seen in the peaceable conduct of the poor in Scotland. About a century ago, he said, they were in the same ignorant and depraved condition as that in which the lower classes of Ireland are now. The only remedy for the evil in Ireland was in spreading education amongst them. He had been in three quarters of the globe, and he never was on a spot where he did not find a Scotchman established; and always in a situation of trust.

Whilst speaking of the extended benefits which infant education is capable of producing, I would humbly suggest its applicability to the missionary system. It would secure to the missionaries the hearts of the rising generation, and make them amends for the mortification they frequently endure from the obduracy and impenitence of the adult heathen. Nor could any better plan be devised in my opinion for the improvement and comfort of the slaves in the West Indies, and others of his ma-jesty's colonies. The children of the slaves should be taught to enjoy moral delights, and instructed with as great care as our own children. This would produce a great change for the better; accompanied with this recommendation, that it would be gradual, and therefore free from the dangers attendant upon all sudden changes. Early good impressions, made in the minds of the sable sons of Africa, would be likely to prove not only of benefit to them, but to ourselves, inasmuch as it would add to the tie of power, the more lasting bond of gratitude.

Having answered, I trust, satisfactorily, the objections to the education of the poor, on the ground of its producing idleness, and likewise in a former place shewn, the duty of taking care of those children whose parents cannot or will not take care of them, I shall, in conclusion notice another objection which has been made, and strange to say, has been allowed much weight, namely, that by taking the children from their parents at so early an age, we estrange their affections from them. I cannot do better than give it refutation in the following anecdote.

The Rev. W. Wilson, vicar of Walthamstow, Essex, has a very excellent Infant School at that place. Having often heard the above objection made, he felt inclined to try whether it had any foundation, and accordingly made the experiment with one of the mothers who resided the farthest from the school; and it should be observed that some of the children came at least a mile and a half. One of the mothers had brought her children to the school, on a very wet morning, this distance, and brought their dinners with them, as she was accustomed to do, when Mr. Wilson addressed her, nearly as follows. It is a very wet morning. *A.* Yes, sir. It is a long way for

you to bring your children this wet morning.
A. Yes, sir, it is, but I do not mind that.—They
are a long time away from you, and perhaps you
do not love them so well as you did when they
were always at home with you. *A.* O, sir, you
are very much mistaken, for I love them better
than ever.—I thought it possible, (replied Mr. W.)
that you might not like them so well. *A.* O dear,
sir, like them so well, (replied the mother,) who
can help liking them? and, taking one of them
up in her arms, she kissed it, and said—I find, sir,
that absence creates love; for, being away from
me all day, I like to hear their little prattle at
night; and they are so full of what they have
heard and seen at school, that it becomes quite
entertaining.

From this we see that the objection commonly
raised is without the least foundation; but to place
the matter beyond all doubt, I was informed by
the same gentleman, that he had an idea of establishing a school at the other end of the town,
for the convenience of those who lived so far; but
the parents of the children begged him not to do
it; stating that they were very well satisfied with
the present school. One woman even said that
she hoped if Mr. W. opened a school next door,
he would permit her to take her children to the
old school; adding, that she was very well satisfied with the school, and that she did not wish
to remove her children on any account whatever.*

---

* I afterwards learnt that this same child, during some
heavy floods, came up to his knees in water, to the school,
and there dried his shoes and stockings; and further, that he
engaged in teaching five children, after school hours, who
could not come to the school. The child in question was
only five years of age.

I am quite satisfied, that if the persons who make these objections would visit the institutions, and make themselves acquainted with the facts that are to be there obtained, they would soon see abundant reason to alter their opinion; and, instead of appearing in the character of objectors, they would become cordial promoters of the plan; for it must be admitted, that no persons can be in a situation to judge of the merits of a thing which they have never seen, and consequently can know nothing at all about. Many persons of the latter class have acknowledged their mistake in plain terms to me, and have confessed how much surprised they have been on witnessing the good effects of the plan.

Every thing that can be urged in behalf of other charitable educational institutions, may be brought forward in behalf of Infant Schools, with this additional recommendation, that they are likely to be more effectual than all others,—inasmuch as they begin earlier, and are therefore more particularly calculated to establish a love of virtue in the souls of the rising generation. I do hope that all who have it in their power will assist in their support and more general establishment. To the ladies of Great Britain I most earnestly and particularly would address my plea on behalf of the infant poor, and I am sure I shall not plead in vain. Ever ready to listen to the cry of the needy and afflicted; when that cry is uttered in the lisping tones of infancy,—they will not, they cannot, turn an indifferent or a deaf ear to its supplication.

CHAPTER IV.

SOME ACCOUNT OF THE ESTABLISHMENT OF INFANT SCHOOLS, AND OF THE INFANT SCHOOL SOCIETY.

"It is not with the experiences of yesterday we come armed to the contest; it is not a speculation that we bring forward to your notice, but an experiment."—BROUGHAM.

I SHALL now proceed to lay before my readers some account of the origin of Infant Schools, and of the society instituted to promote their establishment. The first idea of an Infant School was suggested by the asylums provided by Mr. Owen of New Lanark, for the infant children of the adult part of the population. That they might not be an hindrance to the daily labours of their parents, they were put under the charge of several women, and the whole under the superintendance of one man, Mr. Buchanan. Instead of wandering about the streets unprotected, liable to accidents, or to form bad associations, these children were observed to be taken care of, and made happy; amusement and exercise for them were not forgotten, and they were frequently seen dancing and capering about to the sound of a flute. These asylums for the infant

poor were seen to be so beneficial, that it suggested the propriety of establishing similar institutions in this country. Accordingly, Mr. Buchanan was engaged, and came over from New
Lanark, and a school was opened under his
management on Brewer's Green, Westminster.
The gentlemen who established the above school
were the following:—Henry Brougham, Esq.
M. P.; James Mill, Esq.; John Smith, Esq.
M. P.; the Marquis of Lansdowne; Zaca-
riah Macauly, Esq.; Thomas Babington, Esq.;
Lord Dacre; Sir Thomas Baring; William
Leake, Esq. M. P.; Henry Hase, Esq,; Ben-
jamin Smith, Esq.; John Walker, Esq.; and
Joseph Wilson, Esq. The latter gentleman was
so convinced of the importance of Infant Schools,
that he soon afterwards established one at his
own expense, in Quaker Street, Spitalfields. He
built the school-room, and supplied every thing
that was necessary; and on the 24th of July,
1820, the school was opened. Twenty-six
children were admitted the first day; on the
next day twenty-one; on the 31st sixty-five;
and on the 7th of August thirty-eight; at which
last date I was engaged by Mr. Joseph Wilson
to undertake the management of it.

Thus situated, I commenced, and soon found
that I had a complete desert, as it were, to cultivate; for the children were mostly strangers to
each other, and few of them knew their letters.
The first thing that appeared necessary, was to
form the children into classes; which being done,
I endeavoured to select two children out of each
class to act as monitors; but finding that there
were not more than six children in the whole
school that knew their letters, it was impossible

to derive any assistance from them, in the way of teaching the others. The consequence was, I was obliged to take the children by one class at a time, and having supplied each child with a card, on which the alphabet was printed in large letters, I formed them into a square, and commenced by calling out A, and likewise desiring each child to point with his finger to the letter, which being done, the next letter was called, and so on, till the whole alphabet was repeated. By pursuing this plan, in course of time, I was enabled to find monitors who knew their letters, and by these means adopted a regular system, an account of which will be laid before the reader in the following pages.

Mr. Owen's institution, on the plan of which the school of Brewer's Green was established, was intended merely for an asylum, as I have before said; and therefore in making it subservient to purposes of moral and intellectual cultivation, I had all the difficulty of an original and untried scheme to encounter. That I had much difficulty in so doing I well know; how much success it is not for me to determine. Suffice it to say, with regard to the school in question, that the neighbourhood was in a short time perceptibly improved; and the school became so much respected amongst the poor, that we at length had 220 children in it, the whole of whom came unsolicited on our part; the parents applying of their own free-will to have their children admitted.

Attention now was drawn to the school, as having assumed a systematized method of instructing infants, and visitors from all parts flocked to see the pleasing novelty,—upwards of two hundred children, the whole under six years of age, receiving instruction, and displaying the most perfect order and happiness, though sepa- rated from their parents. All who came pro- fessed themselves not less surprised than gratified; and the consequence was, many other schools began now to be established in various parts. The Rev. W. Wilson, vicar of Walthamstow, Essex, brother to the gentleman above men- tioned, established one at Walthamstow, which exceeded the most sanguine expectations; and an excellent lady, Miss Neave, opened one in Palmer's Village, Westminster, for 160 children; there was also another infant school opened in Duncan Street, Liverpool, a very large one, by the Society of Friends, a people always foremost in doing good; and who, on this occa- sion, if I am rightly informed, collected amongst themselves, in one day, no less a sum than 1000*l.* They went on prospering and increasing at an amazing rate, especially after the formation of the London Infant School Society. How many there may be at present I cannot exactly enumerate; that they must be numerous will be apparent when I say, that since the establishment of the Society, (by whom I was engaged imme- diately on its formation) I have been continually employed in the organization of new schools in various parts of this kingdom, as well as in some parts of Ireland; and that I am now endeavour- ing to promote the establishment of similar schools in Scotland.

Having said thus much as to the origin of the Infant School system, as at present practised, I shall now call the attention of my readers to the formation of the Infant School Society; at a meeting held for that purpose. I need offer no apology for giving a report of the speeches delivered on that occasion. They contain the sentiments of men well qualified to judge upon the matter, and should not therefore be lost to the world.

The Meeting was held at Freemason's Hall, London, on the 1st of June, 1824.

The Marquess of *Lansdown*, in opening the Meeting, said, that he could not do better than state the object and circumstances which had given rise to these schools. A few years ago, it had been suggested to establish in Westminster an Infant School; and this had been followed by similar establishments in various parts of the country. The Schools, however, had completely succeeded, not only in the negative plan they had in view, of keeping the children out of vice and mischief, but even to the extent of engrafting in their minds at that early age those principles of virtue, which capacitated them for receiving a further stage of instruction at a more advanced school, and finally, as they approached manhood, to be ripened into the noblest sentiments of probity and integrity. An objection had been urged, and as he once thought, with great propriety, that, with regard to young children, the most beneficial education they could receive was a domestic one under the superintendence of kind and prudent parents; but upon maturely weighing this objection, it appeared to him that the option pending on the benefits of the Institution, was between some sort of education and no education at all; for it was evident to every body, that in this great town it was impossible for poor parents to give that attention to their children in their early years, which was the very period when they most especially required attention, and therefore far from doing harm by withdrawing these children from the superintendance of their parents, they were rather withdrawn from the streets of this crowded metropolis, where they were exposed to every vice, and which, by gradually maturing as they grow up, would finally lead them to the perpetration of the most atrocious and injurious crimes.   This Society,—acting upon the important truth, that where the seeds of vice might be sown, there might be introduced the seeds of good,—that where evil had taken root there virtue might be planted,—had the satisfaction already of seeing hundreds giving, as it were, security for their future good conduct, by the happiness and content which they at present exhibited, and presenting to the world a fair picture of a well-governed and promising society.

Mr. *Brougham.*—My Noble Friend has already stated the success that has attended these Schools, —has so distinctly remarked upon their advantages,—and encountered the objections that have been made to the system in so able a manner, that very few general observations are left for me to make; but there is one other objection which, as he has not noticed, I will here take upon me to mention—it has been urged by some that we are aiming at carrying education too far; that we are drawing it out to an extravagant length, and that, not satisfied with dispensing education to children who have attained what in former times was thought a proper age, we are now anxious to educate mere infants, incapable of receiving be-

nefit from such instruction. This objection may
be answered in two ways. In the first place, it
should be observed, that the objection comes from
those very persons who object to education being
given to children when they arrive at a more
advanced period, on the ground that their parents
then begin to find them useful in labour, and
consequently cannot spare so much of their time
as might be requisite : surely, then, the education
of the children should commence at that time
when their labour can be of no value to their
parents; but the other answer, in my opinion, is
still more decisive : it is found even at the early
age of seven or eight, that children are not void
of those propensities, which are the forerunners
of vice, and I can give no better illustration of
this, than the fact of a child only eight years old,
being convicted of a capital offence at our tri-
bunals of justice; when, therefore, I find that at
this early period of life, these habits of vice are
formed, it seems to me that we ought to begin
still earlier to store their minds with such tastes,
and to instruct them in such a manner, as to
exclude the admission of those practices that lead
to such early crime and depravity. My Noble
Friend has most justly stated, that it is not with
the experiences of yesterday that we come armed
to the contest : it is not a speculation that we
are bringing forward to your notice, but an experiment. It is now six years since an establishment was first commenced in Brewer-street,
Westminster, where success has always been attendant on our exertions. Though at first it was
nothing but an obscure establishment, where its
success was scrutinized before it was published,
its own merits have caused it to spread and be-

come known, as recommended by experience,
and it is with these feelings that we call with the
more confidence for the public support. In leaving poor children to the care of their parents
neglect is the least that happens; it too frequently occurs that they are turned over to
delegates, where they meet with the worst treatment; so that we do not in fact come so much
into contact with the parents themselves as with
these delegates, who are so utterly unfit for the
office they undertake. It is to carry the experiment further, that we now come before the
public, for the purpose of erecting a central model
school, where masters may be trained for the
purpose of supplying schools elsewhere, and I
hope that you will not separate without affording
such a testimony of your good-will towards this
excellent work, as will insure success to the in-
tentions of forming a central establishment, and
preparing masters. I beg leave to move—" That
this meeting is strongly impressed with a sense of
the many and great benefits, moral and political,
which may be expected to result from the general
establishment throughout the United Kingdom,
and especially in populous towns and villages, of
Infant Schools on the plan of those already formed in Vincent-square, Westminster; in Quaker-
street, Spitalfields; at Walthamstow, Bristol,
and various other places."

Mr. *Wilberforce* said, having witnessed the
happy effects produced by those schools in Westminster, he felt a warm zeal in support of such
institutions. They could not begin too soon to
impress religious principles on the minds of the
young: it was an affecting consideration, that
while great statesmen had been busied in their

closets on some fine scheme or speculation, they had neglected those salutary principles which the Almighty had given to mankind; it was remarkable how eagerly the young mind received the histories in the Bible, and how well they were fitted to work on their dispositions; and when he considered the miserable state of the poor, he could not but feel that the rich were, in some degree, the authors of it, in having neglected to afford them the means of education.

The Motion was then put by the Noble Chairman, and carried unanimously.

Mr. *Smith*, M. P., had agreed to the wish of the Committee, in proposing the second resolution, the object of which was to form a central model school, for training masters and mistresses to educate the children. The real fact was, that the character of all mankind was formed very early—much earlier than might be supposed: at the age of two or three years, dispositions were found in children of a description the most objectionable. In these schools the principles of mutual kindness and assistance were carried as far as could well be conceived, and it was most delightful to regard the conduct of the children towards each other. Instead of opposition, they displayed mutual good-will, inculcated to the greatest degree, so as to destroy in the minds of the children that selfishness which was the bane of our nature. Such effects appeared almost to realise the golden age, for the children appeared always happy, and never so happy as when attending the schools. The whole principle upon which this was conducted, was not fear, but love; from principle alone good could come. When the child was intimidated, its mind was cramped, and it was necessary to give it confidence, before its faculties could be called into action.   There was, consequently, a great difficulty in selecting proper persons to superintend these schools, and therefore the central school was proposed for the purpose of training the instructors into a right course, and teaching them the great secret of mingling patience with firmness, the only way of carrying those points which had gained the admiration of every person who had visited the schools.   The honourable gentleman concluded, by moving— " That for the purpose of extending the knowledge and promoting the adoption of this system, a society be now instituted under the designation of ' The Infant School Society;' the objects of which shall be to establish in some central part of the metropolis, an Institution which, while it dispenses to the adjoining population, may also serve as a model of imitation, and as a seminary for training and qualifying masters and mistresses to form and superintend schools."

Dr. *Thorpe*, in reading this resolution, hoped he might be allowed to trespass a few minutes as a minister of Him who had said, " Suffer little children to come unto me, and forbid them not."— With respect to the utility of these schools, he thought it must be acknowledged by all who cast their eyes on the crowded streets of this city. There could scarcely be a more pitiable sight than to see one infant trusted to the care of a child scarcely older than itself, and exposed to all the contagion of vice that hourly presented itself; and as every parent must be aware of this, he trusted that every parent whom he was now addressing would give this Institution their support. In the National Schools, the masters chiefly complained of the bad habits which they had to unteach—if he might use the expression—the child, before they could begin to teach him any thing, and it was this very mischief that this society proposed to remedy, should it be enabled by its funds so to do.

Sir *James Mackintosh* said, that it had fallen to his lot to have to propose a resolution, and he would begin by saying, that after the able speeches which had fallen from the gentlemen who had preceded him, there was, in fact, nothing left for him to say, but to appeal to their feelings. The claims of this Institution were of such a nature, that they required no recommendation but a full statement of them. The foundation of its happy results had been pointed out to exist in the principles of policy, and of religion paramount to all policy—a religion that appealed to every feeling of human nature. The resolution he was about to propose, including a subscription, he would begin by addressing that softer sex, whose fair persons were the depository of all the gentler affections, and who were the kind and delightful solacers of the human race, and requesting them to promote by their best interests the cause of these little innocent infants, on whom so much of the happiness of society in a great measure rested, as they formed the rising generation. To the gentlemen present he would recommend this charity, as one less attended with perplexity in its operations or doubt as to its utility, than many, which, though established with the best possible motives, frequently failed in effecting the good proposed; but in this the most acute opponent could not discover any mischief that would arise from its success. The objection that it did not do so much good as it was supposed, would sink into nothing before the good that it did accomplish; and where, he would again ask them, could be found a fitter object for benevolence? Money given to the poor might in some instances do harm, but when they were called upon to contribute to the kind temper and good principles of the rising members of society, he thought that none could withstand the plea. The hon. gentleman concluded by moving " That a subscription be now entered into for the purpose of accomplishing this object."

W. Allen, Esq. seconded the Resolution. He had already experienced the happy results produced by the education of the lower classes. By the plans recently acted upon, many thousands of individuals had been instructed, who would otherwise have been totally destitute of education. By that system many children, who had before been considered as a nuisance in the different towns and villages in which they resided, had been rendered useful and respectable members of society. It had been well observed, that in our large National Schools a great want was felt of that early instruction, both moral and religious, which was necessary to predispose the mind to profit by a more extended education. He agreed with his honourable friend, Mr. *John Smith*, that all systems of education should be founded on love and affection; first make a child love you, and then you may teach it what you please. He was attracted to this society particularly, in consequence of the liberal principles upon which they set out ; for he understood that while the morals and religion of the children were strictly attended to, no particular creed or catechism was to be forced upon them. With respect to the great principles of revealed religion, as set forth in the Holy Scriptures, they were all agreed. He felt with his venerable friend, Mr. *Wilberforce*, that the strength of every country depended upon a firm and deep-rooted religious feeling; without this basis all human plans of improvement must fall, and be swept away as a vision. Under the present system of educating young children, love and affection would be cherished, instead of that distant and repulsive feeling which children of different sects would imbibe if educated apart.

Lord *Calthorpe* said, he rose for the purpose of proposing a resolution, for the appointment of a Committee, to whom the management of the objects of the institution would be entrusted. He thought that this was a most meritorious and praiseworthy establishment, for it was of the very last importance that they should rescue the rising generation from the vice and depravity by which they were surrounded. He thought the present system totally in accordance with the dictates of nature. He remembered a passage in Paley, in speaking of children, which always struck him as containing great force and beauty, and was the more pleasing, as it gave the reader a strong idea of the mind of the man who wrote it. He says, " There is always some peculiarly bright spot on the surface of nature which appeals to every mind, and seems to carry a strong conviction with it of the superintendance of Divine Providence; but to my mind nothing so fully conveys the benevolence of the Deity as the pleasures which little children enjoy." He goes on to say, " that grown up persons do, to a certain degree, provide their own gratification and amusements, but the amusements of an innocent, healthy child are

provided by other hands.   I never saw a young
healthy child at its sports without perceiving a
new evidence of the finger of God, and a new proof
of his love, benevolence, and protection." Advert-
ing to the objection made against this plan, he
would ask, whether in the lower classes of society
it was desirable that children should be always
with their parents?   He did not deny that, generally speaking, in society such an intercourse
operated as a sort of mutual check and correction
on both; but he could not help considering it a
little romantic and poetical to expect, that the intercourse between an infant child and an angry
and irritated parent could produce such an effect.
Was it not rather true, that in the case of the labouring classes of society, there was often to be
found such a monstrous inversion of nature, that
from the lips which at first lavished the never-
ceasing caresses of maternal fondness, the child,
at moments of irritation and perhaps of disappointment, often heard language which ought
never to meet its ear, and learned that of which it
ought to have remained for ever ignorant?   This
institution provided a remedy against that evil,
and held forth benefits at which humanity ought
to exult.   There was another point upon which
he entertained sanguine hopes of benefit from this
system of education. If anything had been proved
by the attempts already made to educate poor
children, it was this—that their parents, who appeared inaccessible to all instruction, and who
refused all instruction when offered to them
by others, or when attempted to be influenced
by hope or fear, have by that instinctive pa-
rental fondness to be found in all, listened to
the sacred truths when repeated from the lips of

their offspring, thus accomplishing that, which was thought impossible, by the lips of babes and sucklings. In a nation like this such an institution had peculiar claims on their support. They had tried to provide a remedy for every evil; their hospitals sheltered the aged and distressed; and it behoved them to provide also to rescue young and unprotected children from the blasting contagion of vice and infamy. The Noble Lord concluded by moving that certain gentlemen, whose names were given, should be requested to act as a committee to draw up rules for the society, to receive subscriptions, and to make the further arrangements for carrying the Resolutions of the meeting into effect.

The Reverend *E. Irving* rose. It was a sentence, spoken from the lips of Him, who spake as man never spake, " Unless ye become as little children, ye shall not enter into the kingdom of heaven." In which sentence the greatest and most weighty truth was conveyed. For, therein, they were not only taught that infants were capable of education, and had a right to it, but that they must themselves become like unto little children, before they were fitted for eternal salvation. The infant state was the period at which to commence education. If any one doubted this, let him attempt the education of a grown man, and he would find what slow progress he would make — he would find what slow approaches he would make to his intellect, surrounded, as it necessarily must be, by the prejudices of his calling or other circumstances. He might persevere, but in the end it was to be feared he would find it too late. Let him take a younger subject, say nine or ten years of age (he mentioned this after nine years experience), and it would soon be found what obstructions lay in the way from the rudiments of evil, already far advanced. In short, he must go back, and find the very germ of the child's intellect, before it roots were shot forth into an unhealthy soil, and ere it was engrafted upon from the fulsome plant by which it was surrounded. He would ask could any parents of the lower classes afford time or possess ability to work on these sweet influences? Certainly not. If the mass of the population were stupid or uneducated, who were to blame but the upper classes, who had neglected to educate them at an early period? Those who imbibed vicious principles might, by a little care and attention in youth, have been trained up and confirmed in virtue and morality. He hoped the meeting would persevere in the good work they had undertaken, and they would be the means, under God, of destroying that hydra of discord and confusion which lives and preys upon the bowels of every land on the face of the earth. With a committee, composed as this would be composed, of statesmen, scholars, philanthropists, and men of science and skill, they might expect the most happy results, and he prayed that the LORD GOD, the Father of the spirits of men, would pour down his blessing upon their undertaking and bring it to perfection. The resolution was put and agreed to.

Sir *James Mackintosh* begged to state to the meeting, the state of the subscriptions, which he hoped with their exertions would be rendered adequate to its object. He then read the following names which composed the first list :—Marquess of Lansdown, 52*l.* 10*s.*; J. Smith, 52*l.* 10*s.*

. Wilson, 50*l.*; H. Brougham, 25*l.*; W. Wilson, 0*l.*; Morning Chronicle, 52*l.* 10*s.*; Z. Macauley, 0*l.*; J. Hoare, 21*l.*; Abel Smith, 10*l.*; Robert Owen, 10*l.*; George Strutt, 10*l.*

The Marquess of *Downshire* rose to move a vote of thanks to their Noble Chairman; a resolution in which he felt convinced the Meeting would most heartily concur with him. With respect to the Institution itself, it had his entire concurrence; although, from his situation, it was his duty to assist such establishments in his own country, he should give this as much support as he could consistently with that superior duty. The noble Marquess concluded by moving "That the thanks of the Meeting be presented to the Marquess of Lansdown, for his able conduct in the chair."

Dr. *Lushington* said he always thought that that man would be the greatest benefactor to his country who did most for the suppression of crime; this, he was sorry to say, our legislature neglected in a great degree, while they readily employed themselves in providing for its punishment. Those acquainted with our prisons must know that those found to have sunk deepest into vice and crime were persons who had never received any education, moral or religious. In the Refuge for the Destitute, an exact account was kept, and it was found that of the great mass of culprits sent there by the Magistrates on account of their youth, two-thirds were the children of parents who had no opportunity of educating them. By this institution they would at once promote virtue and prevent vice. It is not necessary now to adduce instances of the folly of hoping to repress crime by severity; look to our

Criminal Code, that sanguinary record of the inflictions of man upon his fellow-creature : that system has now proved ineffectual, and, thank God, we are now entering upon a different course —a system of kindness and benevolence, which will smooth the poor man's path in this life, and teach him to hope for happiness in the next. He had now only further to add, that he was most happy in seconding the vote of thanks to their Noble Chairman, who had ever stood forward in the cause of mercy, of knowledge, and humanity, disregarding the taunts of those who, seeking their own advantage, had pursued different courses; an individual, whose uniform kindness of heart and noble nature, ennobled even the illustrious class, to whom, from birth and parentage he belonged.

The motion was carried unanimously.

The Marquess of *Lansdown* begged to return to the meeting his unfeigned thanks for the honor they had done him : again he repeated, that all he could claim of merit to himself, was not being indifferent to the call of others, or to those feelings of humanity which were placed in every bosom. It would be unnecessary to add one word, had he not received some letters since he had come into the room suggesting means of promoting the object they all had in view; one was from a member of that sex to whom his Honourable and Learned Friend had alluded, whose exertions were never yet wanting in the cause of kindness and benevolence : it was from Miss Neave, who stated that an infant school had been established in Putney, in Surry, on a very cheap plan. The school was in a brick-house, consisting of four rooms, capable of accommodating fifty children, and it was considered that in the villages near London, two of those schools would be more convenient than one on a larger scale. The object of this school was not confined to the instruction of children only, but provided means also of instructing female servants after they had left, in the knowledge suited to their calling, thus combining in the best manner, moral and religious culture, with instruction preparatory to their entrance on the duties of life. The object of the Meeting to-day was to collect all the scattered streams of instruction and direct them into one channel, and he trusted that means would be provided adequate to their wants, and that their exertions would be successful, for nothing could possibly be more meritorious than to increase the knowledge, and consequently the happiness of that very respectable class of society, the mechanics of this country.

Sir *James Mackintosh* then stated, that a considerable addition had been made to the subscriptions already received. He was happy to find that the small subscriptions had been no less gratefully received and applauded than the larger sums. It was to the feeling that dictated the subscriptions they should look, and often they would find that in the eye of reason, when all the circumstances were considered, the smaller donation was entitled to the higher praise. He could only add that if the feelings of any ladies and gentlemen had been awakened by the subscriptions, he would say to them, "Go, thou, and do likewise;" and with a view to that purpose a list would be kept in the committee room for taking down their names.

A liberal subscription was immediately commenced, and before the meeting had separated upwards of 700*l.* was collected.

I shall close the present chapter with an abstract of the first address issued by the Committee after the above meeting, as containing some valuable remarks upon the subject of Infant Education.

"*Infant School Society, London, July* 16 1824. The Infant School Society has been formed to promote the establishment of Schools, or rather Asylums for the Children of the Poor, before the age at which they are capable of engaging in any profitable employment, or at which they may be received into the other Schools, to which they are not usually admitted until they have attained the age of about six years: the proper objects of the Society's care, therefore, are children of both sexes, from two to six years of age.

" It is well known that children of this age generally prove, during the working hours of the day, a heavy incumbrance on parents who are obliged to toil hard for a subsistence. One of the Society's objects is to lighten the pressure of this inconvenience, and to leave the parents, and particularly the mother, more fully at liberty to pursue some gainful occupation for the common benefit of the family.

" So convinced are the poor themselves of the advantage of this kind of relief, that in numerous instances, Dames'-Schools, as they are called, have been established, in which ten, twenty, or thirty infants are placed under the care of an old woman, by whom they are shut up, perhaps in a close apartment, in order to be kept out of harm's way while the parents are at work. And for this accommodation parents are willing to pay from two-pence to four-pence a week for each child. The children are left with the dame, and remain under her care, (with the exception, in most cases, of the dinner hour,) until the evening.

" It is proposed to form Infant Schools, which shall be capable of receiving from 200 to 300 Infants, and which, while they secure the same relief to parents, shall be made subservient to many other purposes, important not only to the children themselves, but through them to their parents, and to the community at large.

" If the period of mere infancy is less fitted, comparatively speaking, for intellectual progress, yet curiosity is even then sufficiently active to enable the superintendant of such an establishment to convey much useful knowledge to his pupils, by means which are calculated to call forth, *without oppressing*, their faculties. No parent, for example, can be ignorant of the effect produced by pictures, whether of animate or inanimate objects, in engaging the attention, and developing the faculties, even of very young children. And this is only one of the many modes by which ideas may be communicated to infants, without the necessity either of resorting to any harsh expedients, or of imposing *any strain* on their faculties.

" The incidental acquisition of useful knowledge, which cannot fail to accompany this course of early tuition, though in itself a circumstance of no mean value, is but of small account, in comparison with that moral culture, with those habits of self-government, and with those feelings of mutual kindness, which form the characteristic tendencies, and indeed the grand recommendation of the whole system.

" The Committee, however, are deeply sensible,

and they wish to impress this sentiment on all who may undertake to form infant schools, that it is by instilling into the infant mind the principles of religion, that the effects even of the most perfect discipline can be rendered permanent, and that those higher ends can be secured for which man is formed, and which infinitely transcend in importance all the temporal advantages, great as they are, to be derived from education. To produce, therefore, in the minds of the children, feelings of reverence and gratitude towards their Creator and Redeemer; to impress upon them a sense of their moral responsibility; to convey to them a knowledge of the leading truths of revealed religion, and to familiarize them with the right examples of piety and benevolence which the scriptures furnish, ought to form leading features of the system of instruction pursued in these infant schools.

" It would be difficult duly to estimate the effects on society, and, amongst many others, the certain diminution of private vice and of public delinquency, which, under the divine blessing, must follow the general adoption and steady prosecution of such a system of infant training.

" At present we behold the streets, and lanes, and alleys, of the metropolis, and other large towns and villages, crowded with squalid children, left, in utter neglect, to wallow in filth, to contract disease, and to acquire habits of idleness, violence, and vice. Almost the first language which many of them learn to lisp, is that of impurity and profaneness. Almost the first science in which many of them are instructed, is that of depredation. Abroad, they are exposed to every vicious seduction; at home, they suffer from the caprice or violence of parents, who are incapable of instructing their ignorance, whose poverty makes them discontented and irritable, and who feel the very presence of their children to be a drawback on their efforts to earn a subsistence.

" If we contrast with this state of things the effect which may be anticipated from the general establishment of infant schools, conducted on the principles which have now been developed, what heart but must exult in the prospect? Let all who regard such expectations as visionary, only take the pains of personally and minutely inspecting those receptacles of infancy which have been already formed at Walthamstow, Whitechapel, Vincent Square, Westminster, Blackfriars, Brighton, Bristol, and Liverpool. Let them view the children, clean, healthy, joyous; giving free scope to their buoyant spirits; their very plays made subservient to the correction of bad and the growth of good dispositions; and the *happiness* they manifestly enjoy *employed* as the means of training them in habits of prompt and cheerful obedience, of mutual kindness, of unceasing activity, of purity and decorum. Again, let them watch the return of these children to their homes at noon, and at night, and witness the pleasurable sensations with which they are received, so different from the scowling looks and harsh tones with which their teazing importunities and interruptions, during the hours of labour, are apt to be met. And let them, moreover, contemplate the striking re-action of the improved manners and habits of the infants, on the older branches of the family. Let them view and consider all this, and they will no longer doubt the beneficial influence of the proposed institutions."

CHAPTER V.

REQUISITES FOR THE ESTABLISHMENT OF AN INFANT SCHOOL.

I SHALL now lay before my readers an account of the things necessary for the establishment of an Infant School; previously to presenting them with the detail of the plan to be pursued in it.

In the first place it is necessary to provide an airy and spacious apartment, with a dry, and, if possible, a large play-ground attached to it. The plot of ground, I conceive, should not be less than fifty feet wide, and one hundred feet long; but if the ground were one hundred and fifty, or two hundred feet long, it would be so much the better, as this would allow one hundred or one hundred and fifty feet for a play-ground; which is of such importance, that I consider the system would be very defective without it, for reasons which will be spoken of hereafter.

There should likewise be a room about fifteen feet square, for the purpose of teaching the children in classes, which may be formed at one end of the large room: this is absolutely necessary. As the master and mistress should live on the premises;

a small house, containing three or four rooms, should be provided for them. The reason for their living on the premises is, that the children should be allowed to bring their dinners with them, as this will keep them out of the streets; and, indeed, of those who do go home to dinner, many will return in a very short time, and if there be no persons on the premises to take care of them, they will be lost; and not only so, but strange boys will come in from the streets, and do a great deal of mischief, if no one be there to prevent it.

The portion of sitting-room that I have allowed for each child is twelve inches. The scholars should sit all round the school-room, with their backs against the wall. A school according to the plan in the frontispiece, will be found large enough for all the purposes of an infant school; but if wished to be more commodious, it may be of the same length as the plan, and instead of twenty-two feet wide, may be made thirty feet wide; this will hold as many children as ought to be collected together in one place, and as many as any man and woman can possibly teach, to do justice to; if it be any longer, it will be difficult for all the children to hear the master. An oblong building is the cheapest, on account of the roof. Economy has been studied in the plan given, without any thing being added that is unnecessary. This, of course, is a matter of opinion, and may be acted upon or not, just as it suits those who may choose to build. The master's house in the plan, it will be seen, projects a little into the play-ground, to afford him an opportunity of seeing the children at play while he is at dinner, that he may notice any improper conduct on the part of the children, and mention it when the accounts of the day are made up.

As children are very apt to get into danger, even when at school, it becomes expedient to exercise the utmost vigilance, in order to prevent the possibility of an accident; for where two hundred children are assembled together, the eldest not seven years of age, it is most certain that if there be danger some will get into it. For this reason, all the doors on the premises should be so secured, that the children cannot swing them backwards and forwards; if they are not, the children will get their fingers pinched, or worse accidents may occur. The forms also should be so placed that the children may not be likely to fall over them. Every thing in short should be put out of the way, that will be likely to occasion danger to children.

The master's desk should be placed at the end of the school, where the class-room is. By this means he will be able to see the faces of all the children, and they can see him, which is extremely necessary, as they may then be governed by a motion of his hand.

The *furniture* necessary for the school consists of a desk for the master; a rostrum, firmly built; seats for the children; lesson-stand; stools for the monitors; slates and pencils; pictures of scriptural subjects; pictures of natural history; alphabets and spelling lessons; brass letters and figures, with boards for them; cubes, geometrical figures, &c.; and the transposition-frame or arithmeticon, as it has been called: to these may be added, little books, &c. The particular use of these will be respectively treated of in the succeeding pages.

The following is a representation of a lesson-post.

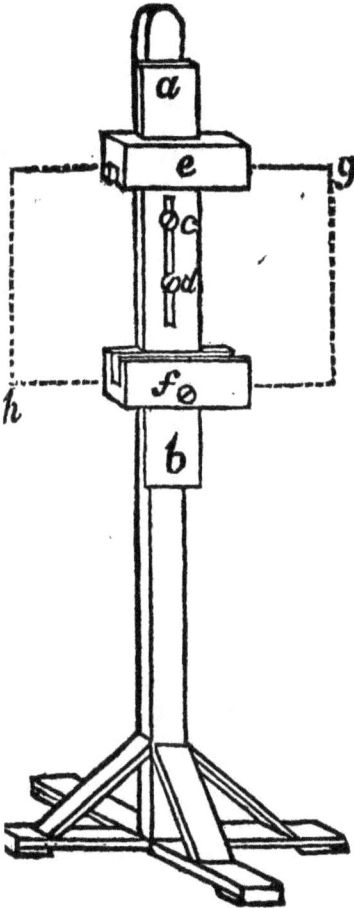

a b is a slip of wood with a groove in it, fixed to the post by means of the screws *c* and *d*, on which slip are two blocks *e* and *f;* the bottom one, *f*, is fixed, with a groove in the upper side, for the lower edge of the board *g h* to rest in; the upper block, *e*, has a groove in the lower side, for the upper edge of the board *g h* to rest in, and rises and falls according to the width of the board, on the slip *a b.*—Instead of being made with feet, the lesson-post is generally, and perhaps better, fixed into the floor of the school-room.

The *lessons*, pasted either on wood or millboard to render them sufficiently stiff, are placed in the grooves of the lesson-post; when they can be stationed in any position which is most convenient, and adjusted to any height, as the master may see proper.

The arithmeticon, of which a representation will be given in a subsequent Chapter, is simple in its construction; but, as will be seen hereafter, a very useful invention. It is indeed indispens-

able in an infant school, as it is useful for teaching the first principles of grammar, arithmetic,
and geometry.

The following is a list of the articles mentioned, with the prices that have been paid for each;
these, however, vary in different parts of the
kingdom.

	£.	s.	d.		£.	s.	d.
Rostrum					1	10	6
Desk for the Master					1	12	0
Lesson Stand . .	0	9	10	{ Ten of these for 100 Children . . }	4	18	4
Frame to affix to the Wall . . . }	0	4	3	Ditto ditto . . .	2	2	6
Stools for Monitors	0	3	2	Twenty of these . .	3	3	4
Seats for Children, at 1s. per ft.				100 Feet	5	0	0
Pegs for Hats, 3d. each				100 Pegs	1	5	0
					19	11	8
100 Engraved Slates, at 7d. each		.		.	2	18	4
1000 Slate Pencils, at 10d. per Hundred		.		.	0	8	4
Pictures of Natural and Scriptural History, on Boards				.	2	3	6
Alphabets and Spelling Lessons . .				.	0	10	0
Brass Letters, Figures, and Board for them				.	2	0	0
Cubes, Geometrical Figures, &c.				.	0	10	0
Transposition Frame .		.	.	.	0	10	0
Little Books, &c. .		.	.	.	0	10	0
			Total . .	£29	1	10

The Play-ground.—Since several schools have
been established without this necessary appendage, I purpose saying a few words on the subject. It appears to me, that without a play-
ground, Infant Schools would be little superior
to what are termed Dames' Schools, where the
children of mechanics are usually sent; at any

rate, as far as regards the health of the children ; indeed, in some instances, they would be worse, on account of the probability of their having more children than these Dames' Schools.

To have one hundred children, or upwards, in a room, however convenient such room might be in other respects, and not to allow the children proper relaxation and exercise, which they could not have without a play-ground, would materially injure their health, which is a thing, in my humble opinion, of the first importance. I would rather see a school where they charged two-pence or three-pence per week for each child, having a play-ground, than one where the children had free admission without one ; for 1 think the former institution would do the most good. The play-ground, likewise, as will be shewn when we come to speak of the moral cultivation of the children, is one of the most useful parts of the system in this respect. It is there the child shews itself in its true character, and thereby gives the master an opportunity of nipping in the bud its evil propensities. I am, therefore, most anxious humbly to recommend that this necessary appendage to an infant school should not be dispensed with. 1 moreover observe, that where there is a play-ground attached to the school, instead of playing in the streets, where scarcely anything but evil is before their eyes, the children will hasten to the school with their bread and butter in their hands, in less than a quarter of an hour after they have left it, knowing that they have an opportunity of playing there the remainder of their dinner time, so that they love the school, and but rarely wish to be anywhere else.

The play-grounds of some schools are paved

with bricks, which I have found to answer very
well, as they absorb the rain so quickly, that ten
minutes after a shower, the place is dry enough
for the children to play in ; which, perhaps, would
not be the case with any other kind of paving.
They are placed flat on the ground, but I should
prefer them being put edgeways, as they would
last many years longer, yet it would take nearly
double the number of bricks by being so placed.
If it be not paved, the ground will be soft, and
the children will make themselves dirty. It
should be so managed that the water may be
carried off, for, if there are any puddles, the children will get into them. Some persons have recommended a few cart-loads of good iron-mould
gravel, there being a sort which will bind almost
like a rock, if well rolled, but the children are
liable to dig holes if it is only gravel : if this is
noticed in time it may be prevented ; but if they
are suffered to dig holes, and no notice be taken
of it at first, it will be very difficult to prevent
them from making a practice of it. If money can
be saved, by any plan, perhaps it is as well to
notice it ; but after having weighed the advantages and disadvantages of gravelling, I am of
opinion, that bricks are preferable. I should
also recommend that fruit trees be planted in the
centre of the play-ground, and likewise round
the walls ; which will delight the children, and
teach them to have respect to private property.
If any person doubts the propriety of this plan,
I can only say we have many play-grounds thus
ornamented ; and instead of proving a temptation
to the children, it has so far become a means of
confirming principles of honesty in them, that
they never touch a single flower or even a leaf

in the garden. There should also be a border of flowers round the play-ground, of such sorts as will yield the most fragrance, which will tend to counteract any disagreeable smell that may proceed from the children, and thereby be conducive to their health, as well as to that of those who have the charge of them. They will, besides, afford the teacher an opportunity of giving the children many useful lessons; for the more he teaches by things, and the less he teaches by signs, the better. These things need be no expense to the establishment, except the purchase in the first instance, for they will afford an agreeable occupation for the master before and after school hours, and prepare him in some measure for the duties of the day; and will afford him an ample opportunity of instilling a variety of ideas into the minds of the children, and of tracing everything up to the Great First Cause. I have witnessed the good effects of these things, which makes me desirous of humbly recommending them to others.

With regard to the expense, I have ascertained beyond a doubt, that according to the plan adopted in Mr. Wilson's school, 300 children may be taken care of, from the age of eighteen months to seven years, and instructed in every thing that such children are capable of learning, for 150*l.* per annum*, which is ten shillings a year for each

---

* It is to be observed, that I am speaking of a free-school. In Mr. Wilson's school the children pay nothing; but some persons have wished that the children should pay a penny or two-pence per week; this of course would considerably diminish the expenditure, and I have no doubt that in country villages, and in decent neighbourhoods, it might be obtained. But in such neighbourhoods as Spitalfields, St. Catherine's,

child.   This includes the salary for the master and mistress; the salary for a third person to do the drudgery; coals, slates, cards, and every other thing requisite for the school, except the rent of the premises.   I QUESTION WHETHER IT DOES NOT COST THE COUNTRY AS MUCH FOR EVERY TWO INDIVIDUALS THAT ARE TRANSPORTED OUT OF IT.   Perhaps I shall be excused in this place for indulging in a few thoughts on the practicability of establishing Infant Schools throughout the United Kingdom by means of a legislative provision.   I have thought that it might be practicable to establish one or two Infant Schools in every parish, by imposing a tax of one shilling a year upon every family, and every servant in place, both male and female.   The family, I should think, would have no objection to pay such a trifling sum, if they had the privilege of sending their children to school for it; and the latter I should conceive would pay it cheerfully, knowing that they themselves might derive many advantages from similar institutions.   The rich would not have any objection surely to pay so trifling a sum, although they should receive no other benefit from the plan, than being saved perhaps the expense of prosecuting individuals, who, probably, had it not been for the good impressions made upon them in an Infant School, might have committed some crime, so as to have rendered such a proceeding necessary.   I should imagine, that

some parts of St. Giles's, Wapping, &c. &c., many of the parents are not able to pay, and many that are, would sooner let their children run the streets than pay a penny: yet the children of the latter persons are the greatest objects of charity; and it is the children of such persons that chiefly fill our prisons.

there is no person possessing the least spark of humanity, who would not rather pay a tax to prevent a child from falling into danger, than to be compelled to pay a tax for the express purpose of punishing him after he had fallen into it. Perhaps no tax could be imposed that would not be considered unjust by some persons, although they would have no objection to reap the benefit arising from it. The only objection I could see to such a plan, would be on the score of religious opinions, for if an attempt were made to insist upon the children being taught any particular religious sentiments, or should the schools be under the superintendence of individuals of any particular religious sentiments, to the exclusion of all others, such an attempt no doubt would be extremely unpopular, and I for one should object to the plan; but if these things should be done upon truly liberal principles, and an opportunity given to both Churchmen and Dissenters to have schools and schoolmasters, according to their own choice, without any interference on the part of the legislature as to these particulars, I do think that such a tax, with the generality of well-disposed persons, would be far from being objectionable. With respect to the collection of this tax, that would be an after consideration; but, no doubt, care would be taken to have no useless drones in the concern; and further, that in its collection, the public should be put to the least expense possible. If the poor, generally speaking, could see the propriety, as well as the necessity, of keeping their children out of the streets, where there is nothing but bad example before their eyes, and of sending them to school at the earliest age, there would be no necessity for a tax, for they

K 2

would cheerfully come forward and voluntarily
throw in their mite; but this is not the case;
many of them do not see the danger until it comes
upon them, therefore it behoves the legislature—
those who are the guardians of us all—to endeavour to avert the danger; and where the poor
will not do that which would evidently be for
the good of themselves as well as of their children, I can see no impropriety in compelling
them to do it, provided that the religious scruples
of many, before mentioned, are not lost sight of;
for we have certainly no right to compel a man
to have his child taught that which he deems to
be erroneous. There are many leading truths
which may be taught children, to which few persons would object, and these might be taught
generally; but where certain points have been
subject to controversy, without coming to any
final decision, such points should be avoided,
and left to the decision of those who are most
interested therein.

I have merely thrown out these suggestions,
as an opinion, the value of which must be estimated by my readers. I can only say, that I
would most willingly pay my share of the tax,
come when it may; but, if never adopted, I shall
not feel grieved, so long as *the public* see the
necessity of taking care of children, and form
schools or asylums for their protection. The
means by which such a desirable object may be
accomplished, is of little consideration; yet every
one who desires its accomplishment, is in duty
bound, to suggest any thing he may deem likely
to facilitate its extension.

CHAPTER VI.

QUALIFICATIONS OF A MASTER AND MISTRESS.

" Delightful task! to rear the tender thought,
  To teach the young idea how to shoot;
  To pour the fresh instruction o'er the mind;
  To breathe th' enlivening spirit, and to fix
  The generous purpose in the glowing breast."
  THOMSON.

PERHAPS no one ever felt his own insufficiency, in any situation, more strongly than I did, whilst in charge of the Spitalfields' Infant School, which induces me to make a few observations on the qualifications of a master and mistress. It is a very common idea, that almost any person can educate little children, and that it requires little or no ability; but it will be found that this is a great mistake, for if it be the business of such a person to lay the foundation of religion and virtue in the infant mind, with every grace that can adorn the Christian character, there must be something more done than merely saying a few printed lessons by rotation, without knowing whether the children really understand what they say. How frequently may we find children, ten or twelve years of age, who cannot answer the most simple question, and who nevertheless have been to school for years. To give the children ideas, is a part of education seldom thought of; but if we really wish to form the character of the rising generation, and to improve the condition of society generally, attention must be paid to these things. Little, I should think, need be said to prove, that few ideas are given in Dames' Schools. There may be a few of them as to which an exception should be made; but generally speaking, where the children of mechanics are usually sent before the age of seven years, no such thing is thought of. The mind of a child is compared, by Mr. Locke, to a sheet of blank paper, and if it be the business of a tutor to inscribe lessons on this mind, it will require much patience, gentleness, perseverance, self-possession, energy, knowledge of human nature, and above all, piety, to accomplish so great a work with propriety and success.

Whoever is in possession of these requisites, may be considered as a proper person to manage an infant school, and whoever has charge of such an institution will find numerous opportunities of displaying each and all of these qualifications. It would be almost useless to attempt to cure the bad tempers of children, if the master should encourage and manifest such evil tempers in his own conduct; for children are not indifferent to what they see in others : they certainly take notice of all our movements, and consequently the greatest caution is necessary. It will be of little purpose to endeavour to inculcate suitable precepts in the minds of the children, unless they see them shine forth in the conduct of the teacher.

How awkward it would sound, if, when a

teacher was explaining to his pupils the sin of swearing, a child should say, " Please, sir, I heard you swear;" and it is just the same as to those faults which some may consider of minor importance, such as the indulgence of angry passions, and the like, in the presence of children.

Persons who have charge of children cannot be too circumspect,—their characters can never be too good, as every trifling fault will be magnified both by parents and children. Indeed the character of such a person is of so much importance, that very often the designs of benevolent individuals are frustrated by appointing improper persons to fill such situations. Patience is a virtue absolutely indispensable, as it will frequently take the master or mistress a whole hour to investigate a subject that may appear of little or no importance ; such as one child accusing another of stealing a trifle, as a plum, a cherry, a button, or any other thing of like value. The complainant and defendant will expect justice done to them by the master or mistress, and in order to do this, much time and trouble will, in some cases, be necessary. Should a hasty conclusion be formed, and the accused be punished for what he has not been guilty of, in such case the child will be sensible that an injury has been done to him, and will feel dissatisfied with his tutors, and consequently will not pay them the respect they ought to have ; besides, it will frequently be found, on examination, that the accuser is really the most in fault, and I think I have convinced many children that this has been the case, and they have retired satisfied with my decision ; for when a child is satisfied that justice will be done to him, he will open his case freely and boldly, but if he has any idea that justice will not be done to him, he will keep one half the facts of the case in his own mind, and will not reveal them. I once formed a hasty conclusion in the case of two children, and happened to decide the very reverse to what I ought to have done, the consequence was that the child endeavoured to do that for himself, which he found I had not done for him, and pleaded his own cause with the opposite party in the play-ground; but finding that he could not prevail on him, and being sensible that he had been wronged, he was so much hurt, that he brought his father the next day, and we reconsidered the case; when it was found, that the child was correct, and that I had decided wrong. Here I found how necessary it was to exercise the utmost patience, in order to enable me to judge rightly, and to convince my little pupils, that I had the greatest desire to do them justice. I compare an Infant School to a little commonwealth, or a world in miniature, the head or governor of which, is naturally the master. An Infant School master or mistress is not to consider anything relating to the rights of his little community as trifling or unimportant. However justly they might be considered such, comparatively, it must be remembered they are matters of moment to the parties concerned, and such therefore they should be esteemed in the mind of him, who is the arbitrator of their rights, and the legislator of the infant state. He will have to act the part of counsel, judge, and jury, and although the children cannot find words to plead their own cause, yet by their looks and gestures, they will convince you they have some internal evidence that you have rightly decided; and it appears to me, that the future conduct of the children in the world, will depend, in a great measure, upon the correctness of the master's decision.

One would suppose, to hear the observations of some persons, that mere automatons would do for masters and mistresses. By such persons the system is considered as everything, while the persons who are to teach it, have been considered as secondary objects; but a system, however perfect in itself, will be productive of little good, unless it be committed to persons possessed of some degree of skill; as the best watch will go wrong, if not properly attended to. We cannot, therefore, be too circumspect in the choice of the persons to whom we commit the care and education of the rising generation. There is something so powerful in virtue and correctness of deportment, that even infants respect it; and this will operate more powerfully on their minds than many imagine. It does not appear necessary to me that children should be kept under excessive restraint by their tutors; they should rather be encouraged to make their tutor their confidant, for by this means he will become acquainted with many things, the knowledge of which it is essential he should possess both as it regards himself, and, as it regards the welfare of his pupils. If the child be kept under excessive restraint, he will seek some other persons to whom he may open his little mind, and should that person be ill-disposed, the most serious consequences will not unfrequently follow. Let it not be supposed, however, that I am vain enough to believe that I am in possession of the qualifications I have been recommending. We must all be prepared to fall short of what we aim at; but I trust, I know the source from whence all assistance is derived, and I am taught to believe, that such assistance will not be withheld from those who diligently seek it. I am well aware that I shall have to render an account of my stewardship to the Almighty, for every child that may have been placed under my care, and I feel that to do so unblameably requires much assistance from above.

Let not those, then, who are similarly circumstanced with myself, think that I address them in the spirit of arrogance, with a pre-conceived opinion of my own sufficiency; I wish that all who teach may be more fit for the situation than I am. I know many who are an honor to their profession, as well as the situation they fill, but I am sorry to say, I think they do not all meet with the encouragement they merit. It is not always those who do their duty the best, that meet with the most encouragement : but there is one thing to be said, if a man's conscience does not upbraid him, he need not care what the world thinks of him, for conscience is a faithful monitor, and will seldom deceive us, if we attend to its dictates.

Without affecting to present a code of laws for the direction of Infant School conductors, I think the following five short rules, will be found worthy of adoption. Experience recommended them to me, and as such I recommend them to others.

1st. Never to correct a child in anger.

2nd. Never to deprive a child of any thing without returning it again.

3rd. Never to break a promise.

4th. Never to overlook a fault.

5th. In all things to set before the children an example worthy of imitation.

And now, as to a matter on which there is some difference of opinion, *viz.* whether women are or are not as fit for conductors of Infant Schools, as men. My decided opinion is, that alone they are not. There should be in every school a master and a mistress. In the first place in an Infant School, the presence of the man, as of a father in a family, will insure a far greater degree of respect and attention on the part of the children. This does not arise from the exercise of any greater degree of harshness or severity than the mother would be capable of using; nor is it to be attributed, as some suppose, to the less frequent presence of the father in the case of many families, but is rather to be accounted for by an intuitive perception of the greater firmness and determination of the character of the man. To those who deny this I would give as a problem for solution, a case by no means unfrequent, and which most of my readers will have witnessed,—a family in which the mother, ruling with " a rod of iron,"—by no means incurring the charge of spoiling the child, by sparing the rod,—is less heeded, less promptly obeyed in her commands, than a father who seldom or never makes use of any offensive weapons. The mother scolds, threatens, scourges, and is at last reluctantly and imperfectly obeyed—the father, either with regard to his own commands, or seconding those of the mother—speaks, and is instantly obeyed. The idea of disputing his authority, or neglecting or disobeying his laws, never once enters the heads of his children. Exactly the same is it in an Infant

School,—the presence of a man ensures attention and gains respect from the children, not only at first, whilst the novelty of such control might be supposed to operate, but, permanently; as I am sure all who have candidly examined the schools where two women preside, and those conducted by a man and a woman, must have seen.

Another objection to the sole government of females in these schools, is—they have not the physical strength, nor, at present, intellectual powers sufficient for the task. In saying this I trust I shall not be suspected of wishing to offend my fair country-women. That they have not sufficient physical strength is the intention of nature; that they are deficient in mental energy is the defect of education. I trust, there-fore, that no offence will be assumed where no blame is attached. It has been a point much disputed, whether there be really an intrinsic difference in the mental powers, and it has been of course differently decided by the respective disputants. With this I shall have nothing to do; but these things are certain; that the minds of both are capable of much greater activity and achievements than has been generally supposed; and that whilst education has not done what it ought for man, it has done infinitely less for woman. This it is, then, which affords an ad-ditional argument in my mind for a master and a mistress. For let it not be supposed, that I would dismiss women altogether from the system —that I think them useless or even dispensable in an Infant School. If, indeed, one or the other must be done without, and I had my choice, I should certainly give my voice for a master; but the perfect system requires both. There is ample opportunity for the exercise of those offices of maternal love, those affectionate kindnesses, of which man is at best but a poor imitator; neither can it be denied that an active intelligent woman is an useful auxiliary to the labours of the man in the duties of the school. The authoritative presence of the man is the more necessary under our system, because it is a grand object to rule without harshness—by that principle of love which is in no degree incompatible with the respect felt for a kind but judicious school-master. Some children, indeed, as far as regards authority, might be very well managed by a mistress only, but then it must be recollected that an Infant School is composed of every variety of temper and disposition ; and even were it otherwise, the objection of intellectual incompetence, before adverted to, would still hold good.

Such, indeed, is the opinion of the unfitness of females for the occupation of teaching, in Scotland, that in many places the very idea of it is scouted; they have scarcely heard of the term *school-mistress*, even for their youngest children, and certain it is that the matters of education are much better conducted in Scotland, than in most other places. If their minds are to be cultivated, and a firm and decided tone given to their characters, say they, what can be the use of sending them to a school conducted by a woman only? And I must candidly say, that I perfectly agree with them on this head; and have therefore deemed it my duty to be thus explicit on the matter.

One thing I must add, by way of conclusion, —to render any person competent, man or woman, to discharge the duties of the situation

efficiently—the *heart* of the teacher must be in
his school. If he have not the zeal of the ama-
teur, the skill of the professor will be of little
avail. The maxim will apply to every species
of occupation, but it is peculiarly true as to
that of an Infant School teacher. To those who
can feel no other interest than that which the
profit gives to the employment, it will soon become one, not only of an irksome, but of a loath-
some kind. But certain I am that it is possible
to feel it as what it is—an employment not only
of a most important nature, but a most interesting
one likewise. It is one which a philosopher
might choose for the study of the human character, and a philanthropist for its improvement.

CHAPTER VII.

HINTS FOR ORGANIZING AND CONDUCTING AN INFANT SCHOOL.

AS I have had considerable practice in the art of teaching infant children in various parts of the kingdom, I hope I may be allowed to give a few hints on the subject of organizing an Infant School, without being considered ostentatious. I have generally found on opening a new school, that the children have no idea of acting together; in order, therefore, to gain this object, it will be found necessary to have recourse to what we call *manual lessons*, which consist in the children holding up their hands, all at one time, and putting them down again in the same manner; putting the right foot out, or the left foot out; putting their hands together, or rising from their seats, all at one time; putting their hands behind them : and many other things of a similar nature.

These lessons we have recourse to in the first instance, because it is calculated to please the infants, by causing them to act together, which is one grand step towards order. After the first day or two, the children will begin to act together, and to know each other, but until this is the case, they will be frequently peevish and want to go home; therefore any method that can be taken, in the first instance, to please them, should be adopted: for unless you can please them you may be sure they will cry. Having induced them to act together, we are then to class them according to their capacity and age, and according as they shew an aptitude, in obeying your several commands, those who obey them with the greatest readiness may be classed together.

I have found it difficult, at all times, to keep up the attention of infants, without giving them something to do; so that when they are saying the tables in arithmetic, we always cause them to move either their hands or feet, sometimes to march round the school: the best way we have yet found out is the putting their hands one on the other every time they speak a sentence. If they are marching they may count one, two, three, four, five, six, &c.

Having classed them, and having found that each child knows its own place in the school, you may select one of the cleverest of each class for a monitor. Some of the children will learn many of the tables sooner than the others; in this case the teacher may avail himself of the assistance of those, by causing each child to repeat what he knows in an audible manner, the other children repeating after him, and performing the same evolutions that he does; by this means the other children will soon learn. Then the master can go on with something else, taking care to enlist as many children as he can to his assistance, for he will find that unless he does so he will injure his lungs, and render himself unfit to keep up the attention of the children, and to carry on the school with good effect.

When the children have learned to repeat several of the tables, and the monitors, to excite their several classes, and to keep them in tolerable order, they may go on with the other parts of the plan, such as the spelling and reading, picture lessons, &c. as described below. But care must be taken that in the beginning too much be not attempted. The first week may be spent in getting them in order, without thinking of any thing else; and I should advise that not more than sixty children be admitted the first week, that they may be reduced to order, in some measure, before any more are admitted, as all that come after will quickly imitate the others. I should, moreover, not advise visitors to come to see an infant school for some time after it is opened, for several reasons; first, because the children must be allowed time to learn, and there will be nothing worth seeing; secondly, it takes off the children's attention, and interferes with the master; and lastly, it may be the means of visitors going away dissatisfied, and thereby injure the cause intended to be promoted.

In teaching infants to sing, I have found it the best way to sing the psalm or hymn several times in the hearing of the children, without their attempting to sing until they have some idea of the tune; because if all the children are allowed to attempt, and none of them know the tune, it prevents those who really wish to learn from catching the sounds.

You must not expect order until your little

L 3

officers are well drilled, which may be done by collecting them together after the other children are gone, and instructing them in what they are to do. Every monitor should know his work, and when you have taught him to know his work, you must expect it to be done. To get good order you must make every monitor answerable for the conduct of his class. It is astonishing how some of the little fellows will strut about, big with the importance of office; and here I must remark, it will require some caution to prevent them from taking too much upon themselves; so prone are we, even in the earliest years, to abuse the possession of power.

The way by which we teach the children hymns, is to let one child stand in the rostrum, with the book in his hand; he then reads one line, and stops until all the children in the school have repeated it, which they do altogether; he then repeats another, and so on successively, until the hymn is finished. This method is adopted with every thing that is to be committed to memory, such as catechisms and spelling; if twenty words are to be committed to memory, it is done in this way; so that every child in the school has an equal chance of learning.

I have mentioned that the children should be classed: in order to facilitate this there should be a board fastened to the wall perpendicularly, the same width as the seats, every fifteen feet, all round the school; this will separate one class from another, and be the cause of the children knowing their class the sooner. Make every child hang his hat over where he sits, in his own class as this will save much trouble. " Have a place for every thing, and every thing in its place."

This will bring the children into habits of order. Do not do any thing for a child that he is able to do for himself, but teach him to put his own hat and coat on, and hang them up again when he comes to school; teach every child to help himself as soon as possible; if a child falls down, and you know that he is able to get up himself, never lift him up; if you do, he will always lie until you come to lift him up: have a slate, or a piece of paper, properly ruled, hanging over every class, let every child's name that is in the class be written on it, with the name of the monitor: teach the monitor the names as soon as you can, and then he will tell you who is absent; have a semicircle before every lesson, and make the children keep their toes to the mark; a bit of iron hoop nailed to the floor is the best: when a monitor is asking the children questions, let him place his stool in the centre of the semicircle, and the children stand round him: let the monitors ask what questions they please, they will soon get fond of asking questions, and their pupils will soon be equally fond of answering them. Suppose the monitor ask, What do I sit on? Where are your toes? What do you stand on? What is before you? What behind you? At first children will have no idea of this mode of exercising the thinking powers. But the teacher must encourage them in it, and they will very soon get fond of it, and be able to give an answer immediately. It is a very pleasing sight to see the infants stand round the monitors, and the monitors asking them any questions they think of. I have been much delighted at the questions put, and still more so at the answers given. Assemble all the very small children together as soon as you can: the first

day or two they will want to sit with their brothers or sisters, who are a little older than themselves. But the sooner you can separate them
the better, as the elder children frequently plague
the younger ones; and I have always found, that
the youngest are the happiest by themselves.

Having said thus much on the subject of organizing the school, and supposing the little flock
reduced into something like order; we are next
to consider the means of securing cleanliness and
decorum. Although the following Rules for this
purpose are given, it must not be supposed, that
they are presented as a model not to be departed
from. If they can be improved upon so much
the better, but some such will be found indispensable.

RULES

*To be observed by the Parents of Children ad-
mitted into the —— Infant School.*

1.

PARENTS are to send their children clean
washed, with their hair cut short and combed,
and their clothes well mended, by half past eight
o'clock in the morning, to remain till twelve.

2.

If any child be later in attendance than nine
o'clock in the morning, that child must be sent
back until the afternoon; and in case of being
later than two in the afternoon, it will be sent
back for the day.

3.

Parents may send their children's dinners with them in the morning, so that the children may be taken care of the whole day, to enable the mother to go out to work.

4.

If a child be absent, without a notice being sent to the master or mistress, assigning a satis‑factory reason for the absence, such child will not be permitted to return again to the school.

Saturday afternoon is half-holiday.

*** It is earnestly hoped, that parents will see their own interest, as well as that of their children, in strictly observing these rules; and they are exhorted to submit to their children being govern‑ed by the master and mistress; to give them good instruction and advice; to accustom them to family prayer; but particularly to see that they repeat the Lord's prayer, when they rise in the morning, and when they retire to rest, and to set before them a good example: for in so doing they may humbly hope that the blessing of Almighty God will rest upon them and their families; for we are assured in the holy Scriptures, that if we train up a child in the way he should go, that when he is old he will not depart from it, *Prov.* xxii. 6. Therefore parents may be instrumental in the promotion of the welfare of their children in this life, and of their eternal happiness in the world to come.

On each of these rules I will make a few re‑marks.

First rule. Some parents are so habitually

dirty, that they would not wash their children from one week's end to another, unless required so to do, and if it be done for them, they will not be so thankful as when compelled to do it themselves; this I have experienced to be the fact.

Second rule. This rule has its advantages; for it would not be right to punish the children when the fault rests with their parents, consequently by sending them home, the real authors of the evil are punished. Many of the parents have told me, that when their children have been at home, they employed themselves in singing the alphabet, or counting, patting their hands, &c. &c.; that it was impossible to keep an infant asleep, and that they were glad to get them out of the way, and have said, they would take care that their children should not be late again.

But there is no rule without an exception. I have found that this rule has its disadvantages; for some of the elder children would, when they wanted a half-holiday, take care to be late, in order to find the door shut, although they were sent in proper time by their parents; this, when detected, subjects them to a pat on the hand, which is the only corporeal punishment we have. If this rule were not strictly enforced, the children would be coming at all hours of the day, which would put the school into such disorder, that we should never know when all the children had said their lessons.

Third rule. This rule is of great service to those parents who go out to work; for by sending their children's dinners with them, they are enabled to do their work in comfort, and the children, when properly disciplined, will be no additional trouble to the teacher, for they will play about the play-ground, while he takes his dinner, without doing any mischief.

Fourth rule. Many persons will keep their children away for a month or two, when nothing is the matter with them, consequently the children will lose almost all they have learned at school : besides this, it keeps a child out, who perhaps would attend regularly, and we should never know how many children were in the establishment; therefore if a parent does not attend to this rule, the child's name is struck off the book.

On the admission of a child into the school, the parents should be supplied with a copy of the preceding rules, as this will prevent them from pleading any excuse; they should be fastened on pasteboard, otherwise they would double them up and put them into their pockets, and forget all about them : but being on pasteboard, they may hang them up in their dwellings. The short exhortation that follows, it is hoped, may have its use, by reminding the parents of their duty to co-operate with those persons who have the welfare both of themselves and their children at heart.

I shall next speak of the *daily routine* of instruction,

If we would be successful in our labours, we must ask for help,—we must solicit aid from that Being who never yet denied it. A minister who wishes to instruct his flock with effect, never fails to ask his Maker to open his mouth and enable him to speak to his audience in a way which they may understand ; and certainly every master or teacher must ask for help, and teach his pupils to do so too, if he would wish to be successful. If the wisest and best of men ask assistance from God to teach their fellow-men, and feel and know it to be necessary so to do, who would not ask assistance to teach infants?

> " To lead them into virtue's path
> And up to truth divine."

If we only had to educate the *head*, the thing might be less necessary. But the promoters of *infant schools* want to touch the *heart;* they want to operate upon the will and its affections as well as on the understanding; they want to make good men rather than learned men—men of *wisdom*, rather than men of *knowledge;* and he who has this work to do will find it no easy task; he will soon see his own weakness, and need of help.

But to proceed. The children being assembled, should be desired to stand up, and immediately afterwards to kneel down, all close to their seats, and as silent as possible : those who are not strong enough to kneel, may be allowed to sit on the ground. This being done, a child is to be placed in the centre of the school and to repeat the following prayer.

" O God, our heavenly father, thou art good to us; we would serve thee; we have sinned and done wrong many times. Jesus Christ died on the cross for us. Forgive our sins for Jesus' sake; may the holy spirit change our hearts, and make us to love God; help us to-day to be good children and to do what is right. Keep us from wicked thoughts and bad tempers; make us try to learn all that we are taught; keep us in health all the day. We would always think of God, and when we die may we go to heaven. God bless our fathers and mothers, and sisters and brothers, and our teachers, and make us obedient and kind, for Jesus Christ's sake. Amen.

The children afterwards repeat the Lord's prayer, and then sing a hymn; immediately after which they proceed to their lessons; which are fixed to what are called lesson-posts. To each of these posts there is a monitor, who is provided with a piece of cane for a pointer. This post is placed opposite to his class; and every class has a post, up to which the monitor brings the children three or four at a time, according to the number of children he has in his class. We have fourteen classes, and sometimes more, which are regularly numbered, so that we have one hundred children moving and saying their lessons at one time. When these lessons are completed the children are supplied with pictures, which they put on the post, the same as the spelling and reading lessons, but say them in a different manner. We find that if a class always say their lesson at one post, it soon loses its attraction; and consequently, although we cannot change them about from post to post in the spelling and reading lessons, because it would be useless to put a child to a reading post that did not know its letters, yet we can do so in the picture lessons, as the children are all alike in learning the objects.—One child can learn an object as quick as another, so that we have many children that can tell the name of different subjects, and even the names of all the geometrical figures, who do not know all the letters in the alphabet; and I have had children whom one would think were complete blockheads, on account of their not being able to learn the alphabet so quickly as some of

M

the other children, and yet those very children
would learn things which appeared to me ten
times more difficult. This proves the necessity
of variety, and how difficult it is to legislate for
children. Instead therefore of the children standing opposite their own post, they go round from
one to another, repeating whatever they find at
each post, until they have been all round the
school. For instance, at No. I. post there may
be the following objects; the horse, the ass, the
zebra, the cow, the sheep, the goat, the springing-
antelope, the camelopard, the camel, the wild
boar, the rhinoceros, the elephant, the hippo-
potamus, the lion, the tiger, the leopard, the civet,
the weazel, the great white bear, the hyena, the
fox, the greenland-dog, the hare, the mole, the
squirrel, the kangaroo, the porcupine, the racoon.
—Before commencing these lessons two boys are
selected by the master, who perhaps are not
monitors; these two boys bring the children up
to a chalk line that is made near No. 1 post,
eight at a time; one of the boys gets eight children standing up ready, always beginning at one
end of the school, and takes them to this chalk
line, whilst the other boy takes them to No. 1
post, and delivers them up to the charge of No.
1 monitor. No. 1 monitor then points to the
different animals with a pointer, until the name
of every one that is on his plate has been repeated; this done, he delivers them to No. 2
monitor, who has a different picture at his post
perhaps the following :—fishmonger, mason, hat-
ter, cooper, butcher, blacksmith, fruiterer, dis-
tiller, grocer, turner, carpenter, tallow-chandler
milliner, dyer, druggist, wheelwright, shoe-maker
baker, printer, coach-maker, bookseller, brick

layer, linen-draper, cabinet-maker, brewer, painter, bookbinder. This done, No. 2 monitor delivers them over to No. 3 monitor, and No. 3 monitor to No. 4, and so on successively, until there are about one hundred children on the move at one time, all saying different objects: every child says the whole of the objects at every post. This great variety keeps up the attention, and their moving from post to post promotes their health.

As a further guide to the master or mistress of Infant Schools, I subjoin a synopsis of a week's course of instruction, which I drew up for my own use.

RULES AND REGULATIONS,

AS OBSERVED AT THE INFANT SCHOOL,

QUAKER STREET, SPITALFIELDS.

TIME.—*Mornings.* School to assemble at Nine o'clock, and to leave at Twelve.

Afternoons. School to assemble at Two o'clock, and to leave at Five.

MONDAY.

Morning. When assembled, to perform the appointed prayer, after which a hymn is to be sung; then slates and pencils are to be delivered to the children; after which they are to proceed with their letters and spelling. At half-past ten o'clock to play, and at eleven o'clock to assemble in the gallery, and repeat the picture lessons on natural history after the monitor in the rostrum.

Afternoon. Begin with prayer and hymn as in the morning; picture lessons on Scripture history to be repeated from the lesson post, and to be questioned on them afterwards in the gallery.

TUESDAY.

Morning. Usual prayer and hymn. Slates and pencils. Letters and spelling from the sides of the school, and from the tins. Play. Gallery; repeat the addition and subtraction tables.

Afternoon. Prayer and hymn. Multiplication table; the monitor asking the question, and the children answering. Reading lessons. Play. Gallery; numeration and spelling with brass figures and letters.

WEDNESDAY.

Morning. Prayer and hymn. Slates and pencils. Letters and spelling. Play. Gallery; master to teach geometrical figures, and musical characters, by chalking on the swing-slate.

Afternoon. Prayer and hymn. Practice, pence and shilling tables. Play. Gallery; master to give lessons on arithmetic. Extempore teaching on men and things, &c. &c.

THURSDAY.

Morning. Prayer and hymn. Slates and pencils. Letters and spelling. Division, weights, measures, and time, from the rostrum. Play. Gallery, same lessons as Monday morning.

Afternoon. Prayer and hymn. From the lesson posts, epitome of geometry, and natural history. Gallery, brass letters and figures. Extempore teaching on men and things, taking care that all such teaching shall be illustrated by substances.

FRIDAY.

Morning. Prayer and hymn. Slates and pencils. Letters and spelling. Tables in arithmetic at the master's discretion. Play. Gallery; lessons on geography, maps, globes, &c.

Afternoon. Prayer and hymn. Scripture pictures on the lesson posts, and questions on them in the gallery.

SATURDAY.

Morning. Prayer and hymn. Slates and pencils. Letters and spelling. Tables of arithmetic from the rostrum. Play. Gallery. Lessons on the transposition frame, and on geometry from the brass instrument.

N. B. If visitors wish any particular lessons to be performed, and the children appear inclined, the master is not bound to adhere to the above rules, neither at any other time if the children appear particularly disinclined.

There are two or three other matters, on which before concluding this chapter, I must speak, as claiming the attention of Infant School conductors. And first,

ON CLEANLINESS.

Although we have spoken of this matter before, as cleanliness is of considerable importance, not only to the children but to those around them, it may not be amiss to take up a little more of the reader's time upon this subject, and to state the different plans that have been devised, in order to make the children as clean as possible. For this end, Mr. Wilson caused a trough to be erected, and a pipe to convey the water into it, but before it had been up one month, it was found, that instead of answering the end intended, it had quite a contrary effect, for the children would dabble in the trough, and make themselves ten times worse than they were, by wetting themselves from head to foot, which, besides, frequently caused them to take cold, of which the parents would complain. Some would take their children away, and take no notice about it; others would come and give the master, what they called " *a good set down.*" It was, therefore, thought necessary to forbid the children washing themselves,

M 3

and to wash all that came dirty. But it was soon found that the dirty children increased so fast, that it required one person's time to attend to them; besides which, it had another bad effect, it encouraged the parents in laziness ;—and they would tell me, if I complained of their sending the children to school dirty, " That, indeed, they had no time to wash their children; there was a trough in the school for that purpose, and the persons who had charge of the school, were paid for it, and ought to do it." In consequence of this, the trough was taken away, and it was represented to the parents, that it was their duty to keep their children clean; that unless they did so they would be sent home to be washed; and if they persisted in sending them without being washed, there would be no alternative left, but to dismiss their children from the school altogether. This offended some of the parents, and they took their children out of the school, but many afterwards petitioned to have them readmitted. I mention this, merely to prevent others, who may be concerned in the establishment of an Infant School, from incurring an unnecessary expense, and to shew that the parents will value the school equally as well if you make them wash their children, as if you did it for them. The plan that we have acted upon to enforce cleanliness, is as follows. As soon as the children are assembled in the school, the monitors cause them to hold out their hands, with their heads up; they then inspect their hands and their faces, and all those who are dirty are desired to stand out, to be inspected by the master, who will easily perceive whether they have been washed that morning; if not, they are sent home to be washed, and if the mother has any decent pride in her, she will take care that it shall not often occur. But it may be found, that some have been washed, and have been playing with the dirt, when coming to school, which some children are very apt to do; in this case they have a pat on the hand, which generally cures them. There is much trouble, at first, to keep the children quite clean; some of their parents are habitually dirty, and in such case the children will partake of the same quality; these children will require more trouble than others, but they will soon acquire cleanly habits, and, with proper management, become as cleanly as any of the other children. As soon as a child is taken into the school the monitor shews him a certain place, and explains to him, that when he wants to go into the yard, he is to ask him, and he will accompany him there. Of course there are separate accommodations for each sex, and such prudential arrangements made, as the case requires, but which it is unnecessary further to particularize.

ON THE ILL CONSEQUENCES OF FRIGHTENING CHILDREN.

IT is common for many persons to threaten to put children into the black hole, or to call the sweep to take them away in his bag, when they do not behave as they ought; but the ill effects of this mode of proceeding may be perceived by the following fact. There is a child in the school, who has been to one of those initiatory schools, where the children of mechanics are usually sent,

called Dames' Schools, which was kept by an
elderly woman, who, it seems, had put this child
into the coal-hole, and told him, that unless he
was a good boy, the black man would come and
take him away; this so frightened the child, that
he fell into a violent fit, and never afterwards
could bear the sight of this woman.   On the
mother getting the child admitted into our school,
she desired me to be very gentle with him, relating
to me all the above story, except, that the child
had had a fit.   About a fortnight after the admission of the child, he came running one day
into the school exclaiming, " I'll be a good boy!
master! master! I'll be a good boy."   As soon
as he caught sight of me, he clung round, and
grasped me with such violence that I really thought
the child was mad; in a few minutes after this he
went off into strong convulsions, and looked such
a dreadful spectacle, that I thought the child
would die in my arms.   In this state he remained
for about twenty minutes, and I expected the
child would be carried out of the school a corpse.
I sent for the mother, but on her arrival I perceived
she was less alarmed than myself; she immediately
said, the child was in a fit, and that I had frightened him into it.   I told her she was mistaken;
that the child had only just entered the school,
and I was ignorant of the cause of his fright ; but
several of my little scholars soon set the matter at
rest, by stating the particulars of the fright, as
they saw it when coming to school.   It seems
that there was a man passing along the street,
who sweeps chimneys with a machine, and just as
the little fellow passed him, he called out sweep;
this so alarmed the child, that he thought the
man was going to take him, and was affected by

his fears in the way I have stated. The child, however, getting better, and the mother hearing what the children said, begged my pardon for having accused me wrongfully, and then told me the whole particulars of his first fright with the woman and the coal-hole. I had the greatest difficulty imaginable to persuade him, that a sweep was a human being, and that he loved little children as much as other persons. After some time, the child got somewhat the better of his fears, but not wholly so; he never had but one fit afterwards. This shows how improper it is to confine children by themselves, or to threaten that they shall be taken away in a bag, &c. Many persons continue nervous all their lives through such treatment, and are so materially injured, that they are frightened at their own shadow.

It is also productive of much mischief to talk of mysteries, ghosts, and hobgoblins, before children, which many persons are too apt to do. Some deal so much in the marvellous, that I really believe they frighten many children out of their senses. I recollect, when I was a child, hearing such stories, till I have actually been afraid to look behind me. How many persons are frightened at such a little creature as a mouse, because the nature of that little creature has not been explained to them in their infancy. Indeed children should have all things shown them, if possible, that they are likely to meet with; and above all, it should be impressed upon their minds, that if they meet with no injury from the living, it is most certain, the dead will never hurt them, and that he who fears God, need have no other fear. It is also common with many persons, to put a

disobedient child into a room by himself. I
cannot approve of this method, as the child is
frequently frightened into quietness without improving its temper in the least; if it be day-time
it is not so bad, but if it be dark the consequences
are often serious, and materially injure the constitution of the child.

———

ON THE DISEASES OF CHILDREN.

IT may, probably, be considered presumption
in me, to speak of the diseases of children, as this
more properly belongs to the faculty; but let it
be observed, that my pretension is not to cure
the diseases that children are subject to, but only
to prevent those which are infectious from spreading. I have found that children between the
ages of two and seven years, are subject to the
measles, hooping cough, fever, ophthalmia, and
the small-pox. This last is very rare, owing to
the great encouragement given to vaccination;
and were it not for the obstinacy of many of the
poor, I believe this disease would be totally
extirpated. During the whole of the time I was
in charge of the Spitalfields' School, I only heard
of three children dying of it, and those had never
been vaccinated. I always made a point of inquiring, on the admission of a child, whether
this operation had been performed, and, if not, I
strongly recommended that it should. If the parents spoke the truth, I had but few children in
the school who had not been vaccinated: this accounts, therefore, for having lost but three children through that disease.

The measles, however, I consider as a very dangerous disorder, and we lost a great many children by this disease, besides two of my own. The symptoms I have generally found as follow. It is preceded with a violent cough, and the child's eyes appear watery ; the child will also be sick. As soon as these symptoms are perceived, I would immediately send the child home, and desire the parents to keep him at home for a few days, in order to ascertain if it has the measles, and if so, it must be prohibited from coming to school until well. This caution is absolutely necessary, as some parents are so careless, that they will send their children when the measles are thick out upon them.

The same may be said with respect to other diseases, for unless the persons who have charge of the school attend to these things, the parents will be glad to get their children out of the way, and will send them with various diseases upon them, without considering the ill-effects that may be produced in the school. Whether such conduct in the parents proceeds from ignorance or not, I am not able to say, but this I know, that I have had many parents offer children for admission, with all the diseases I have mentioned, and who manifested no disposition to inform me of it. The number of children who may be sick, from time to time, may be averaged at from twenty to thirty-five. Out of two hundred and twenty, we have never had less than twenty absent on account of illness, and once or twice, we had as many as fifty.

Soon after I first took charge of the Spitalfields' School, I found that there were five or six children in the school who had the measles ; the consequence was, that it contaminated the whole school, and about eight children died, one of my own being of that number. This induced me to be very cautious in future, and I made a point of walking round the school twice every day, in order to inspect the children; and after the adoption of this plan, we did not have the measles in the school.

The hooping-cough is known, of course, by the child hooping; but I consider it the safest plan to send all children home that have any kind of cough; this will cause the mother to come and inquire the reason why the child is sent home; I then can ascertain from her whether the child has had the hooping-cough or not.

With respect to fever, I generally find the children appear chilly and cold, and not unfrequently they are sick. I do not however feel myself competent to describe the early symptoms of this disorder, but the best way to prevent its gaining ground in the school is to send all the children home who appear the least indisposed; this will be the most likely way to prevent a fever from getting into the school.

As to the ophthalmia, I can describe the symptoms of that disease, having had it myself, together with the whole of my family. It generally comes in the left eye first, and causes a sensation as if something was in the eye, which pricks and shoots, and causes great pain: the white of the eye will appear red, or what is usually called bloodshot; this, if not speedily attended to, will cause blindness; I have had several children that have been blind with it for several days. In the morning the patients are not able to unclose their eyes, for they will be gummed up, and it will be some time after they are awake before they will be able to disengage the eyelids. As soon as I observe these appearances, I immediately send the child home; for I have ascertained, beyond a doubt, that the disease is contagious, and if a child be suffered to remain with it in the school, the infection will speedily spread among all the children.

As children are frequently apt to burn or scald themselves, I will here insert a method for the cure of both. It is very simple, and yet infallible; at least, I have never known it to fail. It is no other than common writing ink. One of my own children burnt its hand dreadfully, and was cured by immediately washing it all over with ink. Several children burnt their hands against the pipe that was connected with the stove in the school-room, and were cured by the same means. One boy, in particular, took hold of a hot cinder that fell from the fire, and it quite singed his hand; I applied ink to it, and it was cured in a very short time. Let any one, therefore, who may happen to receive a burn, apply ink to it immediately, and he will soon witness the good effects of the application.

CHAPTER VIII.

PRINCIPLES OF INFANT EDUCATION.

" We desire to give a moral constitution to the child instead of
a moral custom."

IT is observed by a very celebrated writer, " that
the educator's care, above all things, should be,
first, to lay in his charge the foundation of reli·
gion and virtue."   If, then, this be the first care,
how important is it to take the earliest opportu·
nity of instilling such principles into infant minds,
before they are overcharged with principles of an
opposite nature.   It has likewise been observed,
and perhaps with some truth, " that the human
soul is never idle, that if the mind is not occupied
with something good, it must needs employ itself
about something evil."   The chief end and design
of an infant school, is to keep the mind employed
about what is innocent and useful ; and therefore
teaching children to read, write, and so on, are
regarded as secondary objects.   Many have been
taught to read and write well, and have had,
what is usually called, a good education ; but
inasmuch as they have not been taught their duty
to God, and to each other, they have frequently

launched out into every species of vice, and their education has only served to render them more formidable and dangerous to the rest of the community.

If we inquire the cause why men have been so loose in their principles, and vicious in their conduct, it seems to be, that in the places of education, of all ranks, until lately, too little attention has been paid to religious instruction. " Too many," says Dr. Fuller, " are more careful to bestow wit on their children, rather than virtue, the art of speaking well rather than doing well ;" whereas, their morals ought to be the chief concern ; to be prudent, honest, good, and virtuous, are infinitely higher accomplishments, than being learned, rhetorical, metaphysical, or, that which the world usually calls, great scholars and fine gentlemen ; and a virtuous education for children, is to them a better inheritance, than a great estate.

The business of Infant Education, may properly be divided into three branches : *moral*, *mental*, and *physical.* The first, relating to the inculcation of those principles, and the development of those feelings, which constitute a virtuous character. The second having regard to the proper treatment of those faculties of reason, with which the human being is gifted,—enabling it, not only to discern between good and evil,— and to appropriate the blessings of life to its enjoyment, but likewise to comprehend, to a certain extent, the wonderful and admirable works of the Creator; and the last, relating to the means proper to be taken for preserving the health of the body. The whole tending to the attainment of that state which may be regarded as the perfection of human existence; health of body, activity of mind, and piety and benevo- lence of spirit.

With regard to the moral treatment of children, under the system of education hitherto pursued, I must candidly say,—it has been frequently omitted altogether, and still more frequently has it been erroneous, and consequently, ineffi- cient. Let me ask,—would it be of any benefit to a child's health, to learn it to repeat certain maxims on the benefits resulting from exercise? Neither can it be of any service to the moral health of the child, to learn it to repeat, or to store in its memory, the best maxims of virtue, unless we have taken care to excite an activity of vir- tuous feeling to apply and act upon those pre- cepts. And yet, this has not been the practice. How frequently do we hear persons remark upon the ill conduct of children, " It is surprising they should do so ;—they have been taught better things !" Very likely; and no doubt they have got all the golden rules of virtue, alluded to, carefully stored up in their memories;—but they are like the hoarded treasures of the miser : the disposition to use them is wanted. It is this we must strive to promote in the child. If we can excite a love of goodness, and an activity of vir- tuous feeling, the child will not err, nor lack the knowledge how to do good, even though we were to forget, or neglect, to give it any rules or maxims to go by. It is to the heart we must turn our attention in the moral treatment of children. With this end in view, the first grand object of the master or mistress of an infant school, is to win the love of the children, by banishing all slavish fear. The children are to be invited to regard their teacher, as one who is desirous of promoting their happiness, by the most affectionate means—not by kind words, but by kind actions. One kind action influences a child more than a volume of words. Words appeal only to the understanding, and frequently pass away as empty sounds; but kind actions influence the heart, and, like the genial warmth of spring, that dispels the gloom which has pervaded the face of nature during the chilly season of winter, they disperse the mists which cold treatment has engendered in the moral atmosphere. The fundamental principle of the Infant School system is *love ;* nor should any other be substituted for it except when absolutely necessary. Let the children see that you love them, and *love* will beget *love*, both toward their teacher, and toward each other. Without the aid of example nothing can be done; it is by the force of this magnetic influence alone that sympathetic feelings can be awakened; example acts as a talisman upon the inmost powers of the soul, and excites them to activity; which should be the constant aim of all persons engaged in the important work of education. As we find in the case of vicious principles that they are strengthened by habit, and good principles proportionally weakened; so, on the contrary, immoral dispositions are weakened by the better feelings being continually awakened; and by checking the growth of every evil tendency, and encouraging the growth of all that is estimable, we shall banish that fondness for the delusive pleasures of this world, which is so general, and substitute in its place the comforts of vital goodness,—those high and lasting enjoyments which alone can bring us peace here, and happiness hereafter.

N 3

The great defect in the human character is *selfishness*, and to remove or lessen this, is the grand desideratum of moral culture. How happy were mankind, if, instead of living, each one for himself, they lived really and mutually for each other! The perfection of moral excellence cannot be better described than as the attainment of that state when we could really " love our neighbour as ourselves." If it be a height of perfection unattainable, it is certainly one which we should ever be striving to attain; no one has got so near to it that he can say,—I can get no nearer; and I fear few can say that they have attained the object. The prevalence of self-love in the human character will be very obvious to the observant master or mistress, in the conduct of the children under their care,—and it is this feeling that they must be ever striving to check or eradicate. Nor need they despair, as to those in whom the evil has not been confirmed by habit, of meeting with much success. The children may be brought to feel, that to impart happiness is to receive it *,—that, being kind to their little schoolfellows, they not only secure a return of kindness, but actually receive a gratification themselves, from so doing; that there is more pleasure in forgiving an injury than in resenting it. Some I know will be apt to say,—that after all, this is nothing but *selfishness* or *self-love*. It is an old bone of contention, and I leave those to quarrel over it who please. Every one knows and feels the difference between that which we call *selfishness*, and that which is comprehensively termed by the lips of divine truth,

* See as an illustration of this, which a very young child may understand, the little tale entitled " The Two Halves," in the Appendix.

the "*love of our neighbour.*" If it must be called self-love, I can only say, that it is the proper direction of the feeling which is to be sought.

In the work of moral culture, it will be necessary not only to watch the child's conduct under the restraint of school discipline, and observation; but at those times when it thinks itself at liberty to indulge its feelings unobserved. The evil propensities of our nature have all the wiliness of serpents; and lurk in their secret places, watching for a proper opportunity of displaying themselves, and coming forth. For the purpose of observation the *play-ground* will afford an admirable opportunity; and is on this account, as well as that it affords exercise and amusement to the children, a most indispensable appendage to an Infant School. It is here the child will shew its character in a true light. The play-ground may be compared to the world, where the little children are left to themselves, and where it may be seen what effects their education has produced; for if they are fond of fighting and quarrelling, it is there that they will do it; if they are artful, it is there they will seek to practise their cunning; and this will give the master an opportunity of applying the proper remedy: whereas, if kept in school (which they must be, if there be no play-ground) these evil inclinations will never manifest themselves until they get into the street, and consequently, the master will have no opportunity of attempting a cure. I have seen many children, who behaved very orderly in the school, but the moment they got into the play-ground they manifested the principle of self-love to such a degree, that they would wish all the rest of the children to be subservient to them; and on these refusing to let them bear rule, would begin to use force, in order to compel them to comply. This is conduct that ought to be checked—and what time so proper as the first stages of infancy?

I have had others, who would try every expedient, in order to deprive the weaker and smaller children of their little property, such as marbles, buttons, and the like; and who, when they have found that force would not do, would try hypocrisy, and other evil arts, that are but too prevalent, and of which they see too many examples out of school. All these things have taken place in the play-ground, and yet in the school such children have shown no such disposition; consequently, had it not been for the play-ground, they would not have been detected, and those principles would have gone on ripening, until they had become quite rooted in the character of the child, and would ever after, perhaps, have formed the basis of its conduct through life. I am, indeed, so firmly convinced, from the experience I have had of the utility of a play-ground, from the above reasons, and others, elsewhere mentioned, that I scruple not to say, an Infant School is of little service without one.

In those instances where the play-ground is ornamented with flowers, fruit-trees, &c. (and I would recommend this plan to be invariably adopted) it not only affords the teacher an opportunity of instilling a variety of ideas into the minds of the children, and of tracing every thing up to the Great First Cause, but it becomes the means of establishing principles of honesty. The children should not on any account be allowed to pluck the fruit or flowers; every thing should be considered as sacred; and being thus early ac-

customed to principles of honesty, temptations in
after-life will be deprived of their power. It
must be a source of great grief to all lovers of
children, to see what havoc is made by them in
plantations near London; and, perhaps, grown
persons are not entirely free from this fault, who
are not content with a proper foot-path, but must
walk on a man's plantations, pull up that which
can be of no use to them, and thereby injure the
property of their neighbour. These things ought
not to be, nor do I think they would be so common as they are, if they were noticed a little
more in the training and education of children.
It has been too much the practice with many, to
consider that the business of a school consists
merely in teaching children their letters, but I
am of opinion, that the formation of character is
of the greatest importance, not only to the children, but to society at large. How can we account for the strict honesty of the Laplanders,
who can leave their property in the woods, and
in their huts, without the least fear of it being
stolen or injured; while we, with ten times the
advantages, cannot consider our property safe,
with the aid of locks and bolts, brick walls, and
even watchmen besides? There must be some
cause for all this, and perhaps the principal one
is, the defects in the education of children, and
the total neglect of the infant poor, at a time
when their first impressions should be taken
especial care of; *for conscience, if not lulled into
sleep, but rather called into action, will prove
stronger than either brick walls, bolts, or locks;
and I am satisfied, that I could have taken the
whole of my children into any gentleman's plan-*

*tation, without their doing the least injury what.
ever.*

Another thing I would notice, with regard to *speaking the truth.* There is nothing so delight-ful as the hearing and speaking of truth; for this reason there is no conversation so agreeable as that of the man of integrity, who hears without any design to betray, and speaks without any intention to deceive: this admitted, we should strive to our utmost to induce children to speak the truth. But our success, in a great measure, will depend on the means we take to accomplish that end. I know that many children are fright-ened into falsehood by the injudicious methods adopted by those persons who have the care of them. I have known a mother promise her child forgiveness if it would speak the truth, and, after having obtained confession, has broken her pro-mise. A child, once treated in this manner, will naturally be guarded against a second like de-ception. I have known others who would pre-tend not to punish the child for confession, but for first denying it, and afterwards confessing, I think that children should not be punished on any account after having been promised forgive-ness; truth being of too great importance to be thus trifled with; and we cannot wonder if it is lightly esteemed by children, after the example is set by their parents. Having had several thou-sand children pass through my hands, it has fur-nished me with opportunities of observing the bias of the infant mind, and I must say, that I have not found children so inclined to evil and falsehood as I had heretofore imagined, neither so corrupt as is generally supposed. For if our dealings are fair and honourable with children, we may expect from them much better things. I do believe, when we have ascertained the proper method of treating children, it will be found that they came from the hands of their Creator in a much better state than we generally suppose, and that they are not so prone to vice, cruelty, lying, and many other evils, as is generally believed. Instead of snarling at each other like dogs, I find they will be as kind and good natured to each other as any race of beings on earth: for many of their faults are often committed rather through ignorance than intention. It being my intention to enter somewhat at length into the question of rewards and punishments, as connected with moral culture, I shall devote a separate chapter to it, and shall now proceed to speak of the development of the mental powers.

Before I enter into minute details upon this subject, I must trespass a little upon the attention of the reader, in order to show the necessity of the plan I am about to describe; in doing this it will be proper to quote the words of an excellent author, who says, " From the time that children begin to use their hands, nature directs them to handle every thing over and over, to look at it while they handle it, and to put it into various positions, and at various distances from the eye. We are apt to excuse this as a childish diversion, because they must be doing something, and have not reason to entertain themselves in a more manly way. But if we think more justly, we shall find that they are engaged in the most serious and important study; and if they had all the reason of a philosopher, they could not be more properly employed. For it is this childish employment that enables them to make the proper use of their eyes. They are thereby every day acquiring habits of perception, which are of greater importance than any thing we can teach them. The original perceptions which nature gave them are few, and insufficient for the purposes of life; and therefore she made them capable of many more perceptions by habit. And to complete her work, she hath given them an unwearied assiduity in applying to the exercise by which those perceptions are acquired."

This is the education which nature gives to her children, and since we have fallen upon this subject, we may add, that another part of nature's education is, that by the course of things, children must exert all their muscular force, and employ all their ingenuity, in order to gratify their curiosity and satisfy their little appetites. What they desire is only to be obtained at the expense of labour and patience, and many disappointments. By the exercise of body and mind necessary for satisfying their desires, they acquire agility, strength, and dexterity in their motions, as well as health and vigour to their constitutions; they learn patience and perseverance, they learn to bear pain without dejection, and disappointment without despondency: the education of nature is most perfect in savages, who have no other tutor; and we see, that in the quickness of all their senses, in the agility of all their motions, in the hardiness of their constitutions and in the strength of their minds, to bear hunger, thirst, pain, and disappointment, they commonly far exceed civilized nations. A most ingenious writer, on this account, seems to prefer savage to social life. But it is the intention of nature, that human education should be joined to her institution in order to form the man, and she hath fitted us for human education, by the natural principles of imitation and credulity, which discover themselves almost in infancy, as well as by others which are of later growth.

When the education which we receive from men does not give scope to the education of nature, it is wrongly directed; it tends to hurt our faculties of perception, and to enervate both the body and mind. Nature has her way of rearing men, as she has of curing their diseases: the art of medicine is, to follow nature, to imitate and assist her in the cure of diseases; and the art of education is, to follow nature, to assist and to imitate her in her way of rearing men. The ancient inhabitants of the Baleares followed nature in the manner of teaching their children to be good archers, when they hung their dinner aloft by a thread, and left them to bring it down by their skill in archery.

The education of nature, without any more human care than is necessary to preserve life, makes a perfect savage. Human education joined to that of nature, may make a good citizen, a skilful artizan, or a well-bred man; but reason and reflection must superadd their tutory, in order to produce a Bacon or a Newton.

Notwithstanding the innumerable errors committed in human education, there is hardly any education so bad, as to be worse than none. And I apprehend there is no one, if he were to choose whether to educate a son among the French, the Italians, the Chinese, or among the Esquimaux, would not give the preference to the last. When reason is properly employed, she will confirm the

o

dictates of nature, which are always true and wholesome.

The error of the *past* system (for such I hope I may venture to call it) of *mental development* was, that the inferior powers of the mind were called into activity, in preference to its higher faculties. The object sought was to exercise the memory, and store it with information, which, owing to the inactive state of the understanding and cogitative powers, was seldom or never of any use. To learn and adopt the opinions of others was thought quite enough, without the child being troubled to think for itself, and form an opinion of its own. But this is not as it should be. Such a system is very little likely to produce great or wise men; and is only adapted to the tutory of parrots. Now, the first thing we attempt to do in an infant school is, to set the children thinking,—to get them to examine, compare, and judge, of all those matters which their dawning intellects are capable of mastering. It is of no use to tell a child, in the first place, *what it should think,*—this is at once inducing an idleness of mind, which is but too generally prevalent among adults; owing to this very practice—this erroneous method of proceeding having been adopted by those who had the charge of their first years. Were a child left to its own resources, to discover and judge of things wholly by itself, though an opposite evil would be the consequence, namely, a state of comparative ignorance, yet I am doubtful whether it would be a greater or more lamentable one than that issuing from the injudicious system of giving children dogmas instead of problems, opinions instead of interrogatories. In the one case we should find a mind, uninformed and uncultivated, but with a vigorous and masculine character, holding the little knowledge it possessed, with the power and right of a conqueror; in the other, a memory stored with a heap of useless lumber,—without a single opinion or idea it could call its own,— a mind indolent and narrow, and from long-indulged inactivity, incapable of exertion. Once more, as the fundamental principle of the system, I would say, let the *children think for themselves.* If they arrive at erroneous conclusions, assist them in attaining the truth; but let them, with such assistance, arrive at the truth by their own exertions. Little good would be done, if you should say to a child,—*That* is wrong,—*this* is right, unless you enable the child to perceive wherein the error of the one and the truth of the other consist. It is not only due to the child as a rational being that you should act so, but it is essentially necessary for the development of its intellectual faculties. It were not in the least degree more ridiculous for a master in teaching arithmetic, to give his pupil the problem and answer, without informing him of, or instructing him in, the method of working the question, than it is for a person to give a child results of reasoning, without showing him how the truth is arrived at. Some persons will be ready to exclaim, " Surely the teacher should not withhold from the child the benefit of his knowledge and experience,—the child will have time enough to examine the merits of his information when he grows older and more competent to do so!" To this I answer: in the first place nothing should be submitted to the child which it is not fully competent to understand. To give the child tasks or subjects too difficult for its state of mental power, is a violation of nature; and as foolish and detrimental as though you were to place a hundred pounds weight on its shoulders, when it is incapable of supporting ten. The teacher's experience can only be of service to the child as far as it has relation to a like stage of existence; and as to postponing the period when a child is to think for itself, I can only say, there is no occasion for it. Nature has provided food adapted to the powers of the infant's stomach, and those who would rightly conduct the work of education, should imitate her in providing its intellectual food. That this may be done, I am attempting to show in theory in the pages of this work; and, that it answers equally well in practice, any one who has a doubt, may assure themselves by visiting any one of the schools conducted upon the plan here laid down.

It has been a charge brought against the system, that we are not sufficiently anxious to teach the children to read, &c. Now, though I may venture to say, that under no other plan, do the children acquire a knowledge of the characters of the alphabet, and the formation of words as soon as under the present, yet I am quite ready to concede that I consider their learning to read a secondary object, to that of teaching them to examine into, and find out the nature and property of things, of which words are but the *signs*. It is with *things*, and not *words*, we wish to make our children acquainted. If they first learn the nature and properties of an object, there is no fear of their afterwards enquiring its name; but we too frequently find, that having acquired *names*, they are indifferent and forgetful of the objects represented.

Our first endeavour is, to excite a spirit of enquiry,—to foster that inquisitive spirit which is so natural to young children;—till this is properly done, your information will be unwelcomely received, and it is most likely soon forgotten, but having once stirred up their curiosity, you are more likely to tire of communicating than they of receiving. The skilful teacher will rather indeed leave them with a still craving appetite, than satiate them with a redundancy. I have frequently found the most beneficial results arise from a sudden cessation of a lesson or lecture on an interesting topic. The children have awaited its renewal with the utmost impatience, pondering over what they had already heard, and anticipating what was yet to come with the greatest interest. Give a child a *task*, and you impose a burthen on him,—permit him to learn something and you confer a favour.

Having excited a spirit of enquiry, your next endeavour is to direct it to proper objects. To offer the child such objects for investigation as are suited for its infantile faculties; these of course will be things which have relation to its animal senses; the nature and properties of bodies, ascertainable by the application of those senses, &c. Having induced it to examine for itself, you are now to elicit the ideas exerted by each object respectively; ascertain the child's notion on the subject, and having thus brought it to put its ideas into a definitive shape in language; having taught it to use its reason and judgment freely, and to express its notions fearlessly and candidly,—it matters not how simple the subject—you are to attempt the correction of its erroneous notions, by putting forth your own, in as simple a way as possible. Not so as to induce the child to give up its own opinions and adopt yours in their place, but in such a way as to direct its reasoning process to the attainment of truth; to induce a comparison, and consequent discovery of its own error.

The powers of observation will speedily be improved under such a course of instruction, and in all the subsequent stages of existence, will not fail to constitute an independent and shrewd observer. But some may think we are putting a strain on the child's faculties by the plan recommended, and are overstepping nature's laws, —and that the result must be detrimental to the child, both in mind and body. So far, however, is this from being true, that we have taken nature for our guide. We deprecate that unnatural system, which gave the children tasks beyond their powers, and for which their infantine faculties were not qualified;—we would lead them on in the path which nature has marked out—step by step—taking care that one thing should be thoroughly mastered before another was attempted. Such are the general principles of mental culture I would recommend; their application in detail to the respective branches of education will occupy the greater remaining part of the volume; and I shall now speak of the remaining division of the plan of an Infant School system.

As so much has been written on the necessity of *proper exercise* for children, and as I have more than once incidentally noticed the subject, in the preceding pages, one would have thought

it absolutely unnecessary to have noticed the
subject again : but, " custom, that plague of
wise men, and idol of others," is not so easily
changed; hence a custom, although it may be
quite contrary to reason, is frequently rigidly
adhered to, for no other reason than because it
is a custom.—I trust, however, the time is fast
approaching when every thing connected with
the training and educating of the rising generation will undergo a thorough revision, and that
the legislative body will not think it beneath
their notice to attend to this subject. If we
examine the treatment of horses, dogs, and other
animals, we shall find (strange as it may appear)
that there has been more pains bestowed upon
them than there has been upon the infant poor.
It is not uncommon to see men take horses and
dogs out for an airing, and give them exercise,
but it is very uncommon to see a governess or
master giving their pupils exercise—I mean the
children of the poor. It is true that we may
sometimes see the children of boarding-schools
taking a little exercise, but not nearly so much
as they ought, and when they do, it is turned
to no other account than merely for the walk.
So much are they rivetted to books, and confined
to rooms, that it has never entered the mind of
many masters to teach by things instead of books;
and yet no one will deny, that the wide world
furnishes plenty of lessons, and that many of the
objects in nature would prove the best of *books*,
if they were but read—but no, this is not the
custom. Give a child a book into his hand, and
let him addle his brain over it for two or three
hours, and if he does not learn his task set him

down for a *blockhead;* never mind whether he understands the subject. If he does not learn his task, flog him. No questions allowed by any means. Nothing can be greater impertinence, than for children to desire explanation; let them find it out as well as they can. This is part of the old system; but will it be argued that this is the best method to cultivate and treat the *human* mind? May I hope to be excused when I say, that I think, if only one half the pains were taken to *break in, train, and exercise* the infant poor, that is taken with *gentlemen's horses and dogs,* we should very soon sensibly feel its effects. Of all the causes which conspire to render the life of man short and miserable, no one has greater influence than the want of proper exercise. Healthy parents, wholesome food, and proper clothing, will avail little where exercise is neglected; sufficient exercise will counterbalance several defects in nursing, but nothing can supply the want of it. It is absolutely necessary to the health, the growth, and the strength of children.

The desire of exercise is coeval with life itself. Were this principle attended to, many diseases might be prevented; but while indolence and sedentary employments prevent two-thirds of mankind from either taking sufficient exercise themselves, or giving it to their children, what have we to expect, but diseases and deformity among their offspring? The rickets, a disease which is very destructive to children, has greatly increased in Britain, since manufactures began to flourish, and people, attracted by the love of gain, left the country to follow sedentary employments in great towns. It is amongst these people that this disease chiefly prevails, and not only deforms, but kills many of their offspring.

The conduct of other young animals shews the propriety of giving exercise to children. Every other animal makes use of its organs of motion as soon as it can, and many of them, when under no necessity of moving in quest of food, cannot be restrained without force. This is evidently the case with the calf, the lamb, and most other young animals. If these creatures were not permitted to frisk about, and take exercise, they would soon die, or become diseased. The same inclination appears very early in the human species; but as they are not able to take exercise themselves, it is the business of their parents and nurses to assist them. Children may be exercised in various ways, and the method we take to exercise them is shewn in other parts of this work. It is a pity that men should be so inattentive to this matter; their negligence is one reason why females know so little of it. Women will ever be desirous to excel in such accomplishments as recommend them to the other sex; but men generally keep at such a distance from even the smallest acquaintance with the affairs of the nursery, that many would reckon it an affront were they supposed to know any thing of them. Not so, however, with the kennel or the stables; a gentleman of the first rank is not ashamed to give directions concerning the management of his dogs or horses, yet would blush were he surprised in performing the same office for that being who is to be the heir of his fortunes, and the future hopes of his country.

" Arguments to show the importance of exercise might be drawn from every part of the animal economy; without exercise, the circulation of the blood cannot be properly carried on, nor the different secretions duly performed; without exercise the fluids cannot be properly prepared, nor the solids rendered strong or firm.   The action of the heart, the motion of the lungs, and all the vital functions, are greatly assisted by exercise.   But to point out the manner in which these effects are produced, would lead us into the economy of the human body, which is not our object.   We shall therefore only add, that when exercise is neglected, none of the animal functions can be duly performed; and when this is the case, the whole constitution must go to wreck.   A good constitution ought certainly to be our first object in the management of children.   It lays a foundation for their being useful and happy in life ; and whoever neglects it, not only fails in his duty to his offspring, but to society."

I am sorry to say, that many men have considered it quite beneath their notice, to have any thing to do with infant children, and consequently have permitted their children to be sent to what is called schools, and there to be placed on seats for hours, under the care of some person, who, in many cases, is no more fit to teach and instruct children, than I am fit to be a monarch.   If any man will take his children into his garden or fields, and encourage them to ask questions on the glories, works, and first great Cause of nature, he will soon find out the importance of the thing, and the necessity of his own mind being well cultivated, to be enabled to answer their questions.   Whatever men may think of this subject, they will find ultimately, that the rising generation have never had a fair chance of becoming wise; because they have not had proper exercise, either for their minds or bodies.

While this is the case, let us not complain of weak and thoughtless children, or of weak and thoughtless servants; for the former owe it to the neglect of their parents and the public; and the latter to their not having been taught to think at all—and yet those very persons that object to the education of the poor are the first to complain of thoughtless servants.

It will have been perceived that amusement and exercise form prominent features in the plan I have laid down; and I certainly did hope that in every Infant School they would ever have remained such. A notion, however, that habits of industry must be established, has been the means, I am sorry to say, of a sad perversion of the system in this respect. The time allowed for amusement and exercise has been very much abridged, that the children might learn and practise sewing, knitting, plaiting, &c. Now, no one can be more disposed to the encouragement of industrious habits than I am, but let it not be at the expense of the health of the children; which I am certain in these cases it must be. Deprive the children of their amusement and they will soon cease to be the lively, happy beings we have hitherto seen them, and will become the sickly, inanimate things, we had been accustomed to see and pity, under the confinement and restraint of the Dames' Schools. I do not scruple to say, that if the *play-grounds* of Infant Schools are cut off from the system,— they will from that moment cease to be a blessing to the country.

CHAPTER IX.

ON REWARDS AND PUNISHMENTS.

The magisterial severity of some teachers frightens more
knowledge out of children than they can ever whip into them.

AS man comes into the world with a propensity
to do that which is forbidden, it has been found
necessary, at all times, to enact laws to govern
him, and even to punish him, when he acts contrary to those laws; and where is the person,
who will deny any man a just reward who has
done any act, whereby his fellow-men have been
benefitted? Indeed, it is an old, though homely
maxim, " That the sweet of labour is the hope
of reward." If, then, rewards and punishments
are necessary to make men active, and to keep
them in order, who are expected to know right
from wrong, how can it be expected that children, who come into the world with hereditary
propensities to evil, can be governed without
some kind of punishment? I am aware that I
am not taking the popular side of the question,
by becoming an advocate for punishment, but
notwithstanding this, I must say, that I do not
think any school in England has ever been governed without it; and I think that the many
theories ushered into the world, on this subject,
have not been exactly acted upon. Indeed it
appears to me, that while men continue to be
imperfect beings, it is not possible that either
they, or their offspring, can be governed without

some degree of punishment. I admit that punishment should be administered with prudence, and never employed but as a last resource; and I am sorry to say, that it has descended to brutality in some schools, which, perhaps, is one reason why so many persons set their faces against it altogether.

The first thing that appears to me necessary, is to find out, if possible, the real disposition and temper of a child, in order to be able to manage it with good effect. I admit that it is possible to govern some children without corporeal punishment, for I have had some under my charge whom I never had occasion to punish, to whom a word was quite sufficient, and who, if I only looked displeased, would burst into tears. But I have had others quite the reverse; you might talk to them till you were tired, and it would produce no more effect half an hour afterwards, than if they had not been spoken to at all. Indeed children's dispositions and tempers are as various as their faces; no two are alike; consequently what will do for one child will not do for another; hence the impropriety of having any invariable stated mode of punishment. What should we think of a medical man, who was to prescribe for every constitution alike? The first thing a skilful physician does, is to ascertain the constitution of the patient, and then he prescribes accordingly; and nothing is more necessary, for those who have charge of little children, than to ascertain their tempers and dispositions; having done this, as far as possible, should a child offend, they will, in some measure, know how to apply the necessary cure.

To begin with rewards: the monitors I have generally allowed one penny a week each; this was allowed by Mr. Wilson, in the Spitalfields' School, at my own request, as I found much difficulty in procuring monitors; for, whatever *honors* were attached to the office of a monitor, children of five years old could not exactly comprehend them; they could much easier perceive the use of a penny; and as a proof how much they valued the penny a week above all the honors that could be conferred upon them, I always had a good supply of monitors after the penny a week was allowed. Before this time, they used to say, "Please, sir, may I sit down, I do not like to be a monitor?" Perhaps I might prevail on some to hold the office a little longer, by explaining to them what an honorable office it was; but, after all, I found that the penny a week spoke more powerfully than I did, and the children would say to each other, " I like to be a monitor now, for I had a penny last Saturday; and master says, we are to have a penny every week; don't you wish you were a monitor?" "Yes, I do; and master says, if I be a good boy, I shall be a monitor bye and bye, and then I shall have a penny." I think they richly deserve it. Some kind of reward I consider necessary, but what kind of reward, must, of course, rest entirely with the promoters of the different schools.

With regard to punishments, they are various, according to the disposition of the child. The only corporeal punishment that we inflict, is a pat on the hand, which is of very great service in flagrant cases of misconduct; for instance, I have seen one child bite another's arm, until it has almost made its teeth meet. I should suppose few persons are prepared to say, such a child should not be punished for it. I have seen others, who, when they first came to school, as soon as their mothers had brought them to the door, would begin to scream as if they were being punished, while the mother continued to threaten the child without ever putting one threat into execution. The origin of all this noise, has been, perhaps, because the child has demanded a halfpenny, as the condition of coming to school, and the mother probably has not had one to give him, but has actually been obliged to borrow one in order to induce him to come in at the school door: thus the child has come off conqueror, and sets it down as a maxim for the future that he may do just as he pleases with the mother. I have sometimes made my appearance at this time, to know what all the noise was about, when the mother has entered into a lamentable tale, telling me what trouble she has had with the child, and that he will not come to school without having a halfpenny each time he comes. What is the issue? The moment the child has seen me, all has been as quiet as possible. 1 have desired the child to give me the half-penny, which he has done directly, I have returned it to the mother, and the child has gone into school, as good as any child could do. I have had others, who would throw their victuals into the dirt, and then lie down in it themselves, and refuse to rise up, crying, " I will go home; I want to go into the fields; I will have a halfpenny." The mother answered, " Well, my dear, you shall have a halfpenny, if you will stay at school." " No, I want to go and play with Billy or Tommy;" and the mother at length has taken the churl home again, and thus fed his vanity and nursed his pride, till he has completely mastered her, to that degree, that she has been glad to apply to the school again, and beg that I would take him in hand.

I have found it necessary under such circumstances, to enter into a kind of agreement with the mother, that she should not interfere in any respect whatever: that on such conditions, and such only, could the child be admitted; observing, that I should act towards it as if it were my own, but that it must and should be obedient to me; to which the mother has consented, and the child has been taken in again, and strange to say, in less than a fortnight has been as good, and behaved as orderly as any child in the school. But I should deem myself guilty of duplicity and deceit, were I to say that such children, in all cases, could be managed without corporeal punishment, for it appears to me, that corporeal punishment, in moderation, has been the mode of correcting refractory children, from the earliest ages; for it is expressly stated in the Scriptures, "*He that spareth his rod hateth his son, but he that loveth him chasteneth him betimes;*" and again, "*He that knoweth his Lord's will, and doeth it not, shall be beaten with many stripes.*"*

* The following extract from the "Teacher's Magazine" will shew that corporeal punishment, in moderation, is not contrary to the Scriptures, and I hope will prove a sufficient defence for my *pat on the hand:*—

"The arguments of those whose opinions are *against* the question, appear to me to be both puerile and unsound, and directly at variance with the express declarations of Scripture. In matters where the Scriptures are silent, we are allowed to speculate and to form our own opinions, according to the rules of propriety and common sense. But where the Scriptures exhibit positive injunctions to govern our conduct, we are not at liberty so to act.

"Nothing can be plainer, than that the Sacred Oracles make corporeal correction an essential ingredient in the system of

There is certainly something very pleasing in the sound, that several hundred infant children may

the religious training of the young. Prov. xxii. 15, 'Foolishness is bound up in the heart of a child, but the rod of correction shall drive it from him.' Chap. xix. 18. 'Chasten thy son while there is hope, and let not thy soul spare for his crying.' Chap. xxiii. 13, 14. 'Withhold not correction from the child, for if thou beatest him with the rod he shall not die. Thou shalt beat him with the rod, and shall deliver his soul from hell.' Chap. xxix. 15—17. 'The rod and reproof give wisdom, but a child left to himself bringeth his mother to shame. Correct thy son and he shall give thee rest; yea, he shall give delight unto thy soul.' Chap. xiii. 24. 'He that spareth his rod, hateth his son : but he that loveth him chasteneth him betimes.' These declarations require no comment; and if they *are* the words of inspiration, to argue and reason against their import must be impious. Moreover, both observation and experience testify that where these injunctions are attended to, and judiciously mixed with pious instruction, the happiest effects are produced; while, on the contrary, where these are neglected, and a system of indulgence and relaxation substituted, we see the most deplorable consequences ensue. And, indeed, what else can we expect, when man departs from the wisdom of God *and leans to his own understanding.*

"We know also that the Divine Administration proceeds according to the same method. It is an evident maxim of Scripture, that correction is the greatest proof of paternal love and regard, for, ' whom the Lord loveth he correcteth, even as a father the son in whom he delighteth.' The wisdom of man says, the exercise of the rod or the cane excites evil passions in the breast of him who useth it, and alienates the affections of the children : but what says the wisdom of God? ' Correct thy son and he shall give thee rest: yea, he shall give delight unto thy soul.' But, perhaps, it will be objected, that what is here insisted upon, belongs exclusively to parents, and will not apply to the discipline of Sunday Schools; to which I would answer, that there is no other mode known or acknowledged in Scripture, for the religious training of children, but that given to parents, consequently, those who take upon themselves this charge, sit in the parents' seat, and are obliged to observe the same rules."

P 3

be well managed, kept in good order, and corrected of their bad habits, without *any sort* of punishment. But as I have not been able to attain to that state of perfection in the art of teaching, I shall lay before the reader, what modes of punishment were adopted in the Spitalfields Infant School, and the success that attended them.

The first offence deserving of punishment, which I shall notice, is playing the truant; and I trust I may be permitted to state, that notwithstanding the children are so very young, they do frequently, at first, stay away from the school, unknown to their parents; nor is this to be wondered at, when we consider how they have been permitted to range the streets and get acquainted with other children of similar circumstances to themselves. When this is the case, they cannot be disciplined and brought into order in a moment; it is a work of time, and requires much patience and perseverance to accomplish it effectually. It is well known that when we accustom ourselves to particular company, and form acquaintances, it is no easy matter to give them up; and it is a maxim, that a man is either better or worse for the company he keeps. Just so it is with children; they form very early attachments, and frequently with children whose parents will not send them to school, and care not where they are, so long as they keep out of their way. The consequence will be that such children will persuade another to accompany them, and of course the child will be absent from school; but as night approaches, the child will begin to think of the consequences, and mention it to his companions, who will instruct him how to deceive both his teacher and his parents, and perhaps bring him through his trouble : this will give him fresh confidence, and finding himself successful, there will be little trouble in persuading him to accompany them a second time. I have had children absent from school, two or three half days in a week, and sometimes whole days, who have brought me such rational and plausible excuses, as completely to put me off my guard; but who have been found out by their parents, from having staid out till seven or even eight o'clock at night; the parents have applied at the school, to know why I kept the children so late, and have then informed me, that they had been absent all day. Thus the whole plot has been developed : it has been found that the children were sent to school at eight o'clock in the morning, and had their dinners given them to eat at school; but instead of coming to school, they have got into company with their older companions, who, in many cases, I have found, were training them for every species of vice. Some have been cured of truant-playing by corporeal punishment, when all other means I could devise have failed. Others, by means the most simple, such as causing the child to hold a broom for a given time.

By keeping a strict eye upon them they soon begin to form an attachment with some of their own school-fellows, and ultimately become as fond of their new companions, their book, and school, as they were before of their old companions and the streets. I need scarcely observe, how strong are our attachments formed in early years at school; and I doubt not but many who read this, have found a valuable and real friend in a school-fellow, for whom they would do anything within their power.

There were several children in the school who
had contracted some very bad habits, entirely by
their being accustomed to run the streets; and
one boy in particular, only five years of age, who
was so frequently absent and brought such reasonable excuses for his absence, that it was some
time before I detected him. I thought it best to
see his mother, and therefore sent the boy to tell
her that I wished to see her: the boy soon returned, saying, his mother was not at home: the
following morning he was absent again, and I sent
another boy to know the reason, when the mother
waited on me immediately, and assured me that
she had sent the child to school. I then produced
the slate, which I kept for that purpose, and informed her how many days, and half-days, her
child had been absent for the last month; when
she again assured me, that she had never kept the
child at home a single half-day, nor had he ever
told her that I wanted to see her; at the same time
observing, that he must have been decoyed away
by some of the children in the neighbourhood;
and regretting that she could not afford to send
him to school before; *adding, that the Infant
School was " a blessed institution," and an institution, she thought, much wanted in the neighbourhood.* I need scarcely observe, that both the
father and mother lost no time in searching for
their child, and after a search of several hours,
found him in Spitalfields market, in company
with several other children, pretty well stored
with apples, &c. which they had, no doubt, stolen
from the fruit-baskets that are continually placed
there. They brought him to school, and informed
me that they had given him a good flogging,
which I found to be correct, from the marks that

were on the child: this, they said, they had no
doubt would cure him. But, however, he was
not so soon to be cured, for the very next day he
was absent again, and after the parents had tried
every expedient they could think of, without success, they delivered him over to me, telling me to
do what I thought proper. I tried every means
that I could devise, with as little success, except
keeping him at school after school hours; for I
had a great disinclination to convert the school
into a prison, as my object was, if possible, to
cause the children to love the school; and I knew
I could not take a more effectual method of causing them to dislike it, than by keeping them,
against their will, after school hours. At last, I
tried this experiment, but to as little purpose as
the others, and I was about to send the child out
of the school altogether, as incorrigible. Being
unwilling, however, that it should be said, a child
of only five years of age had mastered us, I at
last hit upon an expedient which had the desired
effect; and I must say, I was extremely glad to
see it. I never knew him absent without leave
afterwards, and what is more surprising, he appeared to be very fond of the school, and became
a very good child. Was not this, then, a brand
plucked from the fire?

I have been advised to dismiss twenty such children rather than retain them by the above means,
but if there be more joy in heaven over one sinner
that repenteth than over ninety and nine just persons who need no repentance, ought not such a
feeling to be encouraged on earth? particularly
when it can be done by means, that are not injurious to the orderly, but, on the contrary, productive of the best effects. The child afterwards went

into the National School, with several others who
were nearly as bad as himself, but they scarcely
ever failed to come and see me when they had a
half-holiday. Notwithstanding they had been
subjected to the objected punishments, the master
of the National School told me that neither of
them had ever been absent without leave, and that
he had no fault to find with either of them. I
have further to observe that the moment I perceived any bad effects produced by any method of
punishment, that moment it was relinquished.

I believe, that there is not a child in the school
who would not have been delighted to *carry the
broom*, if I had called it play; the other children
might have laughed as long as they pleased, for
he would have laughed as hearty as any of them;
and as soon as he had done, I should have had a
dozen applicants, with " Please sir, may I ; please
sir, may I ;" but only change the name, and call
it a *punishment*, and I had no applications whatever; but they all dreaded it as much as they
could a flogging. I am aware, that this plan of
punishment will appear childish and ridiculous;
and, perhaps, it would be ridiculous to use it for
older children, but with such young children I
have found it answer well, and therefore have no
wish to dispense with it; however, I would have
care taken not to encourage the children to ridicule each other while undergoing this or any other
punishment, but (as I always have done) encourage them to sympathize and comfort a child as
soon as his punishment is over; and I can truly
say, that I do not recollect a single instance, when
any child has been undergoing the broom punishment, but that some of the others have come and
attempted to beg him off, with " Please sir, may

he sit down now;" and when asked the reason why they have wished the little delinquent to be forgiven, they have answered, " May be, sir, he will be a good boy." Well, their request has been complied with, and the culprit forgiven; and what have I seen follow? Why, that which has taught me many an important lesson, and has convinced me that *children can operate on each other's mind, and be the means of producing, very often, better effects than adult persons can.* I have seen them clasp the child round the neck, take him by the hand, lead him about the play-ground, comfort him in every possible way, wipe his eyes with their pinafore, ask him if he was not sorry for what he had done; the answer has been, " Yes;" and they have flown to me—" Master, he says he is sorry for it, and that he will not do so again." In short they have done that which I could not do, they have so won the child over by kindness, that it has caused the offender not only to be fond of them, but equally as fond of his master and the school. To these things I attribute the reclaiming of the children I have mentioned; and so far from its being productive of the " *worst effects,*" I have found it productive of the best.

The ill effects of expelling children as incorrigible, may be seen in the case of Hartley, who was executed some years back. He confessed before his execution that he had been concerned in several murders, and upwards of two hundred burglaries; and by the newspaper account, we learn, that he was dismissed from school at nine years of age, there being no school-master who would be troubled with him, when, finding himself at full liberty, he immediately commenced robber. " Hartley's father (the account proceeds) formerly kept the Sir John Falstaff inn, at Hull, in Yorkshire. He was put to school in that neighbourhood, but his conduct at school was so marked with depravity, and so continually did he play the truant, that he was dismissed as unmanageable. He then, although only nine years of age, began with pilfering and robbing gardens and orchards, till at length his friends were obliged to send him to sea. He soon contrived to run away from the vessel in which he had been placed, and having regained the land, pursued his old habits, and got connected with many of the principal thieves in London, with whom he commenced business regularly as a housebreaker, which was almost always his line of robbery."

Should not every means have been resorted to with this child, before proceeding to the dangerous mode of expulsion? for it is not the whole who need a physician, but those that are sick; and I strongly suspect, that if judicious punishment had been resorted to, it would have had the desired effect. I can only say, that there never was a child expelled from the Spitalfields Infant School, as incorrigible. In conclusion, I have to observe that the broom punishment is only for extraordinary occasions, and I think we are justified in having recourse to any means that are consistent with duty and humanity, rather than turn a child out into the wide world.

CHAPTER X.

LANGUAGE.

METHOD OF TEACHING THE ALPHABET, AND IMPARTING IDEAS OF THINGS AT THE SAME TIME.

Can any thing reflect light before it has received it, or any other light than that which it has received?

THE first thing children wish to acquire, as to language, is a knowledge of the names of things, their senses having revealed each object in its true light, they now desire to express their perceptions in sounds or words. This desire is the first thing you have to gratify; you tell them the name of an object, and from that time such name is the representative of the thing in the mind of the child. If the object be not present, but you mention the name, the memory of the child supplies it with an ideal representation of such object,—which thus becomes, as it were, present in the mind of the child. If this matter had been more frequently thought upon by educators, we should I think have found them less eager to make the child acquainted with names of things

Q

of which it has no knowledge or conception. Sounds and signs, which give rise to no idea in the mind of the child, because the child has never seen or known the things represented, are of no other use than to burden the memory. It is the object of our system to give the children a knowledge of things—and then a knowledge of the *words* which represent those things. These remarks do not only apply to the names of visible things; but more particularly to those which are abstract. If I would say, show a child a *horse*, before you tell it the name of the animal; still more would I urge it upon the teacher to let the child see what *love, kindness, religion,* &c. &c. are, before it is told what name to designate these qualities by. If our ignorance as to material things be the result of instructing children in names, instead of enabling them to become acquainted with things; so on the other hand, I believe, we may account in the same way for *virtue* being so frequently a mere word, an empty sound amongst men, instead of an active principle.

Our next endeavour is to teach the children to express their thoughts upon things;—and if they are not checked by injudicious treatment, they will have some thought on every subject. We first teach them to express their *own notions*— we then tell them ours—and truth will prevail, even in the minds of children. Under this plan it will prevail by its own strength; not by the power of coercion, which renders even truth disagreeable and repulsive; the children will adopt it of choice in preference to error, and it will be firmly established in their minds.

It will no doubt be perceived, that for the promotion of the plan here recommended, it will be advisable to connect with our *alphabetical* and *reading lessons,* as much information as we possibly can. By so doing the tedium of the task to the child will be considerably lessened, as well as much knowledge attained. The means of doing this in a variety of ways will no doubt suggest themselves to the intelligent teacher; but, as an illustration of what we mean, the following conversational plan may not be useless.

We have 26 cards, and each card has on it one letter of the alphabet, and some object in nature. The first for instance has the letter A on the top and an apple painted on the bottom. The children are desired to go into the gallery, which is simply seats elevated one above another at one end of the school like stairs; the master places himself before the children in a situation so that they can see him, and he them, and being thus situated, proceeds in the following manner.

Q. Where am I? *A.* Opposite to us. *Q.* What is on the right side of me? *A.* A lady. *Q.* What is on the left side of me? *A.* A chair. *Q.* What is behind me? *A.* A desk. *Q* Who are before me? *A.* We children. *Q.* What do I hold up in my hand? *A.* Letter A for apple. *Q.* Which hand do I hold it up with? *A.* The right hand. *Q.* Spell apple.* *A.* A-p-p-l-e. *Q.* How is an

---

* It is not supposed that all or many of the children will be able to spell this, or the subsequent words, or to give such answers as we have put down, but *some* amongst the older or more acute of them will soon be able to do so; and thus become instructors of the rest. It may be proper to mention, also, that the information on natural history, &c. &c. displayed in some of the answers, is the result of the

apple produced? *A.* It grows on a tree. *Q.* What part of the tree is in the ground? *A.* The root. *Q.* What is that which comes out of the ground? *A.* The stem. *Q.* When the stem grows up strait, what would you call its position? *A.* Perpendicular. *Q.* What is on the stem? *A.* Branches. *Q.* What is on the branches? *A.* Leaves. *Q.* Of what colour are they? *A.* Green.

Q. Is there any thing besides leaves on the branches? *A.* Yes; apples. *Q.* What was it before it became an apple? *A.* Blossom. *Q.* What part of the blossom becomes fruit? *A.* The inside. *Q.* What becomes of the leaves of the blossom? *A.* They fall off the tree. *Q.* What was it before it became blossom? *A.* A bud. *Q.* What caused the buds to become larger and produce leaves and blossom? *A.* The sap. *Q.* What is sap? *A.* A juice. *Q.* How can the sap make the buds larger? *A.* It comes out of the root and goes up the stem. *Q.* Where next? *A.* Through the branches into the buds. *Q.* What do the buds produce? *A.* Some buds produce leaves; some blossoms, and some a shoot? *Q.* What do you mean by a shoot? *A.* A shoot is a young branch, which is green at first, but becomes hard by age. *Q.* What part becomes hard first? *A.* The bottom.

B.

Q. What is this? *A.* B, for baker, for butter, for bacon, for brewer, for button, for bell, &c. &c. [The teacher can take any of these names he

---

instructions in natural history, which the children simultaneously receive, and which is spoken of in a subsequent chapter.

pleases, for instance, the first :] Children, let me hear you spell baker. *A.* B-a-k-e-r. *Q.* What is a baker? *A.* A man who makes bread. *Q.* What is bread made of? *A.* It is made of flour, water, yeast, and a little salt. *Q.* What is flour made of? *A.* Wheat. *Q.* How is it made? *A.* Ground to powder in a mill? *Q.* What makes the mill go round? *A.* The wind, if it is a windmill. *Q.* Are there any other kinds of mills? *A.* Yes; mills that go by water, mills that are drawn round by horses, and mills that go by steam. *Q.* When the flour and water and yeast are mixed together, what does the baker do? *A.* Bake them in an oven. *Q.* What is the use of bread? *A.* For children to eat. *Q.* Who causes the corn to grow? *A.* Almighty God.

C.

Q. What is this? *A.* It is letter C for cow, c-o-w, and for cat, &c. *Q.* What is the use of the cow? *A.* The cow gives us milk to put into the tea. *Q.* Is milk used for any other purpose besides putting it into tea? *A.* Yes, it is used to put into puddings, and for many other things. *Q.* Name some of the other things. *A.* It is used to make butter and cheese. *Q.* What part of it is made into butter? *A.* The cream which swims at the top of the milk. *Q.* How is it made into butter? *A.* It is put into a thing called a churn, in the shape of a barrel. *Q.* What is done next? *A.* The churn is turned round by means of a handle, and the motion turns the cream into butter? *Q.* What is the use of butter? *A.* To put on bread, and to put into pye-crust, and many other nice things. *Q.* Of what colour is butter? *A.* It is generally yellow.

Q. Are there any other things made of milk?
A. Yes, many things; but the principal one is
cheese.   *Q.* How is cheese made?   *A.* The milk
is turned into curds and whey, which is done by
putting a liquid into it called rennet.   *Q.* What
part of the curd and whey is made into cheese?
A. The curd, which is put into a press; and
when it has been in the press a few days it becomes cheese.   *Q.* Is the flesh of the cow useful?
A. Yes; it is eaten, and is called beef; and the
flesh of the young calf is called veal.   *Q.* Is the
skin of the cow or calf of any use?   *A.* Yes, the
skin of the cow is manufactured into leather for
the soles of shoes.   *Q.* What is made with the
calf skin?   *A.* The top of the shoe, which is
called the upper-leather.   *Q.* Are there any other
parts of the cow that are useful?   *A.* Yes; the
horns, which are made into combs, handles of
knives, forks, and other things.   *Q.* What is
made of the hoofs that come off the cow's feet?
A. Glue, to join boards together.   *Q.* Who made
the cow?   *A.* Almighty God.

D.

Q. What is this?   *A.* Letter D, for dog, for
dove, for draper, &c.   *Q.* What is the use of the
dog?   *A.* To guard the house and keep thieves
away.   *Q.* How can a dog guard the house and
keep thieves away?   *A.* By barking to wake the
persons who live in the house.   *Q.* Is the dog of
any other use?   *A.* Yes, to draw under a truck.
Q. Does he do as his master bids him?   *A.* Yes,
and knows his master from any other person.   *Q.*
Is the dog a faithful animal?   *A.* Yes, very faithful; he has been known to die of grief for the
loss of his master.   *Q.* Can you mention an in-

stance of the dog's faithfulness? *A.* Yes; a dog waited at the gates of the Fleet prison for hours every day for nearly two years, because his master was confined in the prison. *Q.* Can you mention another instance of the dog's faithfulness? *A.* Yes; a dog lay down on his master's grave in a church-yard in London for many weeks. *Q.* How did the dog get food? *A.* The people who lived near noticed him, and brought him victuals. *Q.* Did the people do any thing besides giving him victuals? *A.* Yes, they made a house for him for fear he should die with wet and cold. *Q.* How long did he stay there? *A.* Until the people took him away, because he howled dreadfully when the organ played on Sundays. *Q.* Is it right to beat a dog? *A.* No, it is very wrong to use any animal ill, because we do not like to be beaten ourselves. *Q.* Did Almighty God make the dog? *A.* Yes; and every thing else that has life.

E.

Q. What letter is this? *A.* E, for egg. *Q.* What is the use of an egg? *A.* It is useful for many purposes; to put into puddings and to eat by itself. *Q.* Should country children keep an egg if they find it in the hedge? *A.* No, it is thieving; they should find out the owner and take it home. *Q.* Do children ever throw stones at the fowls? *A.* Yes; but they are mischievous children, and perhaps do not go to school. *Q.* What ought children to learn by going to school? *A.* To be kind and good to every body, and every thing that has life.

F.

Q. What letter is this? *A.* Letter F, for frying pan, for father, &c. *Q.* Let me hear you

spell frying-pan.   *A.* F-r-y-i-n-g p-a-n.   *Q.*
What is the use of the frying-pan?   *A.* To fry
meat and pan-cakes.   *Q.* Spell me the names of
the different kinds of meat.   *A.* B-e-e-f, p-o-r-k,
v-e-a-l, m-u-t-t-o-n, l-a-m-b, h-a-m, &c.   *Q.*
Of what shape are frying pans?   *A.* Some circular and some are like an ellipsis.*   *Q.* Are
there any other utensils into which meat is put
that are circular?   *A.* Yes, please sir, my mother
has some circular plates; and please sir, my
mother has some elliptical dishes.   *Q.* Any thing
besides?   *A.* Yes, please sir, my mother has a
circular table; and, please sir, my mother has a
rectangular one, and it is made of deal.

G.

Q. What letter is this?   *A.* Letter G, for goat,
for good girl, &c.   *Q.* Spell goat.   *A.* G-o-a-t.
Q. What is the use of the goat?   *A.* In some
countries people drink the goat's milk; and the
skin is useful to make the upper-leather of shoes.
Q. Are goats fond of going into the valleys and
low places?   *A.* No; they are fond of going up
hills and high places.   *Q.* If a goat is coming
down a high hill which has only one narrow path
merely wide enough for one goat to walk on
without falling down, and another goat is coming
up the same path, what do they do?   *A.* The
goat that is coming up lies down and lets the
other goat walk over him.   *Q.* Why does not one

---

* It may possibly strike some of my readers as strange
that a geometrical question should be put in a conversation
on the alphabet, but it should be remembered that, according to the Infant School system, *language* is not taught
exclusively, but in connection with *number* and *form*;—
questions like the above, therefore, are calculated to excite
their memories, and induce an application of their geometrical knowledge.

of the goats turn round and go back again ? *A.* Because there would not be room, and the one which should try to turn round would fall down and be killed.

H

Q. What letter is this? *A.* Letter H, for horse, for house, &c. *Q.* What is the use of the horse ? *A.* To draw carts, coaches, stages, waggons, fire-engines, &c. *Q.* Spell horse and cart and coach ? *A.* H-o-r-s-e, c-a-r-t, c-o-a-c-h. *Q.* What is the difference between a càrt and coach ? *A.* A cart has two wheels, and a coach has four. *Q.* Tell me some other difference. *A.* The horses in a cart go before each other, but the horses in a coach go side by side. *Q.* What is the use of a fire-engine ? *A.* To put the fire out when the house is on fire. *Q.* Is it right for children to play with the fire ? *A.* No, very wrong; as many children are burnt to death, and many houses burnt down from it. *Q.* Should the horse be cruelly used ? *A.* No; he should be kindly treated, as he is the most useful animal we have. *Q.* Who created him ? *A.* Almighty God.

I.

Q. What letter is this ? *A.* Letter I, for iron, for idleness, &c. *Q.* Spell iron. *A.* I-r-o-n, *Q.* What is the use of an iron? *A.* To iron the clothes after they are washed, and to make them smooth. *Q.* How do they iron the clothes? *A.* Make the iron hot, and then work it backwards and forwards on the clothes. *Q.* Should little children come with clean clothes to school ? *A.* Yes; and clean hands and faces too. *Q.* Is not iron used for other purposes? *A.* Oh, yes; for a great many things, as knives, forks, &c.

J

Q. What letter is this? *A.* J, for jug, for John, &c. *Q.* What is the use of the jug? *A.* To hold water, or beer, or any other liquid. *Q.* What is a jug made of? *A.* Of clay, which is worked round into the shape of a jug, and then burnt, and that hardens it. *Q.* Should children be careful when they are carrying a jug? *A.* Yes; or else they will let it fall and break it. *Q.* Then it is necessary for children to be careful? *A.* Yes; every body should be careful.

K

Q. What letter is this? *A.* Letter K, for kite, &c. *Q.* What is the use of the kite? *A.* For little children to fly. Please sir, my big brother has got a kite. *Q.* What does your brother do with his kite? *A.* Please sir, he goes into the fields when he has got time, and flies it. *Q.* How does he fly it? *A.* Please sir, he has got a long string, which he fixes to another called a loop, and then he unwinds the string, and gets some boy to hold it up. *Q.* What then? *A.* Please sir, then he runs against the wind, and the kite goes up. *Q.* What is the use of the tail of the kite? *A.* Please sir, it will not fly without a tail. *Q.* Why not? *A.* Please sir, it goes round and round without a tail, and comes down. *Q.* Then what do you suppose is the use of the tail? *A.* Please sir, I don't know.—Another child will probably supply the answer. Please sir, to balance it.

L

Q. What letter is this? *A.* Letter L, for lion, &c. *Q.* Spell lion. *A.* L-i-o-n. *Q.* What is the size of a full grown lion? *A.* A full grown lion stands four feet and a half high, and eight feet long. *Q.* How high do you stand? *A.* Please sir, some of us stand two feet, and none of us above three. *Q.* Has the lion any particular character among beasts? *A.* Yes, he is called the king of beasts on account of his great strength. *Q.* When he seizes his prey, how far can he leap? *A.* To the distance of twenty feet. *Q.* Describe some other particulars concerning the lion? *A.* The lion has a shaggy mane, which the lioness has not. *Q.* What other particulars? *A.* The lion's roar is so loud that other animals run away when they hear it. *Q.* Where are lions found? *A.* In most hot countries; the largest are found in Asia and Africa.

M

Q. What letter is this? *A.* Letter M, for Monday, for mouse, &c. *Q.* What is the use of the mouse? *A.* To make the servants diligent and put the things out of the way. *Q.* How can mice make servants diligent? *A.* If people don't put the candles in a proper place the mice will gnaw them. *Q.* Are mice of any other service? *A.* Please sir, if the mice did not make a smell, some people would never clean their cupboards out.*

N

Q. What letter is this? *A.* Letter N, for nut, &c. *Q.* What is a nut? *A.* A thing that is hard, and it grows on a tree. *Q.* What shape is it? *A.* Something in the shape of a marble. *Q.*

* This answer was given by a child four years old; and immediately afterwards another child called out, Please sir, if were not for bugs, some people would not clean their bedsteads.

How can it be eaten, if it is like a marble? *A.* Please sir, it is the kernel that we eat. *Q.* How are nuts produced? *A.* They grow on trees.

O

Q. What letter is this? *A.* Letter O, for orange. *Q.* Of what colour is an orange? *A.* An orange is green at first, but afterwards becomes of a colour called orange-red. *Q.* Do they grow in the ground like potatoes? *A.* No, they grow on trees like apples. *Q.* Can you tell me any thing in the shape of an orange? *A.* Yes, the earth on which we live is nearly of that shape. *Q.* On what part of the earth do we live? *A.* The surface. *Q.* What do you mean by the surface? *A.* The outside. *Q.* Who formed the earth, and preserves it in its proper motions? *A.* Almighty God.

P

Q. What letter is this? *A.* Letter P, for pig, for plum-pudding, &c. *Q.* What is the use of the pig? *A.* Its flesh is eaten, and is called pork. *Q.* What is the use of the hair or bristles? *A.* To make brushes or brooms. *Q.* What is the use of a brush? *A.* Some brushes are to brush the clothes, and others to brush the dirt out of the corners of the room. *Q.* Does a good servant ever leave the dirt in the corners? *A.* No, never; a good servant or any clean little girl would be ashamed of it.

Q

Q. What letter is this? *A.* Letter Q, for quill, &c. *Q.* How are quills produced? *A.* From the wings of geese and other large birds. *Q.* What is the use of the quill? *A.* To form into pens and many other things. *Q.* What is the use of

he pen? *A.* To dip into ink and write with it.
Q. What do you write upon? *A.* Paper. *Q.*
What is paper made of? *A.* Rags.

R

Q. What letter is this? *A.* Letter R, for rabbit,
&c. *Q.* What is the use of the rabbit? *A.* The
lesh of the rabbit is eaten, and is very nice. *Q.*
What does the rabbit eat? *A.* Corn, grass, cab-
bage leaves, and many different herbs. *Q.* What
is the use of the skin? *A.* To make hats, and to
trim boys' caps. *Q.* Are they very numerous?
A. They are to be found in almost all countries.

S

Q. What is this? *A.* Letter S, for shoe, &c.
Q. What is the use of shoes? *A.* To keep the
eet warm and dry. *Q.* Should children walk in
he mud or in the kennel? *A.* No, because that
would spoil the shoes, and wear them out too
oon. *Q.* And why should little children be
areful not to wear them out, any more than they
an help? *A.* Because our parents must work
narder to buy us more.

T

Q. What letter is this? *A.* Letter T, for tea-
kettle. *Q.* What are tea-kettles made of? *A.*
Some are made of tin, and some of copper, and
ome of iron. *Q.* Why are they not made of
wood? *A.* Because the wood would burn. *Q.*
What thing is that at the top? *A.* The handle.
Q. What is underneath the handle? *A.* The
id. *Q.* What is in the front of it? *A.* The
spout. *Q.* What is the use of the spout? *A.*
For the water to come out. *Q.* What is the use
of the handle? *A.* To take hold of. *Q.* Why
do they not take hold of the spout? *A.* Because
it is the wrong way.

U

Q. What letter is this? *A.* Letter U, for umbrella, &c. *Q.* Is letter U a vowel or con-sonant? *A.* A vowel. *Q.* What is the use of the umbrella? *A.* To keep the rain off any body, *Q.* What are umbrellas made of? *A.* Some of silk and some of cotton. *Q.* Which are the best? *A.* Those that are made of silk. *Q.* Is there any thing else in an umbrella? *A.* Yes, whalebone, *Q.* Where does whalebone come from? *A.* Out of a large fish called a whale. *Q.* Who made the whale? *A.* Almighty God.

V

Q. What letter is this? *A.* Letter V, for vine, &c. *Q.* What is a vine? *A.* A thing that grows against the wall and produces grapes? *Q.* Why does it not grow like another tree and support its own weight? *A.* Because it is not strong enough, *Q.* Then it cannot grow and become fruitful in this country without man's assistance. *A.* No; and, please sir, we cannot grow and become fruit-ful without the assistance of Almighty God.*

W

Q. What letter is this? *A.* It is letter W, for wheel. *Q.* Spell wheel? *A.* W-h-ee-l. *Q.* What is the use of wheels? *A.* To make it easier for horses to draw. *Q.* How do you know that? *A.* Please sir, I had a little cart full of stones, and the wheel came off; and please sir, I found it much harder to draw. *Q.* Then if it was not for wheels the horse could not draw so great a weight? *A.* No; and, please sir, people could not go into the country so quick as they do. *Q.* What trade do they call the persons that make wheels? *A.* Wheel-wrights.

* This answer was given by a child five years of age.

X

Q. What letter is this? *A.* Letter X, for Xenophon, a man's name. *Q.* What was the particular character of Xenophon? *A.* He was very courageous. *Q.* What does courageous mean? *A.* To be afraid to do harm but not to be afraid to do good or any thing that is right. *Q.* What is the greatest courage? *A.* To conquer our own bad passions and bad inclinations. *Q.* Is he a courageous man that can conquer his bad passions. *A.* Yes; because they are the most difficult to conquer.

Y

Q. What letter is this. *A.* Letter Y, for yoke, &c. *Q.* Is it a vowel or consonant? *A.* When it begins a word it is called a consonant, but if not a vowel. *Q.* What is a yoke? *A.* Please sir, what the milk people carry the milk pails on. *Q.* What is the use of the yoke? *A.* To enable the people to carry the milk easier.

Z

Q. What letter is this? *A.* Letter Z, for Zealander. *Q.* What is a Zealander? *A.* A man that lives on an Island on the Southern Ocean, called Zealand. *Q.* How do they live? *A.* Principally by hunting and fishing. *Q.* What is hunting? *A.* Following animals to catch them. *Q.* Who made all the animals? *A.* Almighty God.

The method above described, is adapted for the large room, where the children may be taught altogether; but it is necessary to change the scene even in this; for however novel and pleasing a thing may be at first, if it be not managed with prudence it will soon lose its effect. It is, then, to be observed that the mode of teaching described in the preceding chapter is not prac- tised every day, but only twice or thrice a week. The children will take care that the teacher does not altogether forget to teach them, in any way that they have been accustomed to. After let- ting the above plan lay by for a day or two, some of the children will come to the teacher, and say, " Please sir, may we say the picture alphabet up in the gallery ?" If the other children overhear the question, it will go through the school like lightning : " O yes—yes—yes, sir, if you please, do let us say the letters in the gallery." Thus a desire is created in the children's minds, and it is then that they may be taught with good effect.

Another plan which we adopt is in practice almost every day. It is better adapted for what is called the class-room, and is taught thus :— we have the alphabet printed in large letters, both in Roman and Italic characters, on one sheet of paper ; this paper is pasted on a board, or on pasteboard, and placed against the wall; the whole class then stand around it, but instead of one of the monitors pointing to the letters, the master or mistress does it; so that the children not only obtain instruction from each other, but every child has a lesson from the master or mis- tress twice every day.

In spelling, each child is supplied with a card and tin, and they are taught in the following manner. The children are taken into the class- room, a class at a time, when one child leads off as follows :—P-o-s-t. The other children immediately follow, and when they have spelt the word, the leader repeats another, and so on through the card; the children at the same time keeping their finger to the word they are spelling, so that if a child be inattentive it is sure to be detected.

We pursue, likewise, the following method of teaching the writing alphabet. The children who are about five years old are supplied with slates, on which is engraved the whole alphabet, the same as on copper-plate copies, thirteen letters on each side of the slate, some in capital letters, others in text; the children then put the pencil into the engraving, and work it round into the shape of the letter, which they cannot avoid doing as the pencil will keep in the engraved part; in this way they learn not only to read anything written but also to form their letters correctly.

CHAPTER XI.

NUMBER.

VARIOUS METHODS OF TEACHING THE RUDIMENTS OF ARITHMETIC.

"It is not the possessing, but the right management of any valuable advantage, which makes it desirable."

THE advantage of numerical knowledge has never been disputed. Its continual and universal application to the business of life renders it a most indisputable acquisition to all ranks and conditions of men. The practicability of imparting the rudiments of arithmetic to very young children, has been satisfactorily shewn by the infant school system; and it has been found likewise that it is the readiest and surest way of developing the thinking faculties of the infant mind. Since the most complicated and difficult questions of arithmetic, as well as the most simple, are all solvable by the same rules and on the same principles, it is of the utmost importance to give children a clear insight into the primary principles of number. For this purpose we take care to shew them, by visible objects, that all numbers are combinations of unity; and that all changes of number must consist, either of adding to, or taking from, a certain stated number. After this, or rather, perhaps I should say, in conjunction with the instruction by visible objects, we exhibit to the children the *signs* of number, and make them acquainted with their various combinations; and lastly we bring them to the abstract consideration of number; or what may be termed *mental arithmetic*. If you reverse this, which has generally been the system of instruction pursued—if you set a child to learn its multiplication, pence and other tables,—before you have shewn it by *realities*, the combinations of unity which these tables express in words—you are rendering the whole an abstruse, difficult and uninteresting affair to the infant mind; and, in short, giving it knowledge which it is unable to apply.

As far as regards the general principles of numerical tuition, it may be sufficient to state, that we should begin with unity, and proceed very gradually, by slow and sure steps, through the simplest forms of combination to the more comprehensive. Trace and retrace your first steps—the children can never too thoroughly comprehend the first principles or facts of number.

We have various ways of teaching arithmetic in use in the schools; I shall speak of them all, beginning with a description of an instrument of great utility and much used in Infant Schools.

THE TRANSPOSITION FRAME AND THE METHOD OF USING IT.*

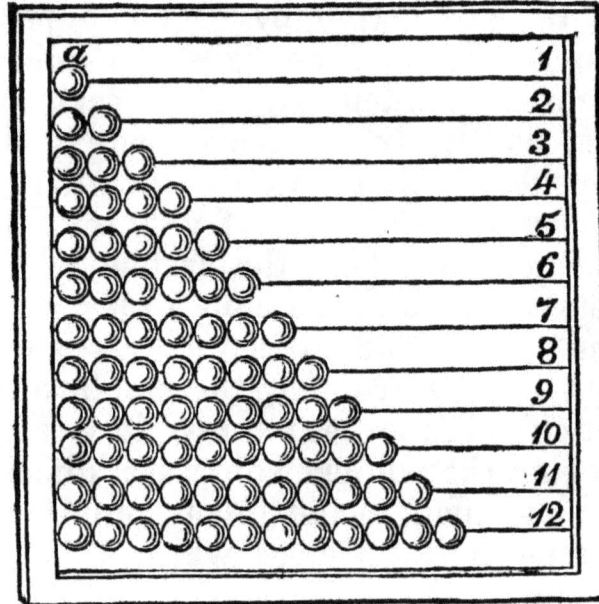

THE frame is 16-in. square, and made of wood, twelve wires pass through it at equal distances; on which wires seventy-eight moveable balls are to be placed beginning with one on the first, two on the second, three on the third, &c. up to tewlve. It is an excellent instrument for an infant school, as with it you may teach the first principles of grammar, arithmetic and geometry.

It is to be used as follows :—Move one of the balls to a part of the frame distinct from the rest. The children will then repeat, "There it is, there it is." Apply your finger to the ball, and set it running round. The children will immediately change from saying, "There it is," to "There it goes, there it goes."

* It is to be understood that this Frame is for teaching the children altogether in the gallery.

When they have repeated " There it goes" long enough to impress it on their memory, stop the ball; the children will probably say, " Now it stops, now it stops." When that is the case move another ball to it, and then explain to the children the difference between singular and plural, desiring them to call out, " There they are, there they are;" and when they have done that as long as may be proper, set both balls moving, and it is likely they will call out, " There they go, there they go," &c. &c.

By the natural position of the balls, they may be taught to begin at the first. The master raising it at the top of the frame, says, What am I doing? Children answer, Raising the ball up with your hand. *Q.* Which hand? *A.* Left hand. Then the master lets the ball drop, saying, "One, one." Raise the two balls, and propose questions of a similar tendency; then let them fall; the children will say, " Twice one:" raise three, and let them fall as before, the children will say, " Three times one." Proceed to raise the balls on every remaining wire, so that they may say, as the balls are let fall, four times one, five times one, six times one, seven times one, eight times one, nine times one, ten times one, eleven times one, and twelve times one

We now proceed as follows; 1 and 2 are 3, and 3 are 6, and 4 are 10, and 5 are 15, and 6 are 21, and 7 are 28, and 8 are 36, and 9 are 45, and 10 are 55, and 11 are 66, and 12 are 78.

Then the master may exercise them backwards, saying, 12 and 11 are 23, and 10 are 33, and 9 are 42, and 8 are 50, and 7 are 57, and 6 are 63, and 5 are 68, and 4 are 72, and 3 are 75, and 2 are 77, and 1 are 78, and so on, in *Addition,* with great variety.

Substraction may be taught in as many ways by this instrument. Thus; take 1 from 1, nothing remains; moving the first ball at the same time to the other end of the frame. Then remove 1 from the second wire, and say, take 1 from 2, the children will instantly perceive that only 1 remains; then 1 from 3, and 2 remain; 1 from 4, 3 remain; 1 from 5, 4 remain; 1 from 6, 5 remain; 1 from 7, 6 remain; 1 from 8, 7 remain; 1 from 9, 8 remain; 1 from 10, 9 remain; 1 from 11, 10 remain; 1 from 12, 11 remain.

Then the balls may be worked backwards, beginning at the wire containing 12 balls, saying, take 2 from 12, 10 remain; 2 from 11, 9 remain; 2 from 10, 8 remain; 2 from 9, 7 remain; 2 from 8, 6 remain; 2 from 7, 5 remain; 2 from 6, 4 remain; 2 from 5, 3 remain; 2 from 4, 2 remain; 2 from 3, 1 remain; and so on, with continual variations; and if the teacher works the frame the right way, the children cannot help receiving correct ideas, as they have ocular demonstration how many balls are left on each wire.

Multiplication. I will now speak briefly of multiplication, as taught by this instrument. The lessons are performed as follows. The teacher moves the first ball, and immediately after the two balls on the second wire, placing them underneath the first, saying at the same time, twice one are two, which the children will readily perceive. We next remove the two balls on the second wire for a multiplier, and then remove two balls from the third wire, placing them exactly under the first two, which forms a square, and then say twice two are four, which every child will discern for himself, as he plainly perceives there are no more. We then move three on the third wire, and place three from the fourth wire underneath them saying, twice three are six. Remove the four on the fourth wire, and four on the fifth, place them as before and say, twice four are eight. Remove five from the fifth wire, and five from the sixth wire underneath them, saying, twice five are ten. Remove six from the sixth wire, and six from the seventh wire underneath them and say, twice six are twelve. Remove seven from the seventh wire, and seven from the eighth wire underneath them, saying, twice seven are fourteen. Remove eight from the eighth wire, and eight from the ninth, saying, twice eight are sixteen. Remove the nine on the ninth wire, and nine on the tenth wire, saying, twice nine are eighteen. Remove the ten on the tenth wire, and ten on the eleventh underneath them, saying, twice ten are twenty. Remove the eleven on the eleventh wire, and eleven on the twelfth, saying, twice eleven are twenty-two. Remove one from the tenth wire to add to the eleven on the eleventh wire, afterwards the remaining ball on the twelfth wire, saying, twice twelve are twenty-four.

Next proceed backwards, saying, 12 times 2 are 24, 11 times 2 are 22, 10 times 2 are 20, &c.

The other rules are to be worked in the same simple manner, which the master must find out by exerting his own thinking powers; and by so exerting himself, he will become qualified to teach the children with better effect, as it would exceed the limits of this work to enter more minutely into the particulars of every rule.

With regard to the teaching of geometry by this frame, it may be necessary to add, that the balls can be variously arranged so as to form different figures in general use. The teacher will perceive, the balls, as they appear in the figure, represent an acute scalene triangle.

To do anything like justice to the instrument, would form a volume of itself; suffice it to say, that it is one of the best instruments that was ever introduced into an infant school, and I do sincerely hope that no nursery will be without it. I shall next proceed to speak of

TEACHING NUMBER BY MEANS OF INCH CUBES OF WOOD.

This plan, is either adapted for teaching children in classes, in the class-room, or in the gallery altogether. The children are formed into a square in the class-room, in the centre of which is placed a table; on this table the cubes are placed, one, two, or three at a time, according to the age and capacity of the children. For example, the master puts down three, and enquires of the children how many there are? The children, seeing three on the table, naturally call out three; the master puts down two more, and enquires as before, how many are three and two, they answer five; he puts five more and asks how many they make. Perhaps some of the children will answer right, and others wrong; he then calls those that answer wrong to the table, and lets them count the cubes, one at a time, until they are correct. He then adds more to those on the table, as far as he thinks proper; say, for example, as far as eighty. The teacher may ask his little pupils how many tens there are in eighty, taking care to place the cubes ten in a row; the children, seeing eight rows will most likely say eight. Then he can ask them how many are eight times ten; the children will answer eighty. They may be cross-examined in this way with good effect, until they begin to be tired, which as soon as the teacher perceives, he must proceed to substract, saying, take 2 from 80, how many remain? Answer, 78. Q. Take 8 from 78, how many remain? A. 70. The teacher may vary his questions in this way as much as he pleases, which will exercise the children's judgment, and also please them. But in order that the children may thoroughly understand what they are about, it is necessary to call a child, and cause him to count them himself, by placing them singly on the table. It must be observed, that it requires much patience, attention, and trouble, to give the children an insight into this part of the system; but the teacher will be amply recompensed for his pains. There are many little children in the different schools, who will readily answer almost any question in the multiplication, pence, addition, and substraction tables. We have 100 of those cubes, and they may be placed in tens, fives, or in any way that the teacher may think will be most advantageous to the scholar; keeping in view that these things present to the children so many *facts* relating to number, which alone can create correct ideas in their minds upon the subject.—The next thing is to make the children acquainted with the signs of number, which can be most effectually done by means of the brass figures.

To assist the understanding, and exercise the judgment, in teaching numeration, slide a figure in the frame, say figure 8. Question. What is this? Answer. No. 8. Q. If No. 1 be put on the left side of the 8, what will it be? A. 81. Q. If the 1 be put on the right side, then what will it be? A. 18. Q. If the figure 4 be put before the 1, then what will the number be? A. 418. Shift the figure 4, and put it on the left side of the 8, then ask the children to tell the number, the answer is 184. The teacher can keep adding and shifting as he pleases, according to the capacity of his pupils, taking care to explain as he goes on, and to satisfy himself that his little flock perfectly understand him. Suppose figures 5476953821 are in the frame; then let the children begin at the left hand, saying units, tens, hundreds, thousands, tens of thousands, hundreds of thousands, millions, tens of millions, hundreds of millions, thousands of millions. After which begin at the right hand side, and they will say five thousand four hundred and seventy-six million, nine hundred and fifty-three thousand, eight hundred and twenty-one; if the children are well practised in this way they will soon learn numeration. Addition is taught with the brass figures by placing one figure over the other; for example, put figure 5 in the frame: the teacher will then enquire what figure it is; some of the children will answer five; if none of them know it, (which will be the case at first,) they must of course be told. Then place the figure 3 over the 5, and ask what the last figure is, and if the children answer correctly, then ask them how many are 3 and 5. Their having answered this question, place another figure over the 3, the figure 6 for example: enquire as before, what figure it is, and then, how many are eight and six when added together; and so on progressively as the teacher may think proper. This may be taught the children when they are in the gallery, or in the class-room. When a sufficient number of figures are up, begin to take away the bottom figures, saying if I take away this figure, how many are left, and so on until they are all taken out of the frame. This will both please, amuse, and edify the little ones. The only remaining branch of numerical knowledge, which consists in an ability to comprehend the powers of numbers, without either visible objects or signs — is imparted as follows:

Addition.

One of the children ascends the rostrum or small pulpit, and repeats aloud, in a kind of chaunt, the whole of the school repeating after him; One and one are two; two and one are three; three and one are four; &c. up to twelve.

Two and two are four; four and two are six; six and two are eight, &c. to twenty-four.

Three and three are six; six and three are nine; nine and three are twelve, &c. to thirty-six.

Substraction.

One from twelve leaves eleven; one from eleven leaves ten, &c.

Two from twenty-four leaves twenty-two; two from twenty-two leaves twenty, &c.

Multiplication.

Twice one are two; twice two are four; &c. &c.

Three times three are nine, three times four are twelve, &c. &c.

Twelve times two are twenty-four; eleven times two are twenty-two, &c. &c.

Twelve times three are thirty-six; eleven times three are thirty-three, &c. &c. until the whole of the multiplication table is gone through.

Division.

There are twelve twos in twenty-four.—There are eleven twos in twenty-two, &c. &c.

There are twelve threes in thirty-six, &c.

There are twelve fours in forty-eight, &c. &c.

Fractions.

Two is the half ($\frac{1}{2}$) of four.

———————— third ($\frac{1}{3}$) of six.

———————— fourth ($\frac{1}{4}$) of eight.

———————— fifth ($\frac{1}{5}$) of ten.

———————— sixth ($\frac{1}{6}$) of twelve.

———————— seventh ($\frac{1}{7}$) of fourteen.

———————— twelfth ($\frac{1}{12}$) of twenty-four; two is the eleventh ($\frac{1}{11}$) of twenty-two, &c. &c.

Three is the half ($\frac{1}{2}$) of six.

———————— third ($\frac{1}{3}$) of nine.

———————— fourth ($\frac{1}{4}$) of twelve.

———————— twelfth ($\frac{1}{12}$) of thirty-six; three is the eleventh ($\frac{1}{11}$) of thirty-three, &c. &c.

Four is the half ($\frac{1}{2}$) of eight, &c.

In twenty-three are four times five, and three-fifths ($\frac{3}{5}$) of five; in thirty-five are four times eight, and three-eighths ($\frac{3}{8}$) of eight.

In twenty-two are seven times three, and one-third ($\frac{1}{3}$) of three.

In thirty-four are four times eight, and one-fourth ($\frac{1}{4}$) of eight.

The tables subjoined are repeated by the same method, each section being a distinct lesson. To give an idea to the reader, the boy in the rostrum says ten shillings the half ($\frac{1}{2}$) of a pound; six shillings and eightpence one-third ($\frac{1}{3}$) of a pound, &c.

Sixpence the half ($\frac{1}{2}$) of a shilling, &c. Always remembering, that whatever the boy says in the rostrum, the other children must repeat after him, but not till the monitor has ended his sentence; and before the monitor delivers the second sentence, he waits till the children have concluded the first, they waiting for him, and he for them; this prevents confusion, and is the means of enabling persons to understand perfectly what is going on in the school.

Numeration, Addition, Substraction, Multiplication, Division, and Pence Tables.

ADDITION AND SUBSTRACTION TABLE.

1 &	2 &	3 &	4 &	5 &	6 &
1 are 2	1 are 3	1 are 4	1 are 5	1 are 6	1 are 7
2 — 3	2 — 4	2 — 5	2 — 6	2 — 7	2 — 8
3 — 4	3 — 5	3 — 6	3 — 7	3 — 8	3 — 9
4 — 5	4 — 6	4 — 7	4 — 8	4 — 9	4 — 10
5 — 6	5 — 7	5 — 8	5 — 9	5 — 10	5 — 11
6 — 7	6 — 8	6 — 9	6 — 10	6 — 11	6 — 12
7 — 8	7 — 9	7 — 10	7 — 11	7 — 12	7 — 13
8 — 9	8 — 10	8 — 11	8 — 12	8 — 13	8 — 14
9 — 10	9 — 11	9 — 12	9 — 13	9 — 14	9 — 15
10 — 11	10 — 12	10 — 13	10 — 14	10 — 15	10 — 16
11 — 12	11 — 13	11 — 14	11 — 15	11 — 16	11 — 17
12 — 13	12 — 14	12 — 15	12 — 16	12 — 17	12 — 18

7 &	8 &	9 &	10 &	11 &	12 &
1 are 8	1 are 9	1 are 10	1 are 11	1 are 12	1 are 13
2 — 9	2 — 10	2 — 11	2 — 12	2 — 13	2 — 14
3 — 10	3 — 11	3 — 12	3 — 13	3 — 14	3 — 15
4 — 11	4 — 12	4 — 13	4 — 14	4 — 15	4 — 16
5 — 12	5 — 13	5 — 14	5 — 15	5 — 16	5 — 17
6 — 13	6 — 14	6 — 15	6 — 16	6 — 17	6 — 18
7 — 14	7 — 15	7 — 16	7 — 17	7 — 18	7 — 19
8 — 15	8 — 16	8 — 17	8 — 18	8 — 19	8 — 20
9 — 16	9 — 17	9 — 18	9 — 19	9 — 20	9 — 21
10 — 17	10 — 18	10 — 19	10 — 20	10 — 21	10 — 22
11 — 18	11 — 19	11 — 20	11 — 21	11 — 22	11 — 23
12 — 19	12 — 20	12 — 21	12 — 22	12 — 23	12 — 24

MULTIPLICATION AND DIVISION TABLE.

2— 2 are 4	4— 5 are 20	6—12 are 72
3 — 6	6 — 24	7— 7 — 49
4 — 8	7 — 28	8 — 56
5 — 10	8 — 32	9 — 63
6 — 12	9 — 36	10 — 70
7 — 14	10 — 40	11 — 77
8 — 16	11 — 44	12 — 84
9 — 18	12 — 48	8— 8 — 64
10 — 20	5— 5 — 25	9 — 72
11 — 22	6 — 30	10 — 80
12 — 24	7 — 35	11 — 88
3— 3 — 9	8 — 40	12 — 96
4 — 12	9 — 45	9— 9 — 81
5 — 15	10 — 50	10 — 90
6 — 18	11 — 55	11 — 99
7 — 21	12 — 60	12 — 108
8 — 24	6— 6 — 36	10 10 — 100
9 — 27	7 — 42	11 — 110
10 — 30	8 — 48	12 — 120
11 — 33	9 — 54	11 11 — 121
12 — 36	10 — 60	12 — 132
4— 4 — 16	11 — 66	12 12 — 144

NUMERATION TABLE.

1	Units.
21	Tens.
321	Hundreds.
4,321	Thousands.
54,321	X of Thousands.
654,321	C of Thousands.
7,654,321	Millions.
87,654,321	X of Millions.
987,654,321	C of Thousands.

PENCE TABLE.

d.	s. d.	d.	s. d.
20 is	1 8	90 is	7 6
30 —	2 6	100 —	8 4
40 —	3 4	110 —	9 2
50 —	4 2	120 —	10 0
60 —	5 0	130 —	10 10
70 —	5 10	140 —	11 8
80 —	6 8	144 —	12 0

Tables of Weights and Measures.

Shillings Table.

s.	l.	s.	s.	l.	s.
20 are	1	0	100 are	5	0
30 ..	1	10	110 ..	5	10
40 ..	2	0	120 ..	6	0
50 ..	2	10	130 ..	6	10
60 ..	3	0	140 ..	7	0
70 ..	3	10	150 ..	7	10
80 ..	4	0	160 ..	8	0
90 ..	4	10	170 ..	8	10

Practice Table.

Of a Pound.

s.	d.		
10	0	are	half
6	8	..	third
5	0	..	fourth
4	0	..	fifth
3	4	..	sixth
2	6	..	eighth
1	8	..	twelfth
1	0	..	twentieth

Of a Shilling.

6d.	are	half
4	..	third
3	..	fourth
2	..	sixth
1	..	twelfth

Time.

60 seconds	1 minute
60 minutes	1 hour
24 hours	1 day
7 days	1 week
4 weeks	1 lunar month
12 cal. mon.	1 year

13 lunar months, 1 day, 6 urs. or 365 days, 6 hrs. 1 year.

Thirty days hath September,
April, June, & November;
All the rest have thirty-one,
Save February, which alone
Hath twenty-eight, except Leap-year
And twenty-nine is then its share.

Troy Weight.

24 grains	1 pennywht.
20 pennywhts.	1 ounce
12 ounces	1 pound

Avoirdupoise Weight.

16 drams	1 ounce
16 ounces	1 pound
28 pounds	1 quarter
4 quarters	1 hund. wt.
20 hund. wt.	1 ton

Apothecaries Weight.

20 grains	1 scruple
3 scruples	1 dram
8 drams	1 ounce
12 ounces	1 pound

Wool Weight.

7 pounds	1 clove
2 cloves	1 stone
2 stones	1 tod
6½ tods	1 weys
2 weys	1 sack
12 sacks	1 last

Wine Measure.

2 pints	1 quart
4 quarts	1 gallon
10 gallons	1 ank. bndy.
42 gallons	1 tierce
63 gallons	1 hogshead
84 gallons	1 puncheon
2 hogshead	1 pipe
2 pipes	1 ton

Ale & Beer Measure.

2 pints	1 quart
4 quarts	1 gallon
8 gallons	1 firkin of ale
9 gallons	1 firk. of beer
2 firkins	1 kilderkin
2 kildrkins	1 barrel
1½ barrel	1 hogshead
2 barrels	1 puncheon
3 barrels	1 butt

Coal Measure.

4 pecks	1 bushel
9 bushel	1 vat or strike
3 bushels	1 sack
12 sacks	1 chaldron
91 chaldron	1 score

Dry Measure.

2 pints	1 quart
2 quarts	1 pottle
2 pottles	1 gallon
2 gallons	1 peck
4 pecks	1 bushel
2 bushels	1 strike
5 bushels	1 sack flour
8 bushels	1 quarter
5 quarters	1 wey or load
5 pecks	1 bshl. water measure
4 bushels	1 coom
10 cooms	1 wey
2 weys	1 last corn

Solid or Cubic Measure.

1728 inches	1 foot
27 feet	1 yard or ld.

Long Measure.

3 barleycorns	1 inch
12 inches	1 foot
3 feet	1 yard
6 feet	1 fathom
5½ yards	1 pole or rod
40 poles	1 furlong
8 furlongs	1 mile
3 miles	1 league
20 leagues	1 degree

Cloth Measure.

2¼ inches	1 nail
4 nails	1 quarter
4 quarters	1 yard
5 quarters	1 English ell
3 quarters	1 Flemish ell
6 quarters	1 French ell

Land or Square Meas.

144 inches	1 foot
3 feet	1 yard
30¼ yards	1 pole
40 poles	1 rood
4 roods	1 acre
640 acres	1 mile

This includes length and breadth.

Hay.

36 pounds	1 trs. of straw
56 pounds	do. of old hay
60 pounds	1 do. of new
36 trusses	1 load

CHAPTER XII.

QUESTIONS AND ANSWERS CONCERNING THE GEOMETRICAL FIGURES.

Useful knowledge can have no enemies, except the ignorant; it cherishes the mind of youth, and delights the aged, and who knows how many mathematicians in embryo, there may be in an Infant School.

AMONG the novel features of the Infant School system, that of geometrical lessons is the most peculiar. How it happened that a mode of instruction so evidently calculated for the infant mind was so long overlooked, I cannot imagine; and it is still more surprising that having been once thought upon, there should any be found incapable of perceiving its utility. Certain it is that the various form of bodies is one of the first items of natural education, and we cannot err when treading in the steps of Nature. It is undeniable that geometrical knowledge is of great service in many of the mechanic arts, and therefore proper to be taught those children who are likely to be employed in some one or other of those arts; but, independently of this, we cannot adopt a better method of exciting a spirit and strengthening their powers of observation. I have seen a thousand instances, moreover, in the conduct of the children, which have assured me, that it is a very pleasing as well as useful branch of instruction. The children, being taught the first elements of form, and the terms used to express the various figures of bodies, find in its application to objects around them an inexhaustible source of amusement. Streets, houses, rooms, fields, ponds, plates, dishes, tables,—in short every thing they see, calls forth their observation as to its form, and afford an opportunity for the application of their little geometrical knowledge. Let it not, then, be said, that it is beyond their capacity — for it is the simplest and most comprehensible to them of all knowledge; — let it not be said that it is useless, since its application to the useful arts is great and indisputable; nor, lastly, let it be asserted that it is unpleasing to them, since it has been shewn to add much to their happiness.

It is essential in this, as in every other branch of education, to begin with the first principles, and proceed *slowly* to their application, and the complicated forms arising therefrom. The next thing is to promote that application of which we have before spoken to the various objects around them. It is this, and this alone, which forms the distinction between a school lesson and practical knowledge; and so far will the children be found from being averse to this exertion, that it makes the acquirement of knowledge a pleasure instead of a task. With these prefatory remarks I shall introduce a description of the method I have pursued, and a few examples of geometrical lessons.

We will suppose that the whole of the children are seated in the gallery, and that the teacher is provided with a large board, having a paper pasted on it, on which are printed the geometrical figures. He first places the board in such a situation before the gallery, that every child may see it, and being provided with a pointer, points to a strait line, asking, What is this? *A.* A strait line. *Q.* Why did you not call it a crooked line? *A.* Because it is not crooked, but strait. *Q.* What are these? *A.* Curved lines. *Q.* What do curved lines mean? *A.* When they are bent or crooked. *Q.* What are these? *A.* Parallel strait lines. *Q.* What does parallel mean? *A.* Parallel means when they are equally distant from each other in every part. *Q.* If any of you children were reading a book that gave an account of some town which had twelve streets, and it said the streets were parallel, would you understand what it meant? *A.* Yes; it would mean that the streets were all the same way, side by side, like the lines which we now see. *Q.* What are those? *A.* Diverging or converging strait lines. *Q.* What is the difference between diverging and converging lines and parallel lines? *A.* Diverging or converging lines are not at an equal distance from each other, in every part, but parallel lines are. *Q.* What does diverge mean? *A.* Diverge means when they go from each other, and they diverge at one end, and converge at the other. *Q.* What does converge mean? *A.* Converge means when they come towards each other. *Q.* Suppose the lines were longer, what would be the consequence? *A.* Please sir, if they were longer they would meet together at the end they converge. *Q.* What would they form by meeting together? *A.* By meeting together they would form an angle. *Q.* What kind of an angle?

A. An acute angle. *Q.* Would they form an angle at the other end? *A.* No, they would go further from each other. *Q.* What is this? *A.* A perpendicular line. *Q.* What does perpendicular mean? *A.* A line up strait, like the stems of some trees. *Q.* If you look, you will see that one end of the line comes on the middle of another line; what does it form? *A.* The one which we now see forms two right angles. *Q.* I will make a strait line, and one end of it shall lean on another strait line, but instead of being upright like the perpendicular line, you see that it is sloping. What does it form? *A.* One side of it is an acute angle, and the other side is an obtuse angle. *Q.* Which side is the obtuse angle? *A.* That which is the most open. *Q.* And which is the acute angle? *A.* That which is the least open. *Q.* What does acute mean? *A.* When the angle is sharp. *Q.* What does obtuse mean? *A.* When the angle is less sharp than the right angle. *Q.* If I were to call any one of you an acute child, would you know what I meant? *A.* Yes, sir, one that looks out sharp and tries to think, and pays attention to what is said to him; then you would say he was an acute child.

Equi-lateral Triangle.

Q. What is this? *A.* An equi-lateral triangle. *Q.* Why is it called equi-lateral? *A.* Because its sides are all equal. *Q.* How many sides has it? *A.* Three sides. *Q.* How many angles has it? *A.* Three angles. *Q.* What do you mean by angles? *A.* The space between two right lines, drawn gradually nearer to each other, till they meet in a point. *Q.* And what do you call the point where the two lines meet? *A.* The angular point. *Q.* Tell me why you call it a tri-angle? *A.* We call it a tri-angle, because it has three angles. *Q.* What do you mean by equal? *A.* When the three sides are of the same length. *Q.* Have you any thing else to observe upon this. *A.* Yes, all its angles are acute.

Isoceles Triangle.

Q. What is this? *A.* An acute-angled isoceles triangle. *Q.* What does acute mean? *A.* When the angles are sharp. *Q.* Why is it called an isoceles triangle? *A.* Because only two of its sides are equal. *Q.* How many sides has it? *A.* Three, the same as the other. *Q.* Are there any other kind of isoceles triangles? *A.* Yes, there are right-angled and obtuse-angled.

[Here the pointer is to be put to the other tri-angles, and the master must explain to the children the meaning of right-angled and obtuse-angled.]

Scalene Triangle.

Q. What is this? *A.* An acute-angled sca-lene tri-angle. *Q.* Why is it called an acute-angled scalene tri-angle? *A.* Because all its angles are acute, and its sides are not equal. *Q.* Why is it called scalene? *A.* Because it has all its sides *unequal.* *Q.* Are there any other kind of scalene triangles? *A.* Yes, there is a right-angled scalene triangle, which has one right angle. *Q.* What else? *A.* An obtuse-angled scalene triangle, which has one obtuse-angle. *Q.* Can an acute triangle be an equi-lateral triangle? *A.* Yes, it may be an equi-lateral, iso-celes, or scalene. *Q.* Can a right-angled tri-angle, or an obtuse-angled tri-angle, be an equi-lateral? *A.* No; it must either be an isoceles or a scalene tri-angle.

Square.

Q. What is this? *A.* A square. *Q.* Why is it called a square? *A.* Because all its angles are right angles, and its sides are equal. *Q.* How many angles has it? *A.* Four angles. *Q.* What would it make if we draw a line from one angle to the opposite one? *A.* Two right-angled isoceles triangles. *Q.* What would you call the line that we drew from one angle to the other? *A.* A diagonal. *Q.* Suppose we draw another line from the other two angles. *A.* Then it would make four triangles.

Penta-gon.

Q. What is this? *A.* A regular pentagon. *Q.* Why is it called a pentagon? *A.* Because it has five sides and five angles. *Q.* Why is it called regular? *A.* Because its sides and angles are equal. *Q.* What does pentagon mean? *A.* A five-sided figure. *Q.* Are there any other kinds of pentagons? *A.* Yes, irregular pentagons. *Q.* What does irregular mean? *A.* When the sides and angles are not equal.

Hexa-gons.

Q. What is this? *A.* A hexagon. *Q.* Why is it called a hexagon? *A.* Because it has six

T

sides and six angles. *Q.* What does hexagon mean? *A.* A six-sided figure. *Q.* Are there more than one sort of hexagons? Yes, there are regular and irregular. *Q.* What is a regular hexagon? *A.* When the sides and angles are all equal. *Q.* What is an irregular hexagon? *A.* When the sides and angles are not equal.

Hepta-gon.

Q. What is this? *A.* A regular heptagon. *Q.* Why is it called an heptagon? *A.* Because it has seven sides and seven angles. *Q.* Why is it called a regular heptagon? *A.* Because its sides and angles are equal. *Q.* What does a heptagon mean? *A.* A seven-sided figure. *Q.* What is an irregular heptagon? *A.* A seven-sided figure, whose sides are not equal.

Octa-gon.

Q. What is this? *A.* A regular octagon. *Q.* Why is it called a regular octagon? *A.* Because it has eight sides and eight angles, and they are all equal. *Q.* What does an octagon mean? *A.* An eight-sided figure. *Q.* What is an irregular octagon? *A.* An eight-sided figure, whose sides and angles are not all equal. *Q.* What does an octave mean? *A.* Eight notes in music.

Nona-gon.

Q. What is this? *A.* A nonagon. *Q.* Why is it called a nonagon? *A.* Because it has nine sides and nine angles. *Q.* What does a nonagon mean? *A.* A nine-sided figure. *Q.* What is an irregular nonagon? *A.* A nine-sided figure whose sides and angles are not equal.

Deca-gon.

Q. What is this? *A.* A regular deca-gon. *Q.* What does a decagon mean? *A.* A ten-sided figure. *Q.* Why is it called a decagon? *A.* Because it has ten sides and ten angles, and there are both regular and irregular decagons.

Rect-angle or Oblong.

Q. What is this? *A.* A rectangle or oblong. *Q.* How many sides and angles has it? *A.* Four, the same as a square. *Q.* What is the difference between a rect-angle and a square? *A.* A rect-angle has two long sides and the other two are much shorter, but a square has its sides equal.

Rhomb.

Q. What is this? *A.* A rhomb. *Q.* What is the difference between a rhomb and a rectangle? *A.* The sides of the rhomb are equal, but the sides of the rectangle are not all equal. *Q.* Is there any other difference? *A.* Yes, the angles of the rectangle are equal, but the rhomb has only its opposite angles equal.

Rhomboid.

Q. What is this? *A.* A rhomboid. *Q.* What is the difference between a rhomb and a rhomboid? *A.* The sides of the rhomboid are not equal, nor yet its angles, but the sides of the rhomb are equal.

Q. What is this? *A.* A trapezoid. *Q.* How many sides has it? *A.* Four sides and four angles, but it has only two of its angles equal, which are opposite to each other.

Q. What do we call these figures that have four sides? *A.* Tetragons, *tetra* meaning four. *Q.* Are they called by any other name? *A.* Yes, they are called quadri-laterals, or quadr-angles. *Q.* How many regular tetragons are there among those we have mentioned? *A.* One, and that is the square, all the others are irregular tetragons, because their sides and angles are not all equal. *Q.* By what name would you call the whole of the figures on this board? *A.* Polygons; those that have their sides and angles equal we would call regular polygons. *Q.* What would you call those whose sides and angles were not equal? *A.* Irregular polygons, and the smallest number of sides a polygon can have is three, and the number of corners are always equal to the number of sides.

Q. What is this? *A.* An ellipse or an oval. *Q.* What shape is the top or crown of my hat? *A.* Circular. *Q.* What shape is that part which comes on my forehead and the back part of my head? *A.* Oval.

The other polygons are taught the children in rotation, in the same simple manner, all tending to please and edify them. They are taught the principle of brick-building, by wooden blocks, made the proper size, so that they may build the front of a house, walls, &c. They may also be taught the principle, in some degree, by which bridges are built, and we have children who can spring an arch, and tell the names of every thing connected with it; in short, there is scarcely any thing of which children are not capable, if we so simplify the things that they can comprehend them. Perhaps it may be thought that I am going into an extreme in attempting to teach infants these things; but if any person doubts the possibility of infants being taught thus, they can satisfy themselves by calling at the schools; and I once more beg leave to remark, that variety forms the most pleasing food for the human mind. And I have found that children are not too young to learn these and many other things still more complicated, but that I have been too old to teach them.

CHAPTER XIII.

PLAN FOR TEACHING INFANT CHILDREN BY THE AID OF PICTURES AND CONVERSATION.

The most barren ground, by manuring, may be made to produce good fruit; the fiercest beasts by art, are made tame; so are moral virtues acquired by education properly applied.

TO give the children general information, it has been found advisable to have recourse to pictures* of natural history, such as of birds, beasts, fishes, flowers, insects, &c. all of which tend to shew the glory of God; and as colours attract the attention of the children as soon as any thing, they eagerly enquire what such a thing is, and this gives the teacher an opportunity of instructing them to great advantage; for when a child of his own free will eagerly desires to be informed, he is sure to profit by the information then imparted.

* See life of Dr. Doddridge :—" His parents brought him up in the early knowledge of religion, before he could read his mother taught him the history of the Old and New Testament, by the assistance of some Dutch tiles in the chimney of the room, where they usually sat; and accompanied her instructions with such wise and pious reflections, as made strong and lasting impressions upon his heart."

We use also pictures of public buildings, and of the different trades; by the former, the children acquire much information, from the explanations which are given to them of the use of the buildings, in what year they were built, &c.; whilst by the latter, we are enabled to find out the bias of a child's inclination. Some would like to be shoe-makers, others builders, others weavers, brewers, &c.; in short it is both pleasing and edifying to hear the children give answers to the different questions. I remember one little boy who said he should like to be a doctor; and when asked why he made choice of that profession, in preference to any other, his answer was, " Because he should like to cure all the sick people." If parents did but study the inclinations of their children a little more than they do, I humbly conceive, that there would be more eminent men in every profession, than there are. It is great imprudence to deter-mine what business children may be adapted for, before their tempers and inclinations are well known; every one, it has been wisely observed, is best in his own profession—that which fits us best, is best; nor is any thing more fitting than that every one should consider his own genius and capacity, and act accordingly.

But as it is possible that a person may be very clever in his business or profession, and yet not be a Christian, it has been thought necessary to direct the children's attention to the Scriptures, even at this early age, and to endeavour, if pos-sible, to lay a solid foundation of piety in the in-fant mind, by teaching them to venerate the Bible, and to fear and love its Divine Author. Many difficulties lie in the way of attaining so desirable an end; the principal one arises not from their

inability to read the Bible, nor from their inability
to comprehend it, but from the apathy of the
heart to its divine principles and precepts. Some
parents are quite delighted if their children can
read a chapter or two in the Bible, and think that
when they can do this, they have arrived at the
summit of knowledge, without once considering
whether they understand one sentence of what they
read, or whether if they understand it, they *feel*
its truth and importance. And how can it be expected that they should either understand or *feel*
its truths, when no previous ground-work has
been laid, at the time when they received their first
impressions, and imbibed their first ideas? Every
man comes into the world without a single innate
idea, yet with a capacity to receive knowledge of
every kind, and is therefore capable of becoming
intelligent and wise. In his infancy he would
take hold of the most poisonous reptile, that might
sting him to death in an instant; would attempt
to stroke the lion with as little fear as he would
the lamb; in short, he is incapable of distinguish-
ing friend from foe. So wonderfully is man formed by his adorable Creator, that he is capable of
increasing in knowledge, and advancing towards
perfection to all eternity, without ever being able
to arrive at it. The first thing that attracts his
attention, even when in the cradle, is a light; and
we may venture to say, the next things that attract his notice, are bright colours; it is for this
reason, that *pictures* of Scripture history have been
selected, such as Joseph and his brethren—Christ
raising Lazarus from the dead — the Nativity —
flight into Egypt — Christ disputing with the doc-
tors—Christ baptized by John—curing the blind
and lame—the last Supper — the Crucifixion —

Resurrection — Ascension, &c. &c. To begin with

Joseph and his Brethren.

The following method is adopted : — The picture being suspended against the wall, and one class of the children standing opposite to it, the master repeats the following passages: " And Joseph dreamed a dream, and he told it to his brethren; and they hated him yet the more. And he said unto them, hear, I pray you, the dream which I have dreamed; for behold, we were binding sheaves in the field, and lo! my sheaf arose and also stood upright; and behold, your sheaves stood round about, and made obeisance to my sheaf."

The teacher being provided with a pointer, will point to the picture and put the following questions, or such as he may think better, to the children :—

Q. What is this? *A.* Joseph's first dream. *Q.* What is a dream? *A.* When you dream, you see things during the time of sleep. *Q.* Did any of you ever dream any thing?

Here the children will repeat what they have dreamed, perhaps something like the following. Please sir, once I dreamed I was in a garden. *Q.* What did you see? *A.* I saw flowers and such nice apples. *Q.* How do you know it was a dream? *A.* Because, when I awoke, I found I was in bed.

During this recital the children will listen very attentively, for they are highly pleased to hear each other's relations. The master having satisfied himself that the children, in some measure, understand the nature of a dream, he may proceed as follows.

Q. What did Joseph dream about first? *A.* He dreamed that his brother's sheaves made obeisance to his sheaf. *Q.* What is a sheaf? *A.* A bundle of corn. *Q.* What do you understand by making obeisance? *A.* To bend your body, which we call making a bow. *Q.* What is binding sheaves? *A.* To bind them, which they do with a band of twisted straw. *Q.* How many brothers had Joseph? *A.* Eleven. *Q.* What was Joseph's father's name? *A.* Jacob, who is sometimes called Israel.

Master.—And it is further written concerning Joseph, that he dreamed yet another dream, and told it to his brethren, and said, behold, I have dreamed a dream more; and behold the sun and the moon and the eleven stars made obeisance to me.

Q. What do you understand by the sun? *A.* The sun is that bright object in the sky which shines in the day-time, and which gives us heat and light. *Q.* Who made the sun? *A.* Almighty God. *Q.* For what purpose did God make the sun? *A.* To warm and nourish the earth and every thing upon it. *Q.* What do you mean by the earth? *A.* The ground on which we walk, and on which the corn, trees, and flowers grow. *Q.* What is it that makes them grow? *A.* The heat and light of the sun. *Q.* Does it require any thing else to make them grow? *A.* Yes, rain, and the assistance of Almighty God. *Q.* What is the moon? *A.* That object which is placed in the sky, and shines in the night, and appears larger than the stars. *Q.* What do you mean by the stars? *A.* Those bright objects that appear in the sky at night. *Q.* What are they? *A.* Some of them are worlds, and others are suns to give them light. *Q.* Who placed them there? *A.* Almighty God. *Q.* Should we fear and love him for his goodness? *A.* Yes, and for his mercy towards us. *Q.* Do you think it wonderful that God should make all these things? *A.* Yes. *Q.* Are there any more things that are wonderful to you? *A.* Yes;—

Where'er we turn our wondering eyes,
   His power and skill we see;
Wonders on wonders grandly rise,
   And speak the Deity.

Q. Who is the Deity? *A.* Almighty God.

Reuben interceding with his Brethren for the Life of Joseph.

Master.—" And Reuben said unto them, shed no blood, but cast him into this pit, that is in the wilderness, and lay no hand upon him; that he might rid him out of their hands, to deliver him to his father again."

Q. Who was Reuben? *A.* One of the brothers of Joseph. *Q.* What is a pit? *A.* A deep hole in the ground. *Q.* What is a wilderness? *A.* A place that is uninhabited, and where nothing grows except thorns and briers.

Master.—My little children, our minds may be compared to a wilderness, and unless they are watered by divine truth which comes from God, they would produce nothing but evil thoughts, which would break forth into bad actions; an evil thought does as much harm to the mind as a thorn would in any part of the body, and if it be brought into action, it not only hurts us, but other persons besides, and therefore children should come to school to have their minds improved, that they may bring forth good thoughts, and good actions, and then, instead of a wilderness, their minds may be compared to a garden.

Q. What kind of a coat had Joseph? *A.* A coat of many colours. *Q.* Did Joseph's brethren say any thing among themselves when they saw Joseph afar off? *A.* Yes; they said one to another, behold this dreamer cometh, come now therefore and let us slay him, and cast him into some pit. *Q.* What is meant by the words slay and cast? *A.* To slay means to kill, and to cast, means to throw his dead body into a pit. *Q.* Did they put him into the pit? *A.* Yes, but there was no water in it, so they put him in alive. *Q.* What was the reason that Joseph's brothers wanted to put him out of the way? *A.* Because of his dreams, and for fear that he should become their master. *Q.* After they had put him in the pit, what did they do? *A.* They sat down and eat bread, and while they were eating it, they saw a number of men with their camels, and they sold him to them. *Q.* What did they do with Joseph's coat? *A.* They killed a kid and dipped the coat in its blood, that Joseph's father might think he had been killed by some wild beast. *Q.* What is a kid? *A.* A young goat. *Q.* What were those men called who bought Joseph? *A.* Ishmaelites. *Q.* Where did the Ishmaelites take him to? *A.* They took him to Egypt, and a man named Potiphar, an officer of Pharaoh, bought him. *Q.* Who was Pharaoh? *A.* The king of Egypt. *Q.* Was Joseph a good servant?

A. Yes, and his master made him head over the other servants. *Q.* Did Joseph remain head servant? *A.* No, his mistress told a falsehood of him, and his master put him into prison. *Q.* Did God forsake Joseph in prison? *A.* No; he was with him, and the keeper of the prison put all the other prisoners under Joseph's care. *Q.* Were any particular prisoners brought in while Joseph was in prison? *A.* Yes, Pharaoh's chief butler and baker. *Q.* What is a butler? *A.* A manservant who takes care of the wine and other things, and an upper servant; and the baker makes the bread for the family. *Q.* Did any thing particular take place while they were in prison? *A.* Yes, the butler and baker both dreamed a dream in one night. *Q.* Who explained the dreams? *A.* Joseph, and he explained them rightly; the butler was restored to his place, but the baker was hanged. *Q.* Did Joseph ask the chief butler any thing? *A.* Yes, he said, think of me when it shall be well with thee, and make mention of me unto Pharaoh. *Q.* Did the chief butler remember Joseph? *A.* No, he forgot him, as is too often the case; but we ought never to forget our friends. *Q.* How long was it before the chief butler spoke of Joseph to Pharaoh? *A.* Two years. *Q.* What caused him to remember? *A.* Because Pharaoh dreamed a dream, and none of his own people could explain it. *Q.* What took place next? *A.* The chief butler told Pharaoh of Joseph, and Pharaoh sent for Joseph, and Joseph explained both his dreams. *Q.* Did Pharaoh believe Joseph? *A.* Yes, and he was so pleased that he gave Joseph a ring, and a gold chain about his neck, and made him ruler over all the other servants. *Q.* How did Joseph first see

U

his brothers? *A.* There was a famine in the land, and Joseph's father sent his brothers to buy corn, and when they saw him they did not know him. *Q.* What does a famine mean? *A.* When there is nothing for people to eat. *Q.* Did Joseph make himself known to his brethren? *A.* Yes, after some time, and then he made a feast for them. *Q.* After Joseph had made himself known to his brethren what did he do? *A.* He sent for his father and told his brothers to say, thus saith thy son Joseph, God hath made me lord over all Egypt, come down unto me directly. *Q.* What did Joseph's brothers say when they came to their father? *A.* They said thy son Joseph is yet alive, and he is governor over all the land of Egypt; and Jacob's heart fainted, for he could not believe them at first. *Q.* Did he believe them at last? *A.* Yes, when he saw the waggons which Joseph had sent to carry him, the spirit of Jacob their father revived. *Q.* Did Jacob consent to go? *A.* Yes; he said it is enough, Joseph my son is yet alive, I will go and see him before I die. *Q.* If we want any more information about Joseph and his brethren, where can we find it? *A.* In the 37th chapter of Genesis, and many of the following chapters.

In this way the teacher may go on, until he has placed before the children the leading facts of the history of Joseph, taking care that the children understand every term used; and he will find the children both instructed and pleased, and himself none the worse for the exercise. He may also ask them the chapter, verse, name of the book, &c.

Lazarus raised from the Dead.

The picture being suspended as before described, we proceed thus :

Q. What is this ? *A.* Jesus Christ raising Lazarus from the dead. *Q.* Who was Lazarus ? *Q.* A man that lived in a town called Bethany, and a friend of Christ's. *Q.* What is a town ? *A.* A place where there are a great number of houses, and persons living in them. *Q.* What do you mean by a friend ? *A.* A person that loves you, and does all the good he can for you, to whom you ought to do the same in return. *Q.* Did Jesus love Lazarus ? *A.* Yes, and his sisters, Martha and Mary. *Q.* Who was it that sent unto Jesus Christ, and told him that Lazarus was sick ? *A.* Martha and Mary. *Q.* What did they say ? *A.* They said, Lord, behold, he whom thou lovest is sick. *Q.* What answer did Jesus make unto them ? *A.* He said, this sickness is not unto death, but for the glory of God. *Q.* What did he mean by saying so ? *A.* He meant that Lazarus should be raised again by the power of God, and that the people that stood by, should see it, and believe on him. *Q.* How many days did Jesus stop where he was, when he found Lazarus was sick ? *A.* Two days. *Q.* When Jesus Christ wanted to leave the place, what did he say to his disciples ? *A.* He said let us go into Judea again. *Q.* What do you mean by Judea ? *A.* A country where the Jews lived. *Q.* Did the disciples say any thing to Jesus Christ, when he expressed a wish to go into Judea again ? *A.* Yes, they said, Master, the Jews of late sought to stone thee, and goest thou thither again? *Q.* What did Jesus Christ tell them? *A.* He told them a great many things, and at last told them plainly that Lazarus was dead. *Q.* How many days had Lazarus lain in the grave before he was raised up? *A.* Four. *Q.* Who went to meet Jesus Christ, when she heard that he was coming? *A.* Martha; but Mary sat still in the house. *Q.* Did Martha say any thing to Jesus, when she met him? *A.* Yes, she said, Lord, if thou hadst been here my brother had not died. *Q.* Did Martha tell her sister that Jesus Christ was come? *A.* Yes, she said, the Master is come, and calleth for thee. *Q.* Did Mary go to meet Jesus Christ? *A.* Yes; and when she saw him, she fell down at his feet, and said, Lord, if thou hadst been here, my brother had not died. *Q.* Did Mary weep? *A.* Yes; and the Jews that were with her. *Q.* What is weeping? *A.* To cry. *Q.* Did Jesus weep? *A.* Yes; and the Jews said, behold, how he loved him. *Q.* Did the Jews say any thing else? *A.* Yes; they said, could not this man that opened the eyes of the blind, have caused that even this man should not have died? *Q.* What took place next? *A.* He went to the grave, and told the persons that stood by, to take away the stone. *Q.* And when they took away the stone, what did Jesus Christ do? *A.* He cried, with a loud voice, Lazarus, come forth; and he that was dead, came forth, bound hand and foot, with grave clothes, and his face was bound about with a napkin.—Jesus saith unto them, loose him, and let him go; and many of the Jews which came to Mary, and had seen these things which Jesus did, believed on him. *Q.* If we wanted any more information about Lazarus and his sisters, where should we find it? *A.* In the Bible. *Q.* What part? *A.* The eleventh and twelfth chapters of John.

I have had children at the early age of four years, ask me questions, that I could not possibly answer; and among other things, the children have said, when being examined at this picture, "that if Jesus Christ had cried softly, Lazarus, come forth, he would have come."—And when asked, why they thought so, they have answered, "Because God can do any thing;" which is a convincing proof, that children, at a very early age, have an idea of the Omnipotence of the Supreme Being. Oh, that men would praise the Lord for his goodness to the children of men!

The Nativity of Jesus Christ.

The picture being suspended as the others, and a whole class being in the class-room, put the pointer into one of the children's hands, and desire the child to find out the Nativity of Jesus Christ. The other children will be on the tip-toe of expectation, to see whether the child makes a mistake; for should this be the case, they know that one of them will have the same privilege of trying to find it; should the child happen to touch the wrong picture, the teacher will have at least a dozen applicants, saying, " Please, sir, may I? please, sir, may I?" The teacher having selected the child to make the next trial, say one of the youngest of the applicants, the child walks round the room with the pointer, and puts it on the right picture; which will be always known by the other children calling out, " that is the right, that is the right." To view the child's sparkling eyes, who has found the picture, and to see the pleasure beaming forth in his countenance, you might imagine, that he conceived he had performed one of the greatest wonders of the age. The children will then proceed to read what is printed on the picture, which is as follows: " The Nativity of our Lord and Saviour Jesus Christ;" which is printed at the top of the picture. At the bottom are the following words: " And she brought forth her first-born son, and wrapped him in swaddling clothes, and laid him in a manger, because there was no room for them in the inn."—We then proceed to question them in the following manner:

Q. What do you mean by the Nativity of Jesus Christ? *A.* The time he was born. *Q.* Where was he born? *A.* In Bethlehem of Judea. *Q.* Where did they lay him? *A.* In a manger. *Q.* What is a manger? *A.* A thing that horses feed out of. *Q.* What was the reason they put him there? *A.* Because there was no room in the inn. *Q.* What is an inn? *A.* A place where persons lodge who are travelling, and it is like a public house. *Q.* What do you mean by travelling? *A.* When you go from one place to another; from London into the country, or from the country into London. *Q.* Is any thing else to be understood by travelling? *A.* Yes, we are all travelling. *Q.* What do you mean by being all travelling? *A.* We are all going in a good road, or else in a bad one. *Q.* What do you mean by a good road? *A.* That which leads to heaven. *Q.* What will lead us to heaven? *A.* Praying to God, and endeavouring to keep his commandments, and trying all we can to be good children. *Q.* Can we make ourselves good *A.*

No, we can receive nothing, except it be given us from heaven. *Q.* What is travelling in a bad road? *A.* Being naughty children, and not minding what is said to us: and when we say bad words, or steal any thing, or take God's name in vain. *Q.* Where will this road lead to? *A.* To eternal misery.

Here we usually give a little advice according to circumstances, taking care always to avoid long speeches, that will tend to stupify the children. If they appear tired, we stop, but if not, they repeat the following hymn, which I shall insert in full, as I believe there is nothing in it that any Christian would object to.

HARK! the skies with music sound!
Heav'nly glory beams around;
Christ is born! the angels sing,
Glory to the New-born King.

Peace is come, good-will appears,
Sinners, wipe away your tears:
God in human flesh to-day
Humbly in the manger lay.

Shepherds tending flocks by night,
Heard the song, and saw the light;
Took their reeds, and softest strains
Echo'd thro' the happy plains.

Mortals, hail the glorious King!
Richest incense cheerful bring;
Praise and love Emanuel's name,
And his boundless grace proclaim.

The hymn being concluded, we put the following questions to the children.

Q. Who was the new-born king? *A.* Jesus Christ. *Q.* Who are sinners? *A.* We, and all men. *Q.* What are flocks? *A.* A number of sheep. *Q.* What are shepherds? *A.* Those who take care of the sheep. *Q.* What are plains? *A.* Where the sheep feed. *Q.* Who are mortals? *A.* We are mortals. *Q.* Who is the glorious king? *A.* Jesus Christ. *Q.* What is meant by Emanuel's name? *A.* Jesus Christ.

Here the teacher can inform the children, that Jesus Christ is called by a variety of names in the Bible, and can repeat them to the children if he thinks proper; for every correct idea respecting the Saviour which he can instil into their minds will serve as a foundation for other ideas, and he will find that the more ideas the children have, the more ready they will be in answering his questions; for man is a progressive being; his progression is his grand distinction above the brutes.

The Flight into Egypt.

Q. What is this? *A.* A picture of the flight into Egypt. *Q.* What does flight mean? *A.* To go from one place to another as quick as possible. *Q.* Who went into Egypt? *A.* Jesus Christ, with Joseph and Mary. *Q.* What made them go into Egypt? *A.* Because an angel told Joseph, in a dream, to go. *Q.* What was the reason of their going? *A.* For fear of Herod, a king. *Q.* How long did they remain in Egypt? *A.* Until an angel appeared to them again, and told them that Herod was dead.

Solomon's Wise Judgment.

Q. What is this? *A.* A picture of Solomon's wise judgment. *Q.* Describe what you mean? *A.* Two women stood before king Solomon. *Q.* Did the women say any thing to the king when they came before him? *A.* Yes; one woman said, O my Lord, I and this woman dwell in one house, and I had a child there, and this woman had a child also, and this woman's child died in the night. *Q.* To whom did the women speak when they said, O my Lord? *A.* To king Solomon. *Q.* What did the woman mean when she said we dwell in one house? *A.* She meant that they both lived in it. *Q.* Did the woman say any thing more to the king? *A.* Yes; she said the other woman rose at midnight, and took her son from her. *Q.* What is meant by midnight? *A.* Twelve o'clock, or the middle of the night. *Q.* What did the other woman say in her defence? *A.* She said the live child was hers, and the other said it is mine; this they spake before the king. *Q.* When the king heard what the women had to say, what did he do? *A.* He said bring me a sword; and they brought a sword before the king. *Q.* Did the king do any thing with the sword? *A.* No; he said divide the child in two, and give half to the one, and half to the other. *Q.* What did the women say to that? *A.* One said, O my Lord, give her the living child, and in no wise slay it; but the other said, let it be neither mine nor thine, but divide it. *Q.* What took place next? *A.* The king answered and said, give her the living child, and in no wise slay it, she is the mother thereof. *Q.* What is meant by slaying? *A.* To kill any thing. *Q.*

To which woman was the child given? *A.* To the woman that said do not hurt it. *Q.* What is the reason that it was called a wise judgment? *A.* Because Solomon took a wise method to find it out. *Q.* Did the people hear of it? *A.* Yes, all Israel heard of it, and they feared the king, for they saw that the wisdom of God was in him to do judgment. *Q.* What is meant by all Israel? *A.* All the people over whom Solomon was king. *Q.* If we want to know any more about Solomon where can we find it? *A.* In the third chapter of the first book of Kings.

Incidental Conversation. — *Q.* Now my little children, as we have been talking about king Solomon, suppose we talk about our own king; so let me ask you his name? *A.* King George the Fourth. *Q.* Why is he called king? *A.* Because he is the head man, and the governor of the nation. *Q.* What does governor mean? *A.* One that governs the people, the same as you govern and manage us. *Q.* Why does the king wear a crown on his head? *A.* To denote that he governs from a principle of wisdom, proceeding from love. *Q.* Why does he hold a sceptre in his hand? *A.* To denote that he is powerful, and that he governs from a principle of truth. *Q.* What is a crown? *A.* A thing made of gold, overlaid with a number of diamonds and precious stones, which are very scarce? *Q.* What is a sceptre? *A.* A thing made of gold, and something like an officer's staff. *Q.* What is an officer? *A.* A person who acts in the king's name; and there are various sorts of officers, naval officers, military officers, and civil officers. *Q.* What is a naval officer? *A.* A person who governs the sailors and tells them what to do.

Q. What is a military officer? *A.* A person who governs the soldiers and tells them what to do. *Q.* What does a naval officer and his sailors do? *A.* Defend us from our enemies on the sea. *Q.* What does a military officer and his soldiers do? *A.* Defend us from our enemies on land. *Q.* Who do you call enemies? *A.* Persons that wish to hurt us and do us harm. *Q.* What does a civil officer do? *A.* Defend us from our enemies at home. *Q.* What do you mean by enemies at home? *A.* Thieves, and all bad men and women. *Q.* Have we any other enemies besides these? *A.* Yes, the enemies of our own household, as we may read in the Bible, and they are the worst of all. *Q.* What do you mean by the enemies of our own household? *A.* Our bad thoughts and bad inclinations. *Q.* Who protects and defends us from these? *A.* Almighty God. *Q.* Are there any other kind of officers besides these we have mentioned? *A.* Yes, a great many more, such as the king's ministers, the noblemen and gentlemen in both houses of parliament, and the judges of the land. *Q.* What do the king's ministers do? *A.* Give the king advice when he wants it. *Q.* And what do the noblemen and gentlemen do in both houses of parliament? *A.* Make laws to govern us, protect us, and make us happy. *Q.* After they have made the laws, who do they take them to? *A.* To the king. *Q.* What do they take them to the king for? *A.* To ask him if he will be pleased to approve of them. *Q.* What are laws? *A.* Good rules for the people to go by, the same as we have rules in our school to go by. *Q.* Suppose the people break these good rules, what is the consequence? *A.* They are taken before the judges, and afterwards sent to prison. *Q.* Who takes them before the judge? *A.* A constable, and afterwards he takes them to prison, and there they are locked up and punished. *Q.* Ought we to love the king? *A.* Yes, and respect his officers. *Q.* Do you suppose the king ever prays to God? *A.* Yes, every day. *Q.* What does he pray for? *A.* That God would be pleased to make him a wise and good man, so that he may make all his people happy. *Q.* What do the Scriptures say about the king? *A.* They say that we are to fear God and honour the king. *Q.* Who was the wisest king? *A.* King Solomon. *Q.* How did he become the wisest king? *A.* He asked God to give him wisdom to govern his kingdom well; and God granted his request. *Q.* Will God give our king wisdom? *A.* Yes, he will give him what is best for him. It says in the Bible, if any man lack wisdom let him ask of God, for he giveth to all men liberally, and upbraideth not. *Q.* What is the best book to learn wisdom from? *A.* The Bible.

Picture of the Last Supper.

Q. What is this? *A.* A picture of the Last Supper. *Q.* What do you mean by the last supper? *A.* A sacrament instituted by Jesus Christ himself. *Q.* What do you understand by a sacrament? *A.* There are two sacraments, baptism and the holy supper, and they are both performed in the church. *Q.* We will speak about baptism presently, but as we have the picture of the holy supper before us, let me ask if it is called by any other name? *A.* Yes, it is said that Jesus kept the passover with his disciples, and when the even was come he sat down with them, and as they did eat, Jesus took bread, and blessed it and brake it, and gave to his disciples, saying, take, eat, this is my body. *Q.* What took place next? *A.* He took the cup, and when he had given thanks, he gave it them, saying, this is my blood, the blood of the New Testament, which is shed for many. *Q.* Did Jesus command this ceremony to be performed in the church? *A.* Yes, he said in another place, this do in remembrance of me, Luke 22, v. 19. *Q.* What ought those persons to remember who do this? *A.* They should remember that Jesus Christ died on the cross to save sinners. *A.* Is any thing else to be understood by the sacrament of the Lord's supper? *A.* Yes, a great deal more. *Q.* Explain some of it. *A.* When they drink the wine they should recollect that they ought to receive the truth of God into their understandings. *Q.* What will be the effect of receiving the truth of God into our understanding? *A.* It will expel or drive out all falsehood. *Q.* What ought they to recollect when they eat the bread? *A.* They should recollect that they receive the love of God into their will and affections. *Q.* What will be the effect of this? *A.* It will drive out all bad passions and evil desires; for it is said, he that eateth my flesh and drinketh my blood, dwelleth in me and I in him, John 6, v. 27. *Q.* Is any thing more to be understood by these things? *A.* Much more, which we must endeavour to learn when we get older. *Q.* How will you learn this? *A.* By reading the Bible and going to church.

Christ Baptized by John.
Q. What is this? *A.* A picture of Jesus

x

Christ being baptized by John. *Q.* Did Jesus
command baptism to be performed? *A.* Yes;
he said, go teach all nations, and baptize them in
the name of the Father and of the Son and of the
Holy Ghost, and as a further proof, Jesus submitted to be baptized himself. *Q.* Describe how
this was done. *A.* It is said in the third chapter
of John, Then cometh Jesus from Galilee to
Jordan unto John, to be baptized of him. *Q.*
What is meant by Jordan? *A.* A river in which
Jesus was baptized. *Q.* When they came to the
river what took place? *A.* John forbad him,
saying, I have need to be baptized by thee, and
comest thou to me? *Q.* Who was John? *A.*
A disciple of Jesus Christ. *Q.* What did Jesus
say when John forbad him? *A.* He said, suffer
it to be so now, for thus it becometh us to fulfil
all righteousness. *Q.* What next? *A.* He went
up straitway out of the water, and the heavens
were opened, and he saw the spirit of God descending like a dove, and lighting upon him. *Q.*
What is a dove? *A.* A bird, which, from its
harmless nature, is considered an emblem or representative of peace.

—————

Such is the method in which we converse with
the children on these subjects; always taking
care to watch their countenances; the moment
they appear tired we stop, and resume at another
opportunity, for I find that one hour's instruction
with the children's hearts, or wills, is better than
twenty hours' instruction when the children are
thinking of something else.

To give an account of the whole of the Scripture pictures would nearly fill a volume, and per-

haps I have trespassed too much on the reader's time already; suffice it to say, that we have twenty-four of these pictures, all of which are used, besides twelve of Natural History, each picture having a variety of quadrupeds, birds, fishes, and flowers. The first thing we do is to teach the children the names of the different things, then to distinguish them by their forms, and lastly, they are questioned on them as follows :—If the animal is a horse, we put the pointer to it, and say,

What is this? *A.* A picture of a horse. *Q.* What is the use of the horse? *A.* To draw carts, coaches, waggons, drays, fire-engines, caravans, the plough and harrow, and boats on the canals, and any thing that their masters want them. *Q.* Will they carry as well as draw? *A.* Yes, they will carry a lady or gentleman on their backs, a sack of corn, or paniers, or even little children, but they must not hit them hard, if they do they will fall off their backs; besides it is very cruel to beat them. *Q.* What is the difference between carrying and drawing? *A.* To carry is when they have the whole weight on their backs, but to draw is when they pull any thing along. *Q.* Is there any difference between those horses that carry, and those horses that draw? *A.* Yes; the horses that draw carts, drays, coal-waggons, stage-waggons, and other heavy things, are stouter and much larger, and stronger than those that carry on the saddle, and are called draught horses. *Q.* Where do the draught horses come from? *A.* The largest come from Leicestershire, and some come from Suffolk, which are very strong, and are called Suffolk punches. *Q.* Where do the best saddle-horses come from? *A.* They

came at first from Arabia, the place in which the
camel is so useful; but now it is considered that
those are as good which are bred in England.
Q. What do they call a horse when he is young?
A. Foal, or a young colt.   *Q.* Will he carry and
draw while he is young?   *A.* Not until he is
taught, which is called breaking of him in.   *Q.*
And when he is broke in, is he very useful?   *A.*
Yes; and please sir, we hope to be more useful
when we are properly taught.   *Q.* What do you
mean by being properly taught?   *A.* When we
have as much trouble taken with us as the horses
and dogs have taken with them.   *Q.* Why you
give me a great deal of trouble, and yet I endeavour to teach you.   *A.* Yes, sir, but before
Infant Schools were established, little children
like us were running the streets.*   *Q.* But you
ought to be good children if you do run the
streets.   *A.* Please sir, there is nobody to tell us
how†, and if the man did not teach the horse, he
would not know how to do his work.

Here we observe to the children, that as this
animal is so useful to mankind, it should be
treated with kindness.   And having questioned
them as to the difference between a cart and a
coach, and satisfied ourselves that they understand the things that are mentioned, we close, by
asking them what is the use of the horse after he
is dead, to which the children reply, that its flesh
is eaten by other animals; (naming them), and
that its skin is put into pits, with oak bark, and
is called tanning; and that when it is tanned it
is called leather; and leather is made into shoes
to keep the feet warm and dry, and that we are

---

* This answer was given by a child five years of age.
† This answer was given by a child of six years of age.

indebted to the animals for many things that we both eat and wear, and above all to the great God for every thing that we possess. I cannot help thinking that if this plan were more generally adopted, in all schools, we should not have so many persons ascribing every thing to blind chance, when all nature exhibits a God, who guides, protects, and continually preserves the whole.

We also examine the children concerning that ill-treated animal, the ass, and contrast it with the beautiful external appearance of the zebra; taking care to warn the children not to judge of things by their outward appearance, which the world in general are too apt to do, but to judge of things by their uses, and of men by their general character and conduct. After having examined the children concerning the animals that are most familiar to us, such as the sheep, the cow, the dog, and others of a similar kind, we proceed to foreign animals, such as the camel, the elephant, the tiger, the lion, &c. &c. In describing the use of the camel and the elephant, there is a fine field to open the understandings of the children, by stating how useful the camel is in the deserts of Arabia; how much it can carry; how long it can go without water; and the reason it can go without water longer than most other animals; how much the elephant can carry; what use it makes of its trunk, &c. All these things will assist the thinking powers of children, and enlarge their understandings, if managed carefully. We also contrast the beautiful appearance of the tiger with its cruel and blood-thirsty disposition, and endeavour to show these men and women in miniature, that it is a dangerous plan to judge of things by outward appearances, but that there is a more correct way of judging, which forms a part of the business of education.

The children are highly delighted with these pictures, and, of their own accord, require an explanation of the subjects. Nay, they will even ask questions that will puzzle the teacher to answer; and although there is in some minds such a natural barrenness, that, like the sands of Arabia, they are never to be cultivated or improved, yet I can safely say, that I never knew a child who did not like the pictures; and as soon as I had done explaining one, it was always, " Please sir, may we learn this? Please teacher, may we learn that?" In short, I find that I am generally tired before the children; instead of having to apply any magisterial severity, they are petitioning to learn; and this mode of teaching possesses an advantage over every other, because it does not interfere with any religious opinion, there being no body of Christians that I know or ever heard of, who would object to the facts recorded in the Bible, being thus elucidated by pictures. Thus a ground-work may be laid not only of natural history, but of sacred history also; for the objects being before the children's eyes, they can, in some degree, comprehend them, and store them in their memories. Indeed there is such attraction in pictures, that you can scarcely pass a picture-shop in London, without seeing a number of grown persons around the windows, gazing at them. When pictures were first introduced into the school, the children told their parents; many of whom came and asked permission to see them; and although the plates are very common, I observed a degree of attention and reverence in the parents, scarcely to be expected, and especially from those who could not read.

By this plan, then, the reader will perceive, that the way may be paved, if I may be allowed the expression, almost to insure a desire in the children to read the Bible when they are able, and by their previous knowledge of the many leading facts contained therein, it is to be hoped that most of them will understand what they read, and consequently read day after day with increased delight, until they have acquired such a love, veneration, and esteem for the sacred writings, as all the powers of evil will never be able to eradicate.

It is generally the case, that what we have always with us, becomes so familiar, that we set little store by it; but on being deprived of it for a time, we then set a greater value on it: and I have found this to be the case with the children. If the pictures we make use of in our schools be exposed all at once, and at all times, then there would be such a multiplicity of objects before the eyes of the children, that their attention would not be fixed by any of them; they would look at them all, at first, with wonder and surprise, but in a short time the pictures would cease to attract notice, and, consequently, the children would think no more of them than they would of the paper that covers the room. To prevent this, and to excite a desire for information, it is always necessary to keep some behind, and to let very few objects appear at one time. When the children understand, in some measure, the subjects before them; these may be replaced by others, and so on successively, until the whole have been seen.

CHAPTER XIV.

————

ON TEACHING BY OBJECTS.

AS I have before said that it is our object to teach the children from objects in preference to books, I will mention a method we adopt for the accomplishment of this purpose. It consists of a number of boards, of which, and their use, the following description will convey an accurate idea.

The boards are about sixteen inches square and a quarter of an inch thick : wainscot is the best as it does not warp. These will go into the groove of the lesson post : there should be about twenty articles on each board, or twenty-five, just as it suits the conductors of the school ; there should be the same quantity of things on each board, in order that all the children may finish at one time ; this will not be the case, if there be more objects on one board than another. I will give an account of a few of our boards, and that must suffice, or I shall exceed the limits I have prescribed to myself.

The first board contains a small piece of gold in its rough state, a piece of gold in its manufactured state, a piece of silver in both states, a piece of copper in both states, a piece of brass in both states, a piece of iron in both states, a piece of steel in both states, a piece of tinfoil, a piece of solder, a screw, a clasp nail, a clout nail, a hob nail, a spike nail, a sparable, and a tack.

These articles are all on one board, and the monitor puts his pointer to each article, and tells his little pupils their names, and encourages them to repeat the names after him. When they finish at one post they go to the next.

The next board may contain a piece of hemp, a piece of rope, a piece of string, a piece of bagging, a piece of sacking, a piece of canvass, a piece of hessian, a piece of Scotch sheeting, a piece of unbleached linen, a piece of bleached linen, a piece of diaper linen, a piece of dyed linen, a piece of flax, a piece of thread, a piece of yarn, a piece of ticking, a piece of raw silk, a piece of twisted silk, a piece of wove silk, figured, a piece of white plain silk, and a piece of dyed silk, a piece of ribbon, a piece of silk cord, a piece of silk velvet, &c.

The next may contain raw cotton, cotton yarn, sewing cotton, unbleached calico, bleached calico, dimity, jean, fustian, velveteen, gause, nankeen, gingham, bed furniture, printed calico, marseilles, flannel, baise, stuff, woollen cloth and wool, worsted, white, black, and mixed.

The next may contain milled board, paste board, Bristol card, brown paper, white paper of various sorts, white sheep skin, yellow sheep, tanned sheep, purple sheep, glazed sheep, red sheep, calf skin, cow hide, goat skin, kid, seal, pig leather, seal skin, wash leather, beaver, &c.

The next may contain about twenty-five of those wood animals which are imported into this country, and are to be had at the foreign toy warehouses; some of them are carved exceedingly well, and appear very like the real animals.

The next may contain mahogany, and the various kinds of wood.

The next may contain prunings of the various fruit trees.

The next may contain the different small articles of ironmongery, needles, pins, cutlery, small tools, and every other object that can be obtained small enough for the purpose.

The lessons are to be put in the lesson post the same as the picture lessons; and the articles are either glued or fastened on the boards with screws or waxed thread.

The utility of this mode of teaching must be obvious, for if the children meet with any of those terms in a book which they are reading, they *understand it immediately*, which would not be the case unless they had seen the *object*. The most intellectual person would not be able to call things by their *proper names*, much less describe them, unless he had been taught, or heard some other person call them by their right names, and we generally learn more by mixing with society, than ever we could do at school; these sort of lessons persons can make themselves, and they will last for many years, and help to lay a foundation for things of more importance, at some future period, when perhaps *vice* will be less encouraged than it is at present, and *virtue* encouraged a little more, for it appears to me that whoever denies that *virtue* is owing to education, denies there is any such thing as virtue, for it proceeds from being *taught*, and he that hinders the teaching of it, does what he can to root it out of the world.

CHAPTER XV.

A METHOD OF GIVING LITTLE CHILDREN
BODILY EXERCISE, IMPROVING THEIR
MINDS, AND PLEASING THEM, AT THE
SAME TIME.—OF SINGING.

Would you make infants happy, give them variety, for novelty
has charms that our minds can hardly withstand.

AS an Infant School may be regarded in the light of a combination of the school and nursery, the *art of pleasing*, forms a prominent part in the system; and as little children are very apt to be fretful, it becomes expedient to divert, as well as teach them. If children of two years old and under are not diverted, they will naturally cry for their mothers; and to have ten or twelve children crying in the school, it is very obvious would put every thing into confusion. But it is possible to have two hundred, or even three hundred children assembled together, the eldest not more than six years of age, and yet not to hear one of them crying for a whole day. Indeed I may appeal to the numerous and respectable personages who have visited Infant Schools, for the truth of this assertion: many of whom have declared, in my hearing, that they could not have conceived it possible, that such a number of little children should be assembled together, and all be so happy as they had found them, the greater part of them being so very young. I can assure the reader, that many of the children who have cried heartily on being sent to school the first day or two, have cried as much on being kept at home, after they have been in the school but a very short time; and I am of opinion that when children are absent, it is generally the fault of the parents. I have had children come to school without their breakfast, because it has not been ready; others have come to school without shoes, because they would not be kept at home while their shoes were mending; and I have had others come to school half dressed, whose parents have been either at work or gossipping; and who, when they have returned home, have thought that their children were lost; but to their great surprise and joy, when they have applied at the school, they have found them there.

Need any thing more be advanced than these facts, to prove that it is not school, or the acquire-ment of knowledge, that is disagreeable to chil-dren, but the system of injudicious instruction there pursued. Children are anxious to acquire knowledge, and nothing can be more congenial to their taste than association with those of their own age; but we ought not to wonder that little chil-dren should dislike to go to school, when, as in most of the dames' schools, forty or fifty, or per-haps more are assembled together in one room, scarcely large enough for one-third of that number, and are not allowed to speak to, or scarcely look at each other. In those places, I firmly believe, many, for the want of proper exercise, become cripples, or have their health much injured, by being kept sitting so many hours; but as children's health is of the greatest consequence, it becomes necessary to remedy this evil by letting them have proper exercise, combined, as much as possible, with instruction; to accomplish which, many measures have been tried, but I have found the following to be the most successful, viz:

The children are desired to sit on their seats, with their feet out strait, and to shut each hand, and then ordered to count a hundred, or as many as may be thought proper, lifting up each hand every time they count one, and bringing each hand down again on their knees when they count another. The children have given this the name of blacksmith, and when asked why they called it blacksmith, they answered, because they hammered their knees with their fists, in the same way as the blacksmith hammers his irons with a hammer. When they have arrived at a hundred, (which they never fail to let you know by giving an extra shout,) then they may be ordered to sit on the ground. They are then desired to take hold of their toes, which being done, they are desired to add up one hundred, two at a time, which they do by lifting up each foot alternately, all the children counting at one time, saying, two, four, six, eight, ten, twelve, and so on. By this means every part of the body is put in motion; and it likewise has this advantage, that by lifting up each foot every time, they keep good time, a thing very necessary, as unless this was the case, all must be confusion. They also add up three at a time by the same method, thus, three, six, nine, twelve, fifteen, eighteen, and so on; but care must be taken not to keep them too long at one thing, or too long in one position.

Having done a lesson or two this way, they are desired to put their feet out strait, and their hands together, and to say, one and one are two, two and one are three, three and one are four, four and one are five, five and one are six, six and two are eight; and in this way they go on until they are desired to stop.

I have specified these methods not as being the only ones practicable, or fit to be adopted, but merely as hints to the judicious teacher, who will doubtless think of many others, conducive to the same end; and the more he can diversify them the better. It is the combination of amuse-ment with instruction, which in my opinion, renders the system so successful; and unimpor-tant or improper even as it may appear to some, is of more real service in the management of young children, than all the methods of restraint and coercion, which have been hitherto but too generally pursued.

The children may also learn the pence and multiplication tables, by forming themselves into circles around a number of young trees where such are planted in the play.ground. For the sake of order, each class should have its own particular tree; that when they are ordered to the trees, every child may know which tree to go to; as soon as they are assembled around the trees, they are to join hands and walk round, every child saying the multiplication table, until they have finished it; they then let go hands, and put them behind, and, for variety's sake, sing the pence table, the alphabet, hymns, &c. &c: thus the children are gradually improved and delighted, for they call it play, and it is of little consequence what they call it, so long as they are edified, exercised, and made happy.

This plan is calculated to impress the lessons on their memories, and is adapted for fine weather, when they can go out to play, as it is called. But as in wet, or snowy weather, they cannot go out of the school, we then have recourse to the mode previously mentioned. Besides it is necessary that children should have exercise in winter, as well as in summer; in wet, as well as in dry weather; for this purpose we have several swings in the school-room, made of cord only, on which the children are allowed to swing, two at a time. The time that they are permitted to be on the swing, is according to what they have to repeat. If it is the pence-table, they say—

> Twenty pence are one and eightpence,
> That we can't afford to lose;
> Thirty pence are two and sixpence,
> That will buy a pair of shoes.
>
> Forty pence are three and fourpence,
> That is paid for certain fees;
> Fifty pence are four and twopence,
> That will buy five pounds of cheese.
>
> Sixty pence will make five shillings,
> Which, we learn, is just a crown:
> Seventy pence are five and tenpence,
> This is known throughout the town.
>
> Eighty pence are six and eightpence,
> That sum once my father spent;
> Ninety pence are seven and sixpence,
> That for a quarter's schooling went.
>
> A hundred pence are eight and fourpence,
> Which is taught in th'infant school;
> Eight pence more make just nine shillings,
> So we end this pretty rule.

As soon as the table is thus gone through, the children who are on the swings get off, and others supply their places, until, probably, the pence table has been said twenty times; then we go on with the multiplication table, until the children have repeated as far as six times six are thirty-six; when the children on the swings get off, and are succeeded by two more on each swing; they then commence the other part of the table, beginning at six times seven are forty-two, until they have finished the table: During this time, it should be borne in mind, all the children are learning, not only those on the swings, but those who are sitting in the school: and it is surprising to see with what alacrity the children will despatch their other lessons, when it is a wet day, in order to get to the swings. In addition to the knowledge acquired by this method, it is admirably calculated to try their courage. Many little boys and girls, who at first are afraid to get on the swings, will soon swing standing on one leg, and perform other feats with the greatest dexterity, at once shewing their increased courage and greater activity. We generally let four or five children come to a swing, and those that can seat themselves first, are entitled to the first turn, for they are never lifted on. In the anxiety to get on the swing, some of them will perhaps get out of temper, especially those who are not disciplined; but when this is detected they are not allowed to swing that day, which soon makes them good natured to each other, and very cautious not to get into a passion. Thus, in some degree, their bad tempers are corrected, which is very desirable. As soon as two children are seated on each swing, to preserve order, the others retire (generally speaking) in the greatest good humour to their seats.

Some will I know be apt to exclaim, surely this is encouraging and fostering bad feelings—creating enmity and ill-will amongst the children; but I say, No,—it is learning them to feel a spirit of generous emulation, as distinguishable from that of ill-nature or envy.

There is a swing for boys who are between five and six years old, another for those between four and five, another for the very little children, and another for the little girls; and on no account are children permitted to swing on the wrong swing, because if this were suffered, the strong would overcome the weak. But when the children opposed to each other, are nearly equal, the most active of them, as I observed before, generally get the first turn, whilst the less agile are driven to cogitation, that what they cannot achieve by activity they may by address and generalship. I have seen children about three years old trying a number of plans, in order to get on the swing, that would have done credit to much older heads. One thing I would particularly mention, which may perhaps appear singular,—we never had a serious accident from the introduction of the swing; and I was informed by Mr. Buchanan, when master of the Westminster infant school, that during the seven years he had been a teacher there, and at Mr. Owen's establishment, at New Lanark, he never knew of any such happening to one of the children.

Beside the swings, in many schools they have a very useful addition to the play-ground. I mean the gymnastic pole. It consists of an upright pole, firmly fixed in the ground; to the summit of which is attached a cross piece of wood, turning on a strong pivot; from each end of this cross piece hangs a piece of rope, by which the children can swing themselves round; and which affords a method of exercise at once healthful and safe.

Although it is most proper for the master in the play-ground to relax altogether the brow of magisterial severity, yet there is no occasion for him to withdraw the influence of love. He will not prove a check to the enjoyment of the children, if, entering into the spirit of their innocent pastimes, he endeavours to heighten their pleasures by a judicious direction of their sports.

Among other amusements, which his ingenuity may suggest, I would mention a geometrical amusement, which is very practicable. First, let a certain number of children stand in a row. Opposite to these let one or more children be placed as directors to order the change of figure. A straight line, we will suppose is the first thing shewn by the position of the children; the next thing to be formed is a *curve*, by the advancement of each end; then a half-circle,—a circle, by joining hands in a ring;—two equal parallel lines, by the division of the number in action;—next a square,—triangle, &c. &c. These changes may either be made at the command of the master, or, as we before proposed, of one or more children acting as officers to direct these geometrical movements.

As a very efficient *amusement* within doors, I must not omit to mention *singing;* I have incidentally noticed it in a preceding part of this volume, but I would most particularly recommend its cultivation to all founders and teachers of Infant Schools. For my own part, I know of nothing in the world which produces such a thrilling sensation of delight as the hearing of a number of infants singing, in a sweet though simple style, the praises of their Maker. It brings forcibly to one's mind the saying of the Psalmist, "Out of the mouths of babes and sucklings thou hast perfected praise." I knew an instance of a reverend gentleman, who was rather averse than otherwise to Infant Schools, being made a sudden convert and a zealous patron of them, from hearing this lisped melody of devotion. He had long been pressed by a friend, who was an active promoter of the system, to visit one of the schools. At length he consented. When they got to the school the children were singing a hymn. The reverend gentleman paused to listen, evidently much affected by the sound of their voices; before they had concluded the hymn, he entered the school, and beheld the infant choir. "Surely," said he, "this must be pleasing to God!" And from that time he became a warm friend and encourager of Infant Schools.

But it is not only hymns which we set to music; we pursue the same plan with regard to many of the lessons; taking care that the tunes selected are at once lively and simple; if they are dull, or too solemn, the children sing them with no spirit, and if they are difficult, the children will not only be longer in learning them, but they will never sing them with ease to themselves or pleasure to others. But, that children are extremely fond of singing, generally, I might almost say, universally, I am quite convinced; nor are they long in learning a tune; those who have quick ears, imparting it to those who are more slow of acquiring it. As to the method of teaching singing, I have spoken of that in a preceding chapter.

CHAPTER XVI.

ON GRAMMAR, AND THE ELLIPTICAL PLAN
OF TEACHING.

"The grand object of Infant Education is to simplify."

IT has been well observed, " that grammar is the first thing taught, and the last learnt." Now, though it is not my purpose to pretend that I can so far simplify grammar, as to make all its rules comprehensible to children, so young as those found in Infant Schools, I do think that enough may be imparted to them to render the matter more comprehensible to them than it is usually found to be, in after years.

The great mystery of grammar results, in my opinion, from not making the children acquainted with the things of which the words used are the signs, and moreover, from the use of a number of hard words, which the children repeat without understanding. For instance, in the classification of words, or the parts of speech, as they are called, *nouns, substantives,* and *adjectives,* convey as terms no idea to the mind of children; and in spite of the definitions by which their import is explained, remain, to the infant mind, as unin-

telligible, as the language of magical incantation.
That the children can easily comprehend the difference between words which express the names
of things, and those which express their qualities;
and between words which express actions, and
those which express the nature of those actions,
is undeniable : and this is just what should be
taught in an Infant School.   In the first place,
let the children be accustomed to repeat the
names of things, not of any certain number of
things, set down on a lesson card, or in a book,
but of any thing, and every thing, in the school-
room, play-ground, &c.—next let them be exercised in telling something relating to those
things — *their qualities;* as for instance, the
school-room is *large, clean,* &c. — the children
are *quiet, good, attentive,* &c. — the pictures are
pretty; the play-ground is *pleasant,* &c.   Having accustomed the children, in this manner, first
to give you the *names* of things, and then to
observe and repeat something respecting them —
you have gained two ends, you have, first, taught
the children to be observant and discriminative;
and secondly, you have taught them to distinguish two distinct classes of words, — or *names*
and *qualities*; and you may now, if you please,
give them terms by which to distinguish these
respective classes, — viz. *substantives* and *adjectives.*   They will no longer be mysterious words,
" signifying nothing," but recognized signs, by
which the children will understand and express
definite ideas.   The next thing you have to learn
them is the distinction betwixt singular and plural, and, if you think proper, masculine and femi-
nine; but before you talk to the children about
plural number, and *masculine gender,* &c. let them

be made acquainted with the realities of which these hard-sounding words are the signs.

Having made the classification of words clear and comprehensible, you next proceed to the second grand class of words, the *verbs*, and its adjunct the *adverbs*. With these you will proceed as with the former; let action be distinguished by words; — the children *walk, play, read, eat, run;* master *laughs, frowns, speaks, sings;* and so on; letting the children find their own examples; then comes the demand from the master for words expressing the manner of action. How do the children *walk?* — *slowly, fastly, orderly.* How do they *read, eat, run?* How does the master *laugh, speak, sing?* The children now find you ADVERBS, and it will be quite time enough to give them terms for the classification they thus intuitively make, when they have a clear idea of what they are doing. When this end is attained, your children have some ideas of grammar, and those clear ones. There is no occasion to stop here. Proceed, but slowly; and in the same method. The tenses of the verbs; and the subdivision into active, passive, and neuter, will require the greatest care and attention which the teacher can use, to simplify them sufficiently for the children's comprehension; as it will likewise to enable them to understand the nature and office of the other classes of words. As, however, it is not my intention to write a grammar here, but merely to throw out a few hints on the subject, I shall leave the further developement of the plan to the ingenuity of those who may think fit to adopt its principles, as above laid down.

I shall now proceed to call the reader's attention to the elliptical plan of teaching; specimens of which I shall subjoin. The manner in which I became acquainted with the plan is as follows:

During the time I was in charge of the Spital-field's Infant School, my friend Dr. Black per-suaded Dr. Borthwick Gilchrist to look in at our infantine establishment, with the whole of which he was so much delighted, that I have since en-joyed the gratification of his acquaintance, and had the benefit of attending Dr. G.'s oriental lectures, in which his inductive system of educa-tion was practically demonstrated to all his stu-dents, and whose minds are thus attracted to this elliptical branch of it through the whole of their daily lesson; a practice commenced thirty years ago, and continued ever since with commensurate success. To illustrate the subject more fully the Dr. has furnished me with a leaf from " the Hin-doostanee Guide," which he authorises me to submit to my readers, as *one* infallible *mode* of teaching children to reflect, if not speak, in spite of that mental apathy which most easily besets every young scholar. The subsequent artless tale will, at once, speak for itself, and few infants who possess the power of either speech or thought, will be long puzzled in filling up all the blanks, on rational principles of concatenated deduction, which a dozen of such stories must, in a limited period, render pleasant, easy, and comprehen-sible by the meanest capacity. I can readily conceive that a great variety of similar exercises may be so formed, as to suit every gradation of intellect, by the novelty, simplicity, facility, and utility of each in gradual succession, from the lowest to the highest forms of any seminary. After a fair trial among all the infants who have come under my own eye, I can truly say that this scheme exceeds my most sanguine expectation.

Dr. G. observes, in a letter sent to me, about the same period, " You have now the whole method before you, and I shall boldly stake all my hard-earned fame, as a practical orientalist, on the salutary consequences that will spring from the adoption of short elliptical tales at your interesting institution."

My usual practice with respect to the elliptical method of teaching, is to deliver some appropriate, simple, extemporaneous tale, leaving out but few words at first, and those such as must obviously strike the children; as they get used to the plan, I make the omissions more frequent, and of words less obvious. The following specimens will render the whole plain to the understandings of my readers.

ELLIPTICAL PLAN OF TEACHING.

A gardener's youngest[a] was walking among the fruit[b] of his father's[c] , he saw a little[d] fly up and sit on one of the[e] of the trees; the[f] lifted a stone, and was going to[g] it at the poor[h] which seemed to[i] - most sweetly thus:

" My[k] is[l] of moss and hair,
The[m] are[n] and shelter'd there;
When[o] soon shall my young[p] fly
Far from the[q] school[r] eye."

[a] Son [b] trees [c] garden [d] bird [e] branches [f] boy [g] throw [h] bird [i] sing [k] nest [l] built [m] eggs [n] laid [o] hatched [p] ones [q] roaming [r] boys.

Z

The^s   eldest^t   who understood the^u
      of birds came up at that moment, and^v
      out, throw down the^w   , you hard.
hearted^x   , and don't^y   the innocent^z
      in the middle of his song; are you not^{aa}
      with his swelling red breast, his beautiful
sharp eye, and above all with the^{bb}   of his
notes, and the familiar^{cc}   he assumes even
in the^{dd}   of a^{ee}   like you? Ask your
youngest^{ff}   here, if she remembers the^{gg}
which her good^{hh}   read to her yesterday of
a veryⁱⁱ   boy, who was very^{kk}   to a
harmless green^{ll}   which he caught^{mm}
for hunger, among theⁿⁿ   in the^{oo}   of
winter.

The following little verses upon the same principle have been found to answer extremely well,
by putting one child in the rostrum, and desiring
him purposely to leave out those words that are
marked, the other children will fill them up as
he goes on.

I must pray
Both   and day.

Before   eat,   I'll   my bread
I must intreat,   From   to door,
That   would bless Rather   steal
To me   meat.   My neighbour's store.

---

^s Gardener's ^t son ^u notes ^v called ^w stone ^x rogue or boy
^y disturb or hurt ^z bird ^{aa} pleased or delighted ^{bb} sweetness
or melody ^{cc} air ^{dd} presence ^{ee} naughty boy ^{ff} sister ^{gg} story
^{hh} mother, aunt, &c. ⁱⁱ naughty or good ^{kk} cruel or kind
^{ll} finch or linnet ^{mm} perishing or dying ⁿⁿ snow ^{oo} depth or
middle.

I must not play
On   own day,
But I   hear
His   in fear.

It   a sin
To   a pin,
Much   to steal
A greater thing.

I must work,
And I must pray,
That   will feed
Me,   by day.

All honest labor,
God   bless;
Let   not live
In idleness.

I   not be
Or   or wild,
I   not be
A   child.

I   not speak
Of -   ill,
But   bear
To   good will.

I'd   die
Than   a lie,
Lest   be lost
Eternally;

I   not kill
A   fly;
It   an act
Of cruelty.

I   not lie,
I   not feign,
I   not take
      name in vain.

Nor may   tongue
Say what   wrong;
I   not sin
A world   win.

In   Bible
I am   read,
And   in God
In all   need;

For   alone
My soul   save,
And raise   body
From   grave.

Oh!   Saviour
Take my
And   not me
From   depart.

Lord,   that I
In faith   die,
And live   thee
Above   sky.

CREATION.

God made the   that looks so blue,
  God made the   so green,
God made the   that smell so sweet,
  In   colors seen.

God made the   that shines so bright,
  And gladdens all I see;
It comes to give us   and light,
  How   should we be!

God made the   bird to fly,
  How   has she sung;
And though she   so very high,
  She won't   her young.

God made the   to give nice milk,
  The horse for   to use;
I'll treat them   for his sake,
  Nor dare his gifts abuse.

God made the   for my drink,
  God made the   to swim,
God made the   to bear nice fruit,
Which does my   so nicely suit;
  O how should I   him!

"O Lord, how manifest are thy works! in wisdom hast thou made them all."—*Psalm* civ. 24.

I subjoin, as an exercise for teachers themselves, the following hymn,—as one calculated to induce reflections on the scenes of nature, and direct the mind to that Being, who is the source of all excellence!—

WRITTEN FOR THE USE OF CHILDREN,

By the Rev. John Black, Woodbridge, Suffolk.

1 Hast   beheld   glorious
Through all   skies his circuit run,
At rising morn,   closing day,
And when he beam'd his noontide   ?

2 Say, didst   e'er attentive
The evening cloud,   morning dew?
Or, after   , the watery bow
Rise in the   a beauteous   ?

3 When darkness had o'erspread the
Hast thou e'er seen the   arise,
And with a mild and placid
Shed lustre o'er the face of night?

4 Hast   e'er wander'd o'er the plain,
And view'd the fields and waving
The flowery mead,   leafy grove,
Where all   harmony   love.

5 Hast thou e'er trod the sandy
And   the restless   roar,
When rous'd by some tremendous
It's billows rose   dreadful form?

6 Hast thou beheld the   stream
Thro' nights dark gloom,   sudden gleam,
While the bellowing thunder's
Roll'd rattling   the heaven's profound?

7 Hast thou e'er   the cutting gale,
The sleeting shower,   biting hail;
Beheld   snow o'erspread the
The water bound   icy chains?

8 Hast thou the various beings
That sport   the valley green,
That   warble on the spray,
Or wanton in the sunny   ?

9 That shoot along   briny deep,
Or   ground their dwellings keep;
That thro' the   forest range,
Or frightful wilds   deserts strange?

10 Hast   the wondrous scenes survey'd,
That all around thee   display'd?
And hast   never rais'd thine
To Him   bade these scenes arise?

11 'Twas GOD who form'd the concave
And all the glorious orbs   high;
    gave the various beings birth,
That people all the spacious

12 'Tis   that bids the tempests
And rolls the   thro'   skies:
His voice the elements
Thro' all the   extends His sway.

13 His goodness   His creatures share,
But Man is His peculiar
Then, while they all proclaim   praise,
Let   his   the loudest

CHAPTER XVII.

———

VARIOUS ANECDOTES OF INFANT SCHOOL CHILDREN.

THE subjoined anecdotes, will not I am persuaded be found unworthy of perusal by those who are interested in the welfare of young children. They will afford the teacher in particular an opportunity of drawing many useful inferences as to the management of infants.

———

PLAYING THE TRUANT.

A little girl, whose mother was dead, was often absent from school. She was never at a loss for excuses, but from their frequency I was at last induced to suspect their truth. None of the children knew where she resided; so I was obliged to send the eldest boy in the school home with her, to ascertain whether or not her stories were true. I gave the boy positive directions to make haste back; but, much to my surprise, I saw no more of him for six hours. When he returned he told me that the little girl refused to shew him where she lived; and had taken him so far, that he at last determined to leave her, but could not find his way back sooner. In the evening I went myself, according to the direction I had entered in the admission book, but found that the family were removed, and the persons in the house could not tell me where they had gone to reside. I saw nothing of the child for the five following days, when a woman, who had the care of her and her little brother, in arms, came to inquire the reason why the girl came home at such irregular hours, stating, that sometimes she came home at half-past eleven, at other times, not till two, and sometimes at three in the afternoon; in short, often an hour after school was over. I told her that the child was frequently absent, and that it was five days since I had seen her. The woman appeared quite surprised, and told me, that she had always sent the child to school at the regular time; that when she came home before the usual time, she said her governess had sent all the children home a little sooner; and if she came home after the time, then she said that there had been some ladies visiting the school, and that the children had been kept for their inspection.

Here I must acknowledge, that I have frequently detained children a little while after school hours, when we have had visitors, but since it furnishes the children with an excuse for going home late, I think it would be better to discontinue the practice; and would hint to those ladies and gentlemen who feel inclined to visit such schools, that they would come between the hours of nine and twelve in the forenoon, or two and four in the afternoon. I have only to observe, that the child I have been speaking of came to school very regularly afterwards.

BENEFICIAL EFFECTS OF PICTURES.

A little boy, the subject of the following anecdote, being six years of age, and forward in his
learning, I considered him fit to be sent to another
school, and sent word to the parents accordingly.
The father came immediately, and said, he hoped
I would keep him until he was seven years of age;
adding, that he had many reasons for making the
request. I told him, that the design of the Institution was to take such children as no other
school would admit, and as his child had arrived
at the age of six, he would be received into the
National School; moreover, as we had a number
of applications for the admission of children much
younger, I could not grant his request. He then
said, " I understand that you make use of pictures in the school, and I have good reason to
approve of them; for," said he, " you must know
that I have a large bible in the house, Matthew
Henry's, which was left me by my deceased mother; like many more, I never looked into it,
but kept it merely for show. The child, of course,
was forbidden to open it, for fear of its being
spoiled: but still he was continually asking me
to read in it, and I as continually denied him:
indeed, I had imbibed many unfavourable impressions concerning this book, and had no inclination to read it, and was not very anxious that
the child should. However, the child was not to
be put off, although several times I gave him a
box on the ear for worrying me; for notwithstanding this usage, the child would frequently
ask me to read it, when he thought I was in a
good humour; and at last I complied with his

wishes. ' Please, father,' said the child, ' will you read about Solomon's wise judgment,' ' I don't know where to find it,' was the reply. ' Then,' says the child, ' I will tell you; it is in the third chapter of the first book of Kings.' I looked as the child directed, and finding it I read it to him. Having done so, 1 was about to shut up the book; which the child perceiving, said, ' Now, please father, will you read about Lazarus raised from the dead;' which was done; and in short, said the father, he kept me at it for at least two hours that night, and completely tired me out, for there was no getting rid of him. The next night he renewed the application, with, ' Please, father, will you read about Joseph and his brethren?' and he could always tell me where these stories were to be found. Indeed, he was not contented with my reading it, but would get me into many difficulties, by asking me to explain that which 1 knew nothing about; and if 1 said I could not tell him, he would tell me that I ought to go to church, for his master had told him, that that was the place to learn more about it, adding, ' and I will go with you, father.' In short, he told me every picture you had in your school, and kept me so well at it, that 1 at last got into the habit of *reading for myself*, with some degree of delight; this, therefore, is one reason why I wish the child to remain in the school." A short time afterwards, the mother called on me, and told me, that no one could be happier than she was, for there was so much alteration in her husband for the better, that she could scarcely believe him to be the same man : instead of being in the skittle-ground, in the evening, spending his money, and getting tipsy, he was reading at home to her and his children, and the money that used to go for gambling, was now going to buy books, with which, in conjunction with the Bible, they were greatly delighted, and afforded both him and them a great deal of pleasure and profit; her object in calling, she said, was once more to return thanks to Mr. Wilson, and myself, for the great benefit that had accrued to the family through the child being in the Infant School.

Here we see a whole family were made comfortable, and called to a sense of religion and duty, by the instrumentality of a child of six years of age. I subsequently made inquiries, and found that the whole family attended a place of worship, and that their character would bear the strictest investigation.

INFANT CRITICS: THE BOY AND TRIANGLE— THE DEAD FLY.

One day some visitors requested I would call out a class of the children to be examined. Having done so, I asked the visitors in what they would wish the children to be examined; at the same time stating that they might hear the children examined in Natural History, Scriptural History, Arithmetic, Spelling, Geography, or Geometry. They chose the latter, and I proceeded to examine the children accordingly; beginning with straight lines. Having continued this examination for about half an hour, we proceeded to enter into particulars respecting triangles; and having discoursed on the difference between isoceles triangles and scalene triangles, I observed that an acute isoceles triangle had all its angles acute, and proceeded to observe that a right-angled scalene triangle had all its angles acute. The children immediately began to laugh, for which I was at a loss to account, and told them of the impropriety of laughing at me. One of the children immediately replied, " Please, sir, do you know what we were laughing at?" I replied in the negative. " Then, sir," says the boy, " I will tell you. Please, sir, you have made a blunder." I, thinking I had not, proceeded to defend myself, when the children replied, " Please, sir, you convict yourself." I replied, " How so?" " Why," says the children, " you said a right-angled triangle had one right angle, and that all its angles are acute. If it has one right angle, how can all its angles be acute?" I soon perceived the children were right, and that I was wrong. Here, then, the reader may perceive the fruits of teaching the children to think, inasmuch as it is shewn that the children of six years of age and under were able to refute their tutor. If children had been taught to think many years ago, error would have been much easier detected, and its baneful influence would not have had that effect upon society which at this day unfortunately we are obliged to witness.

At another time I was lecturing the children in the gallery on the subject of cruelty to animals; when one of the little children observed, " Please, sir, my big brother catches the poor flies and then sticks a pin through them, and makes them draw the pin along the table." This afforded me an excellent opportunity of appealing to their feelings on the enormity of this offence, and among other things I observed that if the poor fly had been gifted with powers of speech like their own, it probably would have exclaimed, *while dead*, as follows : — " You naughty child, how can you think of torturing me so? Is there not room enough in the world for you and me? Did I ever do you any harm? Does it do you any good to put me in such pain? Why do you do it, you are big enough to know better? How would you like a man to run a piece of wire through your body, and make you draw things about? Would you not cry at the pain? Go, then, you wicked boy, and learn to leave off such cruel actions." Having finished, one of the children replied, " How can any thing speak if it is dead?" " Why," said I, " supposing it could speak." " You meant to say, sir, *dying*, instead of *dead*."

It will of course be understood that in this case I purposely misused a word, and the children, being taught to think, easily detected it.

THE DUTIFUL CHILD, OR PROMPT OBEDIENCE.

One of the children happened to kick another. The injured party complained to the person who then had the charge of the school, saying, " Please, sir, this boy kicked me." It being time for the children to leave school, the master waved his hand towards the gate through which the children pass, thoughtlessly saying, at the same time, " Kick away;" meaning that the complainant was to take no more notice of the affair, but go home. The complainant, however, returning to the other child, began kicking him, and received some kicks himself. Mr. Greaves, then secretary of the Infant School Society, was present, and seeing two children kicking each other, he very naturally enquired the reason. " Please, sir," replied the children, " Master told us!" " Master told you," says Mr. Greaves, " that cannot be; I'll ask him." He accordingly enquired into the truth of the affair, and received for answer, " Certainly not." " Yes," said the child, " you did, sir. Did not I tell you just now that a boy kicked me?" " Yes," says the master, " you did." " Then, please sir," says the child, " you told me to go and kick away!" The master immediately re-collected that he had said so.

This fact shews how improper it is to say one thing to a child and mean another. These children were under the influence of obedience, *and in the light of truth*, and being in that light they could see from no other, and very naturally con-cluded the master meant what he had said.

***

THE EFFECTS OF PROMISING WHAT YOU ARE NOT ABLE TO PERFORM. — THE BOY AND THE PAPER BOAT.

One day, when the children were assembled in the gallery, having none of their usual lessons at hand, I took from my pocket a piece of paper, and promised them that if they would answer me every question I put concerning the paper, I would at last make a paper boat. I proceeded in the following manner :—" What is this?" " What colour?" " What is its use?" " How made?" " What made of?" &c. These questions being answered according to their different views ; and having folded the paper into a variety of forms, and obtained their ideas upon such forms, I proceeded to fulfil my promise of forming it into the shape of a boat; but the children, seeing me at a loss, exclaimed, " Please, sir, you can't do it;" which proved a fact, as I had forgotten the plan, and was obliged to make the confession. " Then, sir," rejoined one of the boys, " you should not have promised."

In the course of my observations I had frequently enjoined the children to make every possible use of their thinking powers, but it appears I had at the same time forgotten to make use of my own, and consequently had been betrayed into a promise which I was not able to perform.

———

EARLY RELIGIOUS IMPRESSIONS.

The following anecdote will shew how early impressions are made on the infant mind, and the effects such impressions may have in the dying moments of a child. A little boy, between the age of five and six years, being extremely ill, prevailed on his mother to ask me to come and see him. The mother called, and stated, that her little boy said he wanted to see his master so bad, that he would give any thing if he could see him. The mother likewise said, she should herself be very much obliged to me if I would come: conceiving that the child would get better after he had seen me. I accordingly went, and on seeing the child, considered that he could not recover. The moment I entered the room, the child attempted to rise, but could not. " Well, my little man," said I, " did you want to see me?" " Yes sir, I wanted to see you very much," answered the child. " Tell me what you wanted me for." " I

A A 2

wanted to tell you that I cannot come to school again, because I shall die." " Don't say that," said the mother, " you will get better, and then you can go to school again." " No," answered the child, " I shall not get better, I am sure, and I wanted to ask master to let my class sing a hymn over my body, when they put it in the pit-hole." The child having made me promise that this should be done, observed, " You told me, master, when we used to say the pictures, that the souls of children never die, and do you think I shall go to God?" " You ask me a difficult question, my little boy," said I. " Is it, sir?" said the child, " I am not afraid to die, and I know I shall die." " Well, child, I should not be afraid to change states with you, for if such as you do not go to God, I do not know what will become of such as myself; and from what I know of you, I firmly believe that you will, and all like you; but you know what I used to tell you at school." " Yes, sir, I do; you used to tell me that I should pray to God to assist me to do to others as I would that they should do to me, as the hymn says; and mother knows that I always said my prayers night and morning, and I used to pray for father and mother, master and governess, and every body else." " Yes, my little man, this is part of our duty; we should pray for every one, and I think if God sees it needful, he will answer our prayers, especially when they come from the heart." Here the child attempted to speak, but could not, but waved his hand, in token of gratitude for my having called; and I can truly say, that I never saw so much confidence, resignation, and true dependence on the divine will, manifested by any grown person on a death-bed, much less by a child, under the tender age of seven years. I bade the child adieu, and was much impressed with what I had seen. The next day the mother called on me, and informed me that the child had quitted his tenement of clay; and that just before his departure, had said to her, and those around him, that the souls of children never die; it was only the body that died; that he had been told at school, while they were saying the pictures, that the soul went to God, who gave it. The mother said, that these were the last words the child was known to utter. She then repeated the request, about the children singing a hymn over his grave, and named the hymn she wished to have sung. The time arrived for the funeral, and the parents of the children who were to sing the hymn, made them very neat and clean, and sent them to school. I sent them to the house, whence the funeral was to proceed, and the undertaker sent word that he could not be troubled with such little creatures, and that unless I attended myself, the children could not go. I told him, I was confident that the children would be no trouble to him, if he only told them to follow the mourners, two and two, and that it was unnecessary for any one to interfere with them further, than shewing them the way back to the school. I thought, however, that I would attend to see how the children behaved, but did not let them see me, until the corpse had arrived at the ground. As soon as I had got to the ground, some of the children saw me, and whispered, "There's master;" when several of them stepped out of the ranks to favour me with a bow. When the corpse was put into the ground, the children were arranged around the grave, not one of whom was more than six years of age.

One of them gave out the hymn, in the usual way, and then it was sung by the whole of them, and, according to the opinions of the by-standers, very well. The novelty of the thing caused a great number of persons to collect together; and yet, to their credit, while the children were singing, there was not a whisper to be heard; and when they had finished the hymn, the poor people made a collection for the children, on the ground. The minister himself rewarded one or two of them, and they returned well stored with money, cakes, &c. This simple thing was the means of making the school more known; for I could hear persons inquiring, " Where do these children come from?" " Why, don't you know?" replied others, " from the Infant School, Quaker Street." " Well," answered a third, " I will try to get my children into it; for I should like them to be there of all things. When do they take them in, and how do they get them in?" " Why, you must apply on Monday mornings," answered another; and the following Monday, I had no less than forty-nine applications, all of which I was obliged to refuse, because the school was full.

THE BOY AND THE SONG.

One day, while I was walking in the playground, I saw at one end of it about twenty children, apparently arguing a subject, pro. and con.; from the attitude of several of the orators, I judged it was about something that appeared to them of considerable importance. I wished to know the subject of debate, but was satisfied, that if I approached the children it might put an end to the matter altogether. Some of the by-standers saw me looking very attentively at the principal actor, and, as I suppose, suggested to the party the propriety of retiring to some other spot, for immediately afterwards they all retired behind a partition, which afforded me an opportunity of distinctly hearing all that passed, without being observed by them. I soon found that the subject of debate was a *song*. It seems that one of the children had brought a song to the school, which some of the monitors had read, and having decided that it was an improper thing for the child to have in his possession, one of them had taken it from the owner, and destroyed it; the aggrieved party had complained to some of the other children, who said that it was *thieving* for one child to take any thing from another child, without his consent. The boy, nettled at being called a thief, defended himself by saying that he, as a monitor, had a right to take away from any of his class any thing that was calculated to do them harm; and was, it seems, backed in this opinion by many others. On the other hand, it was contended that no such right existed; and it was doubtful to me for a considerable time, on which side the strength of the argument lay. At last one of the children observed to the following effect:—" You should have taken it to *master*, because he would know if it was bad better than you." This was a convincing argument, and to my great delight, the boy replied—" How much did the song cost?" The reply was, " A halfpenny." " Here, then, take it," says the child, " I had one given me to-day; so now remember I have paid you for it; but if you bring any more songs to school I will tell master." This seemed to give general satisfaction to the whole party, who immediately dispersed to their several amusements. A struggle like this, between the principles of *duty and honesty*, among children so very young, must prove highly interesting to all lovers of children, and exemplifies, beyond a doubt, the immense advantage of early instruction.

THE WHISTLE.

The circumstance I am about to mention, shews how necessary it is to teach by example as well as precept. Many of the children were in the habit of bringing marbles, tops, whistles, and other toys, to the school, which often caused much disturbance; for they would play with them instead of attending to their lessons, and I found it necessary to forbid the children from bringing any thing of the kind. And after giving notice two or three times in the school, I told them that if any of them brought such things, they would be taken away from them. In consequence of this, several things fell into my hands which I did not always think of returning, and among other things a whistle from a little boy. The child asked me for it as he was going home, but having several visitors at the time, I put the child off, telling him not to plague me, and he went home. I had forgotten the circumstance altogether, but it appears the child did not; for some time after, while I was lecturing the children upon the necessity of telling truth, and on the wickedness of stealing, the little fellow approached me, and said, " *Please sir, you stole my whistle.*" " Stole your whistle!" said I, " did I not give it you again?" " No, teacher, I asked you for it, and you would not give it to me." I stood self-convicted, being accused in the middle of my lecture, before all the children, and really at a loss to know what excuse to make, for I had mislaid the whistle, and could not return it to the child. I immediately gave the child a halfpenny, and said all I could to persuade the children that it was not my intention to keep it.

However, I am satisfied that this trifling mistake of mine did more harm than I was able to repair during some time, for if we wish to teach children to be honest, we should never take any thing from them without returning it again. Indeed, persons having charge of children can never be too cautious, and should not on any account whatever break a promise; for experience has taught me that most children have good memories, and if you once promise a thing and do not perform it, they will pay very little attention to what you say afterwards.

Having now concluded all that I have to say on Infant Schools, I would in conclusion breathe forth a sincere petition to the throne of Divine Truth and Goodness, for the prosperity and spread of the system, in which I am sure I shall be joined by all who have been convinced of its beneficial effects in promoting the present and everlasting welfare of human beings.

Mysterious are thy ways, O God; yet who was ever disappointed that asked of thee in a right spirit? Prosper then thy work which is begun in the world, we beseech thee, O Lord; may thy gracious providence so encircle and protect the rising generation, that there may be no more complaining in our streets. Protect them, O Lord, from the many dangers that surround them, as soon as they draw their breath in this vale of tears, and put into the hearts of those who have the means to consider the state of the infant poor, to give them the assistance they need. Grant that thy blessed example may be followed by many, for thou didst desire that children should come unto thee, and not be forbidden, and thou didst take them up in thine arms and bless them, declaring that of such is the kingdom of heaven. May thy creatures, therefore, not be ashamed to notice little children, but co-operate, hand and heart with each other, and endeavour to teach them all good. May difference of sentiment and opinion be laid aside and forgotten; and may all join hand and heart in endeavouring to rescue the infant race from danger; that so these tender plants may be nurtured with the dew of thy divine blessing, and be thus made fit subjects for thy heavenly kingdom, where the wicked cease from troubling, and the weary are at rest. May thy divine influence descend abundantly upon all those who have hitherto turned their attention to infant children; may they feel great pleasure in doing good; may they receive thy grace and protection abundantly, and when their days of probation are ended, may they find a place in thy heavenly mansions, and there glorify thee throughout the boundless ages of eternity. Amen.

CHAP. XVIII.

REMARKS ON NATIONAL AND SUNDAY SCHOOLS.

ALTHOUGH it has been the special design of the present work to speak of the first efforts of *art* in assisting the proper development of the mental and moral faculties, I shall take the liberty of indulging in a few remarks on the method at present adopted in the more advanced stages of education; as seen in our National and Sunday Schools. I need, I am sure, offer no other apology for so doing, than the fact, that it is in these institutions, the infant poor must complete their education — it is in these schools, the budding faculties must either ripen, or perish — and the moral principles become confirmed or weakened. Certain I am, that it is the wish of all concerned in these praiseworthy institutions *to do their best* for the attainment of this object — the welfare and improvement of the rising generation of the poor classes; and therefore I the less reluctantly offer a few thoughts on the subject, which it is my humble opinion may not be altogether useless.

With regard to National Schools, I must say, there is too much form, and too little of the spirit of instruction, to be found in their management; the minor faculties are attended to in pre-

ference to the higher ones: it is the memory alone
which is called into action : the understanding is
suffered to lie in a state of torpid inactivity.
Their lessons, their plan of using them, and their
discipline altogether, are of that monotonous nature, that the children always seem to me to be
dosing over them. I know it will be pleaded that
the number to be taught at once, renders this defect unavoidable; that it is impossible to teach a
large body of children, in such a way as to secure
the attention and activity of the whole. And it is
so far true, as to its being impossible to detect
and reform every idle pupil, who finds an opportunity of indulging his idleness in the divided
attention of his teacher;—but I do think, if it be
impossible to cure the evil, it may be in a great
degree prevented. Make your system interesting,
lively, and inspiriting, and your scholars will
neither be able nor willing to slumber over it.
Every one knows what an effect is produced on
the physical faculties, by a succession of the
same sound—for instance, by the long-continued
chiming of a single bell; it induces a drowsiness,
which we find it impossible to resist, except by
turning our attention to another subject; but, let
a number of bells strike out into a merry peal—
how quickly we are aroused—how lively we become—whilst their various *changes* secure the
attention and interest, which their pleasing and
spirited tones first excited. And just so it is with
the mind in the matters of education; you must
give a variety of tones, a newness of aspect to
your lessons, or you will never be able to keep up
a lively attention in your scholars. For this purpose I would particularly recommend to the attention of all concerned, the chapters in this volume,

on geometry, conversation, pictures, and likewise that on the elliptical method. By adopting the plan recommended in these chapters, the children will have something to do, — and to do that something they must be *active*. The first object of the teacher is to excite a thirst for knowledge; not to pour unwelcome information into the mind.

It will probably be said, that however well adapted the plan recommended may be for the infantine scholars for whom it was designed, yet, it does not follow that it may be equally advantageous for those of a more advanced age; and if by this it is meant, that the very same lessons, &c. are not equally applicable in both cases, I perfectly agree with the truth of the objection; but it is the *principle* of education that I recommend, and would affirm to be as applicable to children of the most advanced age, as to those of the youngest. It is not sufficient to store the memory, we must give employment to the understanding. It is not sufficient to talk to the children of piety and of goodness; we must present them with a living example of both, and secure an imitation of such example.

As applicable to Sunday Schools, I would particularly recommend the use of picture lessons on scripture subjects, for the use of the junior classes, to be used as a sort of text for conversation, suited to the state of their mental faculties. I am convinced that the knowledge acquired by this method is likely to make a deeper and more lasting impression, than that imparted in a less interesting mode. Nor should the lessons on natural history be neglected, in my humble opinion, in the system of Sunday School instruction; inasmuch as, the more the children know of the wonders of creation, the greater must be their reverence of the Almighty Creator; in addition to which it will enable the teachers to supply variety, a thing so agreeable, and, indeed, indispensable, in the instruction of children. For these reasons, I think it could not justly be considered as either a mis-employment or profanation of the Sabbath-day. For the elder children, moreover, it would be advisable to have occasional class lectures, simplified for the occasion, on astronomy, natural history, &c.; and although it might be unadvisable to occupy the hours of the Sabbath-day with the delivery of them, they might be given, in some week-day evening, and should be made the medium of reward to good behaviour; such children as had misbehaved themselves being proscribed from attending. When thus seen in the light of a privilege, they would not fail to be interesting to the little auditors, as well as conducive to good behaviour.

It is with some degree of reluctance and apprehension, I touch upon another topic — that of religious doctrine. As schools for gratuitous instruction have been established by most of the religious sects extant, it is obvious that some dissimilarity of sentiment on religious subjects must exist, as imparted in such schools. Let it not be supposed, that I would cast a censure on any religious body for establishing a school devoted to such a blessed purpose. On the contrary, I rejoice to see, that however various their theories may be, their opinion of Christian practice, as evinced in such actions, is the same. But, one thing I would say, to each and to all — let a prominence be given to those fundamental truths of love and goodness which Christianity inculcates.

Let the first sounds of religion which salute the ears of infancy be that heavenly proclamation, which astonished and enraptured the ears of the wakeful shepherds, " Peace on earth and good-will towards men." It was the herald-cry by which salvation was ushered into the world, and surely no other can be so proper for introducing it into the souls of children. I must candidly own that I have occasionally witnessed a greater desire to teach particular doctrines, than the simple and beautiful truths which form the spirit of religion; and it is against this practice I have presumed to raise a dissentient voice.

I would further beg leave here to recommend to the attention of all engaged in the work of instruction, in classes, where the children are of a somewhat advanced age, the ingenious method pursued by Mr. Stoat, master of the Islington Parochial Charity Schools, and which he has denominated the system of circulating classes.

I have not the little work at present by me which Mr. Stoat has published, explaining and recommending his plan; but the spirit of it may be learnt from the following account. It is the present practice in most schools to arrange the scholars in their classes, according to their attainments and merits, the best or cleverest scholar being reckoned and placed as the first boy. To the ambitious, or rather I should say, the active and emulous, this station of honour is of course an object of desire, and its attainment the object of their continual endeavours; but, having attained this station, having achieved all that it is possible for industry or ability to achieve,—there being no further point of attraction,—the attention and merit of the possessor are frequently found to

become stagnant; nay, he could almost wish himself at the bottom of his class again, that he might
again have something to win — something to gain
by his ability or perseverance. This is one evil
of the usual method of the permanent arrange-
ment of classes. In the next place, by such ar-
rangement all the meritorious are found together
in the top stations of the classes, and all the idle
and inattentive at the bottom; the former, who
need no spur, finding one in the emulous spirits
of those near them, and the latter, who require
excitement, and the influence of different characters, being left in contented ignominy and
degradation, because shared with others as bad
as themselves. Nothing, it is obvious, can be
more desirable, or more likely to produce good
effects, than the reverse of this; viz. the inter-
mingling of the active and meritorious with those
of opposite character; by the Circulating Classes
of Mr. Stoat this object is attained, along with a
remedy to the evil before complained of, namely,
the cessation of interest and activity likely to
take place in the mind of the scholar, when he
finds that he has no higher post to attain to, than
that which he then holds. The method of the
circulating classes is as follows: each class is arranged in a circle, at one point of which is affixed
a post, which may be termed the post of honour.
On this post are suspended a certain number of
medals, which are of course badges of honour;
now, one side of this post may be said to be the
highest place in the circle, and the other the
lowest; but there is in fact no highest place, for
as soon as a scholar has attained to the highest
place in the class, he passes the post, with the
reward of one medal, and is then, of course, in

the lowest place; if he again attain to the top of the class, he gains another medal, and once more passes the post into the lowest place; and so on, during the whole of the time the class is assembled; at the close of school-hours the number of medals gained by each scholar is registered on a slate, which thus affords a record of the respective merits of the scholars. Thus, it will be perceived, the inert spirits of the school are continually coming in contact with those of the active, whilst the latter have never attained to a point, where exertion can attain for them no further honours or reward. Another peculiarity of method adopted by Mr. Stoat is — that the interrogative system is much used, and that the questions are asked, as well as the answers given, by the scholars themselves. The plan, in both respects, is applicable to all schools, wherein the children are taught in classes, to Sunday Schools, National Schools, and schools for the higher classes; and I would most urgently recommend to all concerned in the work of education, to make the experiment, as I am certain that its extension must be alike productive of benefit to master and scholars.

In conclusion, I would observe that as the foregoing remarks have been kindly made, in such manner it is my hope they will be received, and I wish it to be distinctly understood, that I am a well-wisher towards the established church, and that nothing I have said in these pages, can in any way be construed as tending to weaken, pull down, or undermine the *truth* as there professed, —*the grand object is not to pull down, but to build up:* and whoever sounds a false alarm, or contends that Infant Schools will have this tendency, I have no doubt (to say the least) that they will find

themselves ultimately mistaken. 1 most heartily
wish that wherever there is a National School,
there may be an Infant School, in its immediate
vicinity.

CHAP. XIX.

———

A FEW HINTS FOR PARENTS ON THE SUBJECT OF NURSERY EDUCATION.

~~~~~~~~~~~~

I WILL introduce this subject in the words of Mr. Black, an individual to whom parents and teachers are under considerable obligations.

" Many persons, eminent by their charitable acts, and who express themselves generally desirous of aiding in any plan which may contribute to the improvement and happiness of the poorer classes, have, nevertheless been unwilling to assist in the establishment of Infant Schools, fearful that the superior method pursued in these schools should render the children educated therein much better informed than the children of the richer classes, who might thus be supplanted in numerous lucrative and honorable situations in after-life.

" From this circumstance one of the two following conclusions must be drawn : either, that the system of education pursued in the higher schools is very faulty and imperfect; or that the fears of those ladies and gentlemen are entirely groundless.

" If the first be true, then, it cannot be denied, that the consequences, feared by the richer classes, must necessarily take place, if, either from prejudice or apathy, they continue the same faulty and imperfect method of education which, by the expression of these fears, they positively declare is usually pursued in the higher schools; but the remedy is easy. Let the same good principles of tuition be introduced into nurseries, and into those schools to which the children of the rich are sent —and the latter will not fail to maintain their patrimonial ranks in society. They need then have no fear lest the poorer classes should become too intellectual, but, on the contrary, they will soon find that their own welfare, security, and happiness will not only be assured by, but will increase in proportion as the poorer classes gain knowledge, for by the method of instruction pursued in the *Infant Schools*, the knowledge there acquired is necessarily accompanied by the practice of industry, sobriety, honesty, benevolence and mutual kindness; in fine, by all the moral and religious virtues*."

* To assist in this better method of instruction, the following works have lately been published, and are sold by Messrs. Longman, Rees, Orme, Brown, and Green, Paternoster Row.

1st. The Student's Manual, being an Etymological and Explanatory Vocabulary of Words derived from the Greek, 2s. 6d.

2nd. An Etymological Dictionary of Words derived from the Latin, 6s. 6d.

3rd. An Introductory Latin Grammar, for the use of Parents and Preparatory Preceptors, 2s. 6d.

4th. Companion to the Parents' Latin Grammar, being a Translation, word for word, of an interesting account, in Latin, of various Animals, 2s.

5th. The Paidophilean System of Education, applied to the French Language, 2 vols. 6s. 6d.

Specimens of these different works will be found in the Appendix.

That the system of instruction recommended in the foregoing pages is equally applicable for the children of the rich as for those of the poor, there can be no doubt; and it might be adopted either in schools established on its principles or in the nursery. It is, indeed, obvious that it might be carried to a much greater extent, where the means of so doing would not be wanting. Many things might be taught, which it is neither advisable nor practicable to teach in the schools established for the instruction of poor children.

Whilst the elements of number,* form, and language, may be taught by the means and after the manner recommended in the preceding chapters on the respective subjects; there are other branches of knowledge, which might enter into the scope of nursery instruction, with great advantage to the children.

As an introduction to *botany* I would make the children acquainted with the progress of vegetation, *not from words, but from observation.* I would have three or four garden-pots, filled with mould, introduced into the nursery at a proper

---

* I would here take an opportunity of recommending to parents and teachers two little works which have fallen under my notice. The first, entitled " Butter's Gradations in Reading and Spelling," is certainly well adapted for a first book for infants, inasmuch as it is constructed upon very judicious principles of easy gradation, and is therefore likely to facilitate the progress of the scholar, by conducting him from words of the simplest construction to those of greater difficulty. The other little book is entitled " Intellectual Arithmetic;" and is written on a plan at once novel and ingenious; by which the first rules of arithmetic are so simplified, and their application rendered so plain and obvious, that they may be understood by the most infantile capacity. Both works may be had of the booksellers mentioned in the title-page of the present work.

season of the year; the children should be asked, what is in the pots.—" Dirt," or " mould," will of course be the reply. They should then be shewn the seeds, which are to be deposited in the mould, and assuming in the eyes of the children a prophetic character, the mother or governess should inform them of the process of vegetation, and that about a certain time a pretty flower will make its appearance in the pots; the seeds should then be deposited in the mould, and the pots placed in a proper situation. It would not be improper to let the children themselves sow the seed; thus convincing them of their power of being useful, and becoming the instrument of so great a wonder, as the transformation of a seed into a flower. During the time the seed is lying unperceived beneath the mould, the children should frequently be sent to look " if the pretty flower has come up,"—or questioned as to what they were told concerning it. At length, the green shoot will make its appearance just peeping above the mould, to the no small surprize and gratification of the little observers. They will mark with attentive eagerness the progress of its growth, the appearance of the bud, and the gradual development of " the pretty flower"—till they are fully convinced of the wisdom of the parent or teacher who foretold all which has happened; and made acquainted with the process of vegetation; not from words, but from observation. Certain it is, that such a lesson could not be wholly useless. In the first place it might be made the means of impressing them with ideas of the Almighty power, highly conducive to piety; secondly, it would beget a habit of observation; thirdly, it would be likely to produce a love of flowers and the vege-

table world, favourable to their future pursuits
in the science of botany; and lastly, it would inspire their little breasts with a love and respect
of the parents or teachers who were wise and
kind enough to teach them so many true and wonderful things.

As an efficient and amusing introduction to
natural history, I would have every nursery provided with a microscope, by means of which the
minds of the children might be excited to wonder
and admiration, at the amazing beauty and per-
fectness of the insect world, and the astonishing
construction of various substances, as seen through
this instrument. So far would this be from be-
getting habits of cruelty, that it would be very
likely to check them. Many children who would
be loath to torture a large animal, such as a cat,
a dog, or a bird, feel no compunction at ill-using
a fly, because it appears to them so insignificant
an animal; but had they once witnessed, by
means of a microscope, the wonderful and perfect conformation of the insect, I am persuaded
they would be less inclined to make the distinction.

Various devices might be made use of to teach
the first truths of *astronomy*. So simple a device
as an apple, with a wire run through its centre,
turned round before a candle, might serve to
explain the phenomena of day and night, whilst
the orrery, with the accompaniment of a simple and familiar lecture, — (it should be much
more so, indeed, than any I have heard or read)
—would make them acquainted with those stu-
pendous facts which strike us with astonishment
and awe. It has been well observed by Dr.

Young, with respect to the wonders of astronomy —

> " In little things we search out God — in great
> " He seizes us."

One thing I would here notice — that it should
be a constant practice to remind the children,
that in the apple and the orrery, they see only a
resemblance to the earth and the heavenly bodies
— that *they* are vast in size and distance, beyond
their comprehensions; at the same time leading
them to an actual observation of the heavens by
means of a telescope. This would be a high treat
to the children, and productive of correct notions;
which are but too apt to be lost where we are
under the necessity of teaching by signs so infinitely unlike, in size and nature, as the candle
and the apple, and the brass balls and wires
of the orrery, to the earth and the heavenly orbs.
For giving the children their first lessons in
geography, I would have a floor-cloth in every
nursery, painted like a map, but of course not
filled up so perfectly as maps for adults necessarily are. It should contain a correct delineation
of the position of a certain space of the globe,
we will say for instance of England; let the
children then be told to proceed from a certain
spot, to go through certain counties, towns, &c.
and to fetch a piece of cloth from Yorkshire, or a
knife from Sheffield, cheese from Cheshire, butter
from Dorset, lace from Huntingdonshire, &c. &c.
The lessons thus given would be at once amusing
and instructive, both to the governess and children. If preferred, these maps might be painted
of a less size, to cover a table. No difficulty

culty would be found to get a set of such table-covers or floor-cloths painted, if the public would once encourage the plan.

I would also have an oblong tray made to hold water, large enough to cover a table. In this I would fasten pieces of cork, cut out in the shape of land, according to the best maps, while other small bits of cork should represent the mountains and hills on the surface of the respective islands. By application to the toy-makers, a sufficient number of animals might be got to stock the respective islands, &c. with their appropriate inhabitants; whilst the manufactures and many of the natural products of the different places might be readily supplied by the ingenuity of the parent or governess. A little boat should then be provided, and a voyage to a given part undertaken; various islands might be touched at, and various commodities taken on board or exchanged, according to the mercantile instructions the children should receive; whilst brief accounts might at first be read or given of the climate, productions, and inhabitants of the respective places; till the little scholar should be able to conduct the voyage, purchase or exchange commodities, and give an account of the various countries and their inhabitants, &c. by himself. Certain I am that more might be acquired, by this method, of geographical knowledge, in one week, than by the old method in a twelvemonth: and what the children did learn they would always remember. I might extend these suggestions to the size of a small volume, had I space to do so; but the limits of my present volume forbid; at a future period, should my active employments permit, I may resume the subject of *nursery hints* in an extended and separate form.

There are, indeed, many excellent works already published on the subject; but as by the suggestions and contributions of many, every plan is likely to be perfected, no one is justified in withholding any thing likely to promote the desired object.

APPENDIX.

PRACTICAL LESSONS FOR INFANT SCHOOLS.

(ORIGINAL AND SELECT.)

HYMNS.

THE GOODNESS OF GOD.

THE God who reigns above the sky
  Sees all that children do;
We cannot from his presence fly;
  And he can hear us too.

'Tis God who ev'ry blessing sends
  That little children need,
And finds for them so many friends
  Who teach them how to read:

They teach us likewise how to pray,
  And sing his praises thus;
Then let us do so, that he may
  Bless both those friends and us.

THE SAME SUBJECT.

When first the morning light we see,
  And from our beds arise;
We to our God should thankful be,
  Who ev'ry want supplies.

'Twas God who made the pretty sun,
  That gives all day its light;
And it was God who made the moon,
  And stars which shine at night.

The fish that in the water swim,
  The beasts upon the land;
Were all created first by him,
  And shew his mighty hand.

The food we eat, the clothes we wear,
  'Tis God alone can give;
And only by his love and care,
  Can little children live.

Then let us ever caution take,
  His holy laws to keep;
And praise him from the time we wake
  Until again we sleep.

OBEDIENCE TO TEACHERS.

Little children must obey,
Every thing their teachers say;
God is watching all day long,
Whether they do right or wrong.

And wherever they may be,
Every action he can see;
At home, at school, by day, by night,
Children still are in his sight.

When children do not as they're bid,
And for their naughty ways are chid,
He from the heavens is looking down,
And sees their conduct with a frown.

But when good children strive to please
Their teachers, God their goodness sees;
He marks their actions, and the while,
Is looking on them with a smile.

Then little children, all of you,
Do as God would have you do;
And always think, where'er you be,
Whate'er you're doing—God can see.

RELIANCE ON GOD.

If all my earthly friends should die,
   And leave me mourning here;
Since God regards the orphan's cry,
   O what have I to fear?

If I am rich, he'll guard my heart,
   Temptations to withstand;
And make me willing to impart
   The bounties of his hand.

If I am poor, He can supply,
   Who *has* my table spread;
Who feeds the ravens when they cry,
   And fills his poor with bread.

And, Lord, whatever grief or ill
   For me may be in store,
Make me submissive to thy will,
   And I would ask no more.

Then still, as seasons hasten by,
   I will for heaven prepare;
That God may take me when I die,
   To dwell for ever there.

ENCOURAGEMENT FOR LITTLE CHILDREN.

God is so good that he will hear
   Whenever children humbly pray:
He always lends a gracious ear
   To what the youngest child can say.

His own most holy book declares
    He loves good little children still;
And that he answers all their prayers,
    Just as a tender father will.

He will not scorn an infant tongue
    That thanks him for his mercies given;
And when by babes his praise is sung,
    Their cheerful songs ascend to heaven.

Come, then, dear children, trust his word,
    And seek him for your friend and guide;
Your little voices will be heard,
    An·l you shall never be denied.

THE BIBLE.

This is a precious book indeed,
Happy the child that loves to read!
'Tis God's own word, which he has given
To shew our souls the way to heaven.

It tells us how the world was made;
And how good men the Lord obey'd;
Here his commands are written, too,
To teach us what we ought to do.

It bids us all from sin to fly,
Because our souls can never die;
It points to heaven where angels dwell,
And warns us to escape from hell.

Be thankful, children, that you may
Read this good Bible every day:
'Tis God's own word, which he has given
To shew your souls the way to heaven.

LESSONS ON ANIMALS.

THE HORSE.

Come, children, let us now discourse
About the pretty noble Horse;
And then you soon will plainly see
How very useful he must be.

He draws the coach so fine and smart,
And likewise drags the loaded cart,
Along the road or up the hill,
Though then his task is harder still.

Upon his back men ride with ease,
He carries them just where they please;
And though it should be many a mile,
He gets there in a little while.

With saddle on his back they sit,
And manage him with reins and bit,
The whip and spur they use also,
When they would have him faster go.

And be the weather cold or hot,
As they may wish he'll walk or trot:
Or, if to make more haste they need,
Will gallop with the greatest speed.

When dead his shining skin they use,
As leather for our boots and shoes;
Alive or dead, then, thus we see,
How useful still the Horse must be.

THE DOG.

The Cow, the Sheep, the Horse, have long,
Been made the subject of our song;
But there are many creatures yet,
Whose merits we must not forget.

And first the Dog, so good to guard,
His master's cottage, house, or yard,—
Dishonest men away to keep,
And guard us safely while we sleep.

For if at midnight, still and dark,
Strange steps he hears, with angry bark,
He bids his master wake and see,
If thieves or honest folks they be.

At home, abroad, obedient still,
His only guide his master's will;
Before his steps, or by his side,
He runs or walks with joy and pride.

He runs to fetch the stick or ball,
Returns obedient to the call;
Content and pleas'd if he but gains
A single pat for all his pains.

But whilst his merits thus we praise,
Pleas'd with his character and ways,
This let us learn, as well we may,
To love our Teachers and obey.

THE COW.

Come, children, listen to me now,
And you shall hear about the Cow;
You'll find her useful, live or dead,
Whether she's black or white or red.

When milk-maids milk her morn and night,
She gives them milk so fresh and white;
And this, we little children think,
Is very nice for us to drink.

The curdled milk they press and squeeze,
And so they make it into cheese;
The cream they skim and shake in churns,
And then it soon to butter turns.

And when she's dead, her flesh is good,
For *beef* is our true English food;
But though 'twill make us brave and strong,
To eat too much, we know, is wrong.

Her skin, with lime and bark together,
The tanner tans, and makes it leather;
And without *that* what should we do,
For soles for every boot and shoe?

And last of all, if cut with care,
Her horns make combs, to comb our hair;
And so we learn — thanks to our teachers,
That Cows are good and useful creatures.

THE SHEEP.

Hark now to me, and silence keep,
And we will talk about the sheep;
For sheep are harmless, and we know
That on their backs the wool does grow.

The sheep are taken once a year,
And plung'd in water clean and clear;
And there they swim, but never bite,
While men do wash them clean and white.

And then they take them, fat or lean,
Clip off the wool, both short and clean,
And this is call'd, we understand,
Sheering the sheep, throughout the land.

So then they take the wool so white,
And pack it up in bags quite tight;
And then they take those bags so full,
And sell to men that deal in wool.

The wool is wash'd and comb'd with hand,
Then it is spun with wheel and band:
And then with shuttle very soon
Wove into cloth within the loom.

The cloth is first sent to be dyed;
Then it is wash'd and press'd and dried:
The tailor then cuts out with care
The clothes that men and boys do wear.

LESSONS ON WEIGHTS, MEASURES, &c.*

AVOIRDUPOISE WEIGHT.

Sixteen drams are just an ounce
   As you'll find at any shop;
Sixteen ounces make a pound,
   If you should want a mutton chop.

Twenty-eight pounds are the fourth
   Of an hundred weight call'd gross;
Four such quarters are the whole
   Of an hundred weight at most.

Twenty hundred make a ton.
   By this rule all things are sold
That have any waste or dross:
   And are bought so, too, I'm told.

When we buy or when we sell
   We do it in our Maker's sight,
Whose laws command, you all know well,
   That we should practice what is right.

* For the poetical lessons under this head, I am indebted to
the kindness of Mr. Carol, master of the Stratford Infant
School.

APOTHECARIES' WEIGHT.

Twenty grains make a scruple,—some scruple to take;
Though at times it is needful, just for our health's sake,
Three scruples one drachm, eight drachms make one ounce,
Twelve ounces one pound for the pestle to pounce.
By this rule is all medicine mix'd, though I'm told,
By Avoirdupoise weight 'tis bought and 'tis sold.
But the best of all physic, if I may advise,
Is temperate living and good exercise.

LONG MEASURE—SPACE.

Take barley-corns of mod'rate length,
   And three you'll find will make an inch:
Twelve inches make a foot;—if strength
   Permit, I'll leap it and not flinch.

Three feet's a yard, as understood
   By those possess'd with sense and soul;
Five feet and half will make a rood,
   And also will a perch or pole.

Forty such poles a furlong make,
   And eight such furlongs make a mile,
O'er hedge, or ditch, or seas, or lake;
   O'er railing, fence, or gate, or stile.

Three miles a league, by sea or land,
   And twenty leagues are one degree;
Just four times ninety degrees a band
   Will make, to girt the earth and sea.

But what's the girt of hell or heav'n?
   (No nat'ral thought or eye can see,)
To neither girt or length is giv'n;
   'Tis without space—Immensity!

Still shall the good and truly wise,
   The seat of heav'n with safety find;
Because 'tis seen with inward eyes,
   The state resides within their mind.

DRY MEASURE.

Two pints will make one quart
  Of barley, oats, or rye,
Two quarts one pottle are of wheat
  Or any thing that's dry.

Two pottles one gallon
  Two gallons one peck fair,
Four pecks one bushel heap or brim
  Eight bushels one quarter are.

If when you sell, you give
  Good measure shaken down,
Through motives good, you will receive
  An everlasting crown.

ALE AND BEER MEASURE.

Two pints will make one quart,
  Four quarts one gallon strong:—
Some drink but little, some too much,—
  To drink too much is wrong.

Eight gallons one firkin make,
  Of liquor that's call'd ale:
Nine gallons one firkin of beer,
  Whether 'tis mild or stale.

With gallons fifty-four,
  A hogshead I can fill:
But hope I never shall drink much,
  Drink much, whoever will.

WINE, OIL, AND SPIRIT MEASURE.

Two pints will make one quart,
  Of any wine I'm told:
Four quarts one gallon are of port,
  Or claret new or old.

Forty-two gallons will
  A tierce fill to the bung:
And sixty-three's a hogshead full
  Of brandy, oil, or rum.

Eighty-four gallons make
  One puncheon fill'd to brim :
Two hogsheads make one pipe or butt,
  Two pipes will make one tun.

A little wine within
  Oft cheers the mind that's sad;
But too much brandy, rum, or gin,
  No doubt is very bad.

From all excess beware,
  Which sorrow must attend;
Drunkards a life of woe must share,—
  When time with them shall end.

TIME OR CHRONOLOGY.

Sixty seconds make a minute;
  Time enough to tie my shoe:
Sixty minutes make an hour,
  Shall it pass and nought to do?

Twenty-four hours will make a day;
  Too much time to spend in sleep,
Too much time to spend in play,
  For seven days will end the week.

Fifty and two such weeks will put
  Near an end to every year;
Days three hundred sixty five
  Are the whole that it can share.

Except in leap year, when one day
  Added is to gain lost time;
May it not be spent in play,
  Neither any evil crime.

Our time is short we often say;
   Let us then improve it well;
That eternally we may
   Live where happy angels dwell.

MONEY.

Two farthings one halfpenny make,
A penny four of such will take;
And to allow I am most willing
That twelve pence always make a shilling;
And that five shillings make a crown,
Twenty a sovereign, same as pound.
Some have no cash, some have to spare —
Some who have wealth for none will care.
Some thro' misfortune's hand brought low,
Their money gone, are filled with woe,
But I know better than to grieve;
If I have none I will not thieve:
I'll be content whate'er's my lot,
Nor for misfortunes care a *grout.*
There is a Providence, whose care,
And sov'reign love I crave to share;
His love is *gold without alloy;*
Those who possess 't have *endless joy.*

FOUR SEASONS OF THE YEAR.

On March the twenty-first is Spring,
When little birds begin to sing:
Begin to build and hatch their brood,
And carefully provide them food.

Summer's the twenty-first of June,
The cuckow changes then his tune;
All nature smiles, the fields look gay,
The weather's fair to make the hay.

September, on the twenty-third
When sportsmen mark at ev'ry bird,
Autumn comes in; the fields are shorn,
The fruits are ripe: so is the corn.

Winter's cold frosts and northern blast,
The season is we mention last;
The date of which in *truth*, we must
Fix for December—twenty-first.

FIVE SENSES.

All human beings must, (with birds and beasts)
To be complete, five senses have at least,
The sense of hearing's to the ear confined :
The eye, we know, for seeing is designed.

The nose to smell an odour sweet or ill,
The tongue to taste what will the belly fill.
The sense of feeling is in ev'ry part
While life gives motion to a beating heart.

FOUR SEASONS OF HUMAN LIFE.

Our days four seasons are at most,
    And Infancy's the time of Spring :
Oh! with what trouble, care, and cost,
    Must we be taught to pray and sing.

In Summer as our growth proceeds,
    Good fruit should hang on every branch;
Our roots be clear'd from evil weeds,
    As into science we advance.

Our Autumn is the season, when
    Temptations do our mind assail :
Our fruits are proved in manhood; then
    Let not sin, death, and hell prevail.

For Winter brings old age and death,
    If we've good fruits laid up in store;
Soon as we gasp our latest *breath*,
    We land on a *triumphant shore.*

THE MASTER'S DAILY ADVICE TO HIS SCHOOL.

If you'd in wisdom's ways proceed,
You intellectual knowledge need.
Let science be your guiding star,
Or from its path you'll wander far.

'Tis science that directs the mind,
The path of happiness to find.
If *goodness* added is to *truth*,
'Twill bring reward to ev'ry youth.

THE GOOD CHILDREN'S MONEY-BOX.

All pence by the gen'rous deposited here,
When holidays come, I will equally share
Among all good children attending this school.
I should wish not to find a dunce or a fool.
Then listen, all you, who a prize hope to gain,
Attend to your books, and you'll not hope in vain.

THE MASTER.

GRAMMATICAL LESSON.

THE ARTICLES.

Three little words we hear and see
In frequent use,—*a, an,* and *the;*
These words, so useful, though so small,
Are those which articles we call.

The first two, *a* and *an,* we use,
    When speaking of *one thing* alone;—
For instance, we might wish to say,
    An oak, *a* man, *a* dog, *a* bone.

An oak, *a* man,—means *any* oak,
  Or *any* man of all mankind;
A dog, *a* bone,—means *any* dog,
  Or *any* bone a dog may find.

The, speaks of either one or more,
  The cow, *the* cows,—*the* pig, *the* pigs;
The plum, *the* plums—(you like a score,)
  The pear, *the* pears,—*the* fig, *the* figs.

This article we only use,
  Whenever it may be our wish
To speak of some determined thing,
  As thus: *the* bird, *the* ox, *the* fish.

By which we mean, not *any* bird
  That flying in the air may be,
Nor *any* ox amongst the herd,
  Nor *any* fish in stream or sea;

But some one certain bird or ox,
  Or fish, (let it be which it may,)
Of whom we're speaking, or of whom
  We something mean to write or say.

Remember these things, when you see
The little words—*a, an,* and *the.*

---

*MORAL LESSON.**

THE TWO HALVES.

"What nice plum-cakes," said JAMES to JOHN,
" Our mother sends! Is your's all gone?"

---

* The following tale though not adapted for the younger children of an Infant School, and too long to be committed to memory by the older ones, might be read to such by the master, and would serve as an admirable theme for conversation. It is likewise well adapted for a tale for family circles.

" It is," JOHN answer'd; " is not thine ?"

" No, JOHN, I've sav'd one half of mine;
It was so large, as well as nice,
I thought that it should serve for twice.
Had I eat all to-day, to-morrow,
I might have mourn'd such haste in sorrow :
So half my cake I wisely took,
And, seated in my favourite nook,
Enjoy'd, alone, the *double pleasure*,
Of present and of future treasure."

" I, too," said JOHN, " made up my mind
This morning, when our mother kind
Sent down the cakes, so nice and sweet,
That I but half to-day would eat,
And half I ate; the other half——"

JAMES stopp'd his brother with a laugh;
" I know what you're about to say,—
The other half you gave away.
Now, brother, pray explain to me,
The charms which you in *giving* see.
Shew me how *feasting* foes or friends
Can for your *fasting* make amends."

" A poor old man," said JOHN, " came by,
Whose looks implor'd for charity.
His eyes, bedimm'd with starting tears,
His body bow'd by length of years,
His feeble limbs, his hoary hairs,
Were to my heart as silent prayers.
I saw, too, he was hungry, though
His lips had not inform'd me so.
To this poor creature, JAMES, I gave
The half which I had meant to save.
The lingering tears, with sudden start,
   Ran down the furrows of his cheek,
I knew he thank'd me in his heart,
   Although he strove in vain to speak.
The joy that from such acts we gain
I'll try for your sake to explain.

First, God is pleas'd, who, as you know,
   Marks every action that we do;
That God "from whom all blessings flow,"
   So many, JAMES, to me and you.

Our mother, next, had she but seen
    Her gift of kindness so employ'd?
Would *she* not, JAMES, well pleas'd have been,
    And all my feelings then enjoy'd?
The poor old man, was he not pleas'd?
    Must not his load of sorrow be,
Though but for one short moment, eas'd,
    To think, " Then some one feels for me."
But still you ask, of all this pleasure
    How much will to *the giver* fall?
The whole, rich, undiminish'd treasure,—
    He feels, *he* shares the joy of *all*.

We eat the cake, and it is gone;
What have we left to think upon?
Who's pleas'd by what we then have done!
How many, pray, JAMES, more than one?
The joys by sympathy supplied
Are many, great, and dignified.
But, do not on my word rely,
Whilst you, dear JAMES, the fact may try;
And if you do not find it true,
I'll next time eat *both halves* with you!

QUESTIONS & ANSWERS,

FORMING

AN EPITOME

OF WHAT HAS BEEN PREVIOUSLY ADVANCED

ON THE SUBJECT OF

𝕴𝖓𝖋𝖆𝖓𝖙 𝕾𝖈𝖍𝖔𝖔𝖑𝖘.

―――――

Q. Is there reason to believe that juvenile delinquency has of late years increased? A. The Reports of Committees appointed to inquire into the subject, the daily journals, and the state of our prisons, bear undeniable testimony to the melancholy truth.

Q. Ought we therefore to suppose that our present means to prevent this evil, such as our Sunday Schools, National Schools, Bible and Tract Societies, with similar institutions, are of no use? A. Certainly not; there is no doubt the evil would be much further extended, were it not for the counteracting effects of such institutions.

Q. How can we account for the prevalence and growing extent of the evil? A. Partly from the neglect of the parents,—in some cases wilful, in others unavoidable,—to prevent their children from the contamination of the streets; and partly from the organized system of tuition of young delinquents which is known to exist.

Q. What is the remedy most likely to prove efficient? A. The establishment of Infant Schools; whereby the children of the poor may be preserved from evil company, and the principles of honesty and virtue instilled into their infant minds.

Q. What objections are made to the establishment of Infant Schools? A. Some persons are of opinion that it will make the poor idle and proud.

Q. Is there any ground for such an opinion? A. Not the

least; the ignorant are generally the most idle, and true wisdom teaches us to think humbly of ourselves.

Q. Can a child gain too much experimental knowledge in the first eight or ten years of its life to render it unfit for a Christian servitude?—A. Certainly not; if the Christian spirit be generated in an influential manner during the early period of existence, it is impossible that too much knowledge can accompany it to unfit the mind to endure a Christian servitude, since one of the first feelings which this spirit engenders is " to learn in whatever state we are, therewith to be content."

Q. Will such a natural mode or manner of education break down the various orders of society?—A. No; it will tend rather to restore order, where, for want of this natural mode of development, it has been violated. The poor will become morally satisfied with their condition, when they find that they have something beyond the mere gratification of their animal nature to take delight in; and the rich, from being excited to greater mental exertion, will rise in the scale of morality in the same proportion: thus will mutual good feeling, which is the bond of union in society, subsist among all ranks — each rendering to each that respect which is due to the station of life in which it has pleased Providence to place him.

Q. What is the immediate use of an Infant School? A. To develop all the powers of the mind at a much earlier period than it has hitherto been considered possible to do so, and thus prepare the children for a moral progress, for which it is desirable they should be sent to establishments so organized as to complete, in accord with their original destination, their full development.

Q. What are its first requisites, as it regards efforts and means? A. A spacious and airy school room, proper materials for instruction, and active thinking teachers, who are fully impressed with the moral importance of their undertaking, and feel most deeply interested in its success.

Q. Is it for very young children of both sexes? A. Yes, since they are found to be capable of equal development.

Q. How does it differ in spirit and practice from the National Schools? A. The fundamental principle of the Infant School system is love; it should be the constant endeavour of the master to win the affections of the children, and thus cause them to feel pleasure in submitting to his will; their attention should be excited by external natural objects, no part, however trivial, being suffered to pass unnoticed; they are by this minute mode of instruction led to a habit of observation and thought, from which the most beneficial results may be expected. The National Schools, on the contrary, deaden the faculties of the children, by obliging them to commit to memory the observation of others, few of which they comprehend: they are never invited to think for themselves, and the injurious consequences arising from this radical defect, cannot but be felt through life.

Q. What good influence is it expected to have on the child's moral condition, or more properly its heart? A. The better feelings of the child must gradually become most prominent, since they are constantly excited, while the bad passions are put and kept in subjection by this more and more predominating influence.

Q. What good consequences can result to the parents from it, in a moral or physical respect? A. In a moral respect the good example of their children cannot fail to influence them beneficially, and the habits of cleanliness which they are required to adopt, as also the relief which they experience from the absence of their children during several hours in the day, must contribute to their physical improvement.

Q. What kind of persons are fit as educators of the best dispositions, tempers, and inclinations of children? A. Those who make vital Christianity the basis of all their actions, and who consider that practice and precept must be cemented together by affection.

Q. Should the schools consist of 150 children or less numbers? All patrons of such institutions must of course be guided in this respect by the various circumstances connected with the places in which they are established; but where no obstacle presents itself, 150 is considered the *most* desirable number for a school: it is however better that this number should be increased than diminished.

Q. What kind of a building is proper? A. A light, airy, roomy, cheerful place, which the mind can use to give to itself agreeable sensations.

Q. Where should the schools be placed? A. In the midst of a dense poor population.

Q. What is the new discipline that is to be observed in this mode of training, to banish all slavish fear? A. The children are invited to regard their master as one who is desirous of promoting their happiness by the most affectionate means, and this point being once gained, they invariably submit with great willingness to his direction: it is therefore only when the children first enter the schools, that instances of disobedience occur, and in such cases it has been found necessary to have recourse to a trivial punishment, but this is always as mild as possible.

Q. What are the hours of attendance? A. From 9 to 12 and from 2 to 5, or from 8 to 6, if the parents desire it, and give to the child its dinner.

Q. What are the general expences? A. Rent, taxes, coals, pictures, utensils, repairs.

Q. What is given to the master and mistress? A. From £52. upwards a year, according to the number of children, situation of the place, circumstances of the family, and talents of the individuals.

Q. What to a mistress only? A. From 26*l*. to 40*l*. a year, more if she has a family and any of them to help her.

Q. To what age should the children be retained in the school? A. Until they are admitted into the National Schools.

Q. What are the best dimensions of a school room and how is it to be fitted up? A. 80-ft. long by 22 wide, with seats all round and a rising platform at the end, lesson posts, stools, benches, rostrum, master's desk, slates, pictures, letters, lessons, bell, whistle, pointers, cubes, arithmeticon, maps, hoops, swings, wooden bricks.

Q. Is it necessary to have a class room for the instruction of particulars? A. Yes, for those children, who have made greater progress than the rest, and are in consequence capable of receiving higher development.

Q. Are the materials of instruction new, or the application, or the end for which they are to be applied? A. Only the application, and the end for which the materials are to be applied, are new.

Q. Are the children to teach each other as much as they possibly can in that part which is purely mechanical? A. Yes, in that part which is merely mechanical, and in that only.

Q. Does such confinement injure the health, strength and activity of the body? A. Not in the least, since the minds of the children receive none but pleasurable sensations, and these effectually contribute to corporeal as well as mental improvement: there is also abundance of time between the school hours allowed for recreation.

E E

Q. Can the powers of the human mind be so feeble as not to bear affectionate excitement? A. In the Scriptures we are told at the creation the Almighty said, let us make man in our image, after our likeness, and also that God is love; as every child partaking of its heavenly parent's nature must have a portion of this spirit, and becoming desirous of more, its powers can never be too feeble to be affectionately excited and governed.

Q. Is it possible to awaken in the soul, in its first opening, the moral bias, the human sympathy?—A. If it be affectionately excited and governed, I conceive that this feeling must be the essential result.

Q. What have been the moral consequences in the schools already established?—A. A love of virtue, and an abhorrence of vice; few instances of juvenile depravity having occurred among those who have attended these schools.

Q. Where was the system in its full development first tried?—At the Spitalfields' School.

Q. What must be done to promote it in Ireland?—A. Invite the higher classes of the Irish to witness the good effects which have already been produced in this country by the establishment of the system, and by these facts excite them to put it in practice in their own country, upon the same universal basis.

Q. Is it open to children of every sect? A. Yes, it is the ardent desire of its most zealous supporters that it should be regarded as a universal benefit, and therefore that no children should be rejected on account of the accidental religious sentiments of their parents.

Q. Is it a preparation as well for religion as for useful knowledge and practical industry? A. This is its intention, and from it the most beneficial results are anticipated.

Q. Is the system only for the children of the poor? A. No, it is equally calculated to form all the powers of the mind of the children of the rich.

Q. Is the memory the chief faculty that is to be employed? A. Certainly not: this mode of cultivation must necessarily tend to weaken the other faculties, and leave the mind destitute of its own resources within itself; since all that it possesses has been borrowed from others, and instead of exercising its highest powers it is obliged to have constant recourse to the temporary aid which it thus receives.

Q. Is the system intended to educe both a moral and an intellectual good? A. The immoral dispositions are constantly weakened by the better feelings being continually awakened: a right direction is also given to the powers of the understanding, which are all kept in daily exercise, hence both a moral and an intellectual result may fairly be expected.

Q. Are such schools to realize in the child as much as possible the best and deepest feelings of happiness? A. Yes; by checking the growth of every evil tendency and encouraging the growth of all that is estimable, by banishing a fondness for the delusive pleasures of this world, which its votaries are continually in search of, and by diffusing through the mind the comforts of religion, those high and lasting enjoyments, which alone can bring us peace.

Q. Why have they not been established before? A. Because the higher classes of society have not hitherto been sufficiently alive to the promotion of further good, and it is only by degrees that they are now awaking from their slumbers, and are willing to go forward.

Q. Are the dame-schools sufficient for the purposes of young children? A. No; since it has been proved that infants demand and are capable of extensive mental development, it cannot be supposed that ignorant and inactive old women are competent to undertake so important a charge.

Q. Should the parents be required to pay so much a week for each child or per family? A. This is quite immaterial.

Q. Why is it good that the parents should pay a trifle for the care and instruction of their children? A. Because they set a higher value on the improvement which their children manifest; and being sensible of the real benefit which is thus conferred on them, they are stimulated to greater exertion for the support of their families, and the exercise of stricter economy in the management of their pecuniary means.

Q. Should not the teachers be placed under the affectionate superintendance of one individual? A. Certainly; if the teachers be subject to continual distraction from the interference of various individuals, they cannot feel sufficiently at ease to exercise the kindly feelings, and excite similar ones among the children.

Q. Must the master be governed by a set of strict rules, or left somewhat to his own discretion? A. It being supposed that every care has been taken to select a suitable person, it is better that he should be allowed to use his own discretion, and act according to the circumstances under which he is placed.

Q. Are many books wanted; and why? A. No: it is better to invite the children by means of external objects.

Q. Are pictures preferable to books; and why? A. Yes; because by fresh demonstration things are more deeply fixed in the mind than by a mere relation of stale facts.

Q. Must natural objects be as much introduced as possible for the mind of the child to act upon? See last answer.

Q. Are the children allowed some little time to play? A. Yes; several hours.

Q. Are they to be provided with play things that promote exercise? A. Yes; and with this, instruction should as much as possible be combined.

Q. Are many punishments used? A. No, few punishments are used: it is considered, that disobedience will sufficiently punish itself.

Q. Is industry of any kind intended to be introduced? A. Yes; those who are practically engaged in promoting this system have continual opportunities of improving upon it, and this among others has been suggested and will be introduced as soon as possible.

Q. Why are the rational faculties of observation, thought, and expression, to be cultivated before those artificial powers of reading, writing and cyphering? A. Because in mental as well as physical operations, it is highly necessary that the foundation should be securely laid before the workmen proceed to form the superstructure.

Q. Should the deaf and dumb as well as the blind be admitted into these schools? A. Yes; both have been admitted into the Spitalfields School, and have derived much mental benefit.

Q. Should the natural formation of the powers precede as much as possible artificial instruction? A. Certainly; if this mode be not adopted, the building will soon fall a prey to the storms and tempests to which it must be continually exposed.

Q. Why has there been so little attention paid to the natural expansion of the powers, and so much to the artificial description of them? A. Because the educated part of society have not been sufficiently developed to make so valuable a discovery; they have hitherto mistaken signs for things, effects for causes, and borrowed knowledge for experimental:

they have been content to skim the surface of things without diving to their foundation.

Q. Must we, if human sympathy be the result wanted, quit in a great measure our artificial course of rewards and punishments? A. Yes; the child must be led to seek its own mental improvement solely for the sake of the enjoyment which this cultivation will afford it; the being whose powers have been thus unfolded, will not require artificial means to excite its continuance in this path: it will feel for the deficiencies of others and exercise its energies in promoting the same natural course which has led to such happy results in itself.

Q. Is not singing an essential part of the effort and means to awaken and excite human sympathy? A. Yes; since it has a tendency to excite the finer feelings of our nature, to produce a sympathetic harmony throughout the assembly, and raise the soul from earth to heaven.

Q. Does not one kind action influence a child more than volumes of words? A. Yes; words appeal only to the understanding, and consequently pass away in empty sound; but kind actions influence the heart, and like the genial warmth of spring that dispels the gloom which has pervaded the face of nature during the chilling season of winter, they disperse the mists which cold treatment has engendered in the mental atmosphere.

Q. Is the master's example of the first importance in these schools to quicken the slumbering tie that binds man to man? A. Yes; without the aid of example the best precepts will be unavailing: it is by the force of this magnetic influence alone that sympathetic feelings can be awakened; example acts as a talisman upon the inmost powers of the mind, and excites them to self activity, which should be the constant aim of all persons engaged in the important work of education.

Q. Out of what rank in life should the persons be chosen who are to conduct such kindred schools? A. This is immaterial provided they be competent to the undertaking, and do not engage in it for the mere sake of emolument.

Q. Is there anything done or learnt in these schools which should prevent the children of Roman Catholic Parents from being sent? A. No; the children are too young to become imbued with any peculiar religious sentiment, and it has therefore been considered advisable for none to be refused admittance because their parents may belong to some particular sect.

Q. Should these schools be conducted in such a manner as not to wound the prejudices of any persons? A. Yes; since it is very desirable that all should participate in the benefits of these institutions.

Q. Can the same mode of natural intuitive development be introduced into the colonies for the children of the Negroes? A. Certainly; as I should conceive that these children are as capable of intellectual development as Europeans.

Q. Could not a master and mistress who have a family, be found, that would establish the system in Sierra Leone? A. Whenever it shall be thought advisable to send such persons, there can be no doubt but many may be found who would be willing to go out for this purpose.

Q. Would it not be well for our missionaries to imbue themselves with the spirit on which the method is established before they go forward in their occupation? A. Undoubtedly; the strongest manifestation we can give of our love to God is by the encouragement of a universal feeling of love towards the well being of our fellow-creatures : this is the spirit which should actuate every missionary, and he will derive from an acquaintance with this mode of development, much useful knowledge to aid him in his christian course.

Q. Is there any necessity of bringing the powers of the soul into activity by the excitement of emulation? A. No; by pursuing a judicious course, it is possible to draw forth all the powers of the soul without this excitement: in the new system, therefore, it has never been allowed, as its general tendency is to raise the passion of envy in one party and self-sufficiency in the other.

Q. Are there any kind of rewards necessary to awaken attention, if children are actively, intelligibly and affectionately excited? A. But few; the mind which is thus trained receives so high a bias that its chief delight consists in continually seeking its own improvement.

Q. Why are the habits of the children of the rich less disposing to intellectual pleasures than the habits of the children of the poor? A. Because indulgence is the parent of both mental and corporeal disease.

Q. Are the heads of the Established Church active promoters of these schools? A. Many highly respectable clergymen have visited the school in Spitalfields, and are now actively engaging themselves in establishing schools in their own parishes, and in endeavouring to excite others to follow their example: there is therefore no reason to doubt that, as soon as the system shall become more generally known, the dignitaries of the church will become zealous promoters of it.

Q. Does the good success of the system in its effect on children depend more on habits than on rules?—A. Most assuredly on habits: it is the good example of the master which influences the children, and becomes a living rule.

Q. Are children more delighted with this mode of training them than with the old system of constraining fear?—A. Yes; the happy countenances of the children whose minds are being thus unfolded, prove, most satisfactorily, the truth of this assertion.

Q. Will it cause a necessity for some change in the national mode of instruction?—A. It will most probably cause a gradual alteration to take place in the national mode, as every unprejudiced person must acknowledge the superiority of the new system of mental development, and rejoice to see it substituted for mechanical discipline.

Q. Why are the precepts which are stored up in the memory of children, so little influential on self-improvement? —A. Because they act merely on the animal nature, and consequently cannot operate in the promotion of mental activity, which is the second origin of every degree of civilized improvement.

Q. At what age is a child sensible of shame, or ashamed of punishment?—A. As soon as it is capable of observing anything, however trivial.

Q. Is a child as sensible of right and wrong as he is of sickness and health?—A. Undoubtedly: conscience, which is ever awake, acts as a monitor at all times; in the young as well as the old, this spirit is in constant activity, and it is only when we dislike to listen to its dictates that we endeavour to persuade ourselves that our unerring and ever-present guide is slumbering.

Q. Do not children imitate, imbibe, or adopt virtues as soon as vices; and why?—A. Yes, this imitative faculty is inherent in us, and since virtuous impressions may be fixed at a very early period of life, it is highly necessary that this moral colouring should be given in the first opening of the bud.

Q. Is the love of virtue engendered in the heart in conjunction or connexion with the love of knowledge? — A. Certainly: virtue being the parent of knowledge, it is impossible that the love of the latter can exist independently of the former.

Q. Must a child rise or fall in its natural condition according to the good or bad example it has to imitate, imbibe, or adopt?—A. Most assuredly, according to the quality of the impulse which it thus receives, so will it be stimulated to the practice of good or evil:—how essential, therefore, is it that the appointed guardians of infancy should keep a constant-watch over themselves, and be alive to the dictates of conscience.

Q. Are outward circumstances able to oppress entirely the activity of the natural genius?—No; although they may operate greatly in opposing its progress, they can never render it entirely inactive.

Q. Is there not an intuitive excitive power in the child which acts independently of all outward circumstances?— A. Yes; were not this power intuitive, it would be overpowered by the force of disadvantageous outward circumstances.

Q. Is corporeal punishment of any use when a sense of shame does not attend it?—A. Not of the least use; since its only tendency is to harden the feelings of the child, and to create in it a hatred towards those who inflict it.

Q. Are good manners to be cultivated in the child and to be made as habitual as possible?—A. Good manners are not absolutely essential to our happiness; but as they are at all times pleasing, it is right that they should be cultivated: though the intrinsic value of the marble be not increased, it becomes more agreeable to the eye when it has received the finished polish of a master-hand.

FRENCH LANGUAGE.

THE PAIDOPHILEAN SYSTEM OF EDUCATION,

APPLIED TO

THE FRENCH LANGUAGE.

In 2 vols. 12mo. price 6s. 6d. published by Messrs. Longman and Co. Paternoster-row, London.

THE System here pursued spares to the student the time so unprofitably passed in writing exercises, and the tedious research in turning over the leaves of a dictionary, frequently not finding the words required, and, if found, uncertain which signification to select from a variety, widely differing from each other;—as well as the ennui of endeavouring to comprehend the numerous, difficult, and frequently useless, rules of grammar;—evils consequent upon the general plan of instruction.

By the aid of these two volumes alone, several hundred pupils have gained a better knowledge of the French language in twelve lessons than is generally gained in a twelvemonth, and in twenty-four lessons have been enabled to understand any book of history or on general subjects in the French language.

SPECIMEN OF THE WORK.

C'est l'homme de tous les siècles, comme de tous les
It is   the man   of   all   the   ages,   as

pays. Tous les sages de l'antiquité ont pens-é, ont parl-é,
countries.   ————————y have thought,   spok-en,

ont ag-i pour lui; ou plutôt il a véc-u avec eux, il a
act-ed   for   him;   or   rather he has liv-ed with them, he has

enten-du leurs leçons, il a été le témoin de leurs grands
heard   their   —ss-—,   been   witness   their

exemples. Plus attentif encore à exprim-er leurs mœurs
—-a————   More   ————-ve still   to search-out   mani ers

qu' à admir-er leurs luminères, quel aiguillon leurs
than to   lights (wisdom) what   spur   their

paroles ne laiss-ent elles pas dans son esprit? quelle sainte
words not leave they not in his mind? what holy

jalousie leurs actions n'allum-ent elles pas dans son cœur?
———y   not kindle they not   heart?

Ainsi nos pères   s' anim-ai-ent à la vertu; une noble
Thus our fathers each-other did animate   —i——e; a

émulation les port-ai-t à rend-re à leur tour Athènes et
     them did-carry   in their turn   and

Rome jalouses de leur gloire; ils voul-aient surpass-er les
———y: they were-wishing

Aristide en justice, les Phocion en constance les Fabrice
———s in   ———s in ———y ———ii

en modération, et les Caton même en vertu. Que si les
     and ———s even   But if

exemples de sagesse, de grandeur d'ame, de générosité,
—-a——— wisdom,   of soul,   ———a——y,

d'amour de la patrie, devienn-ent plus rares que jamais,
love   country, become more   than ever,

c'est parce que la mollesse et la vanité de notre âge ont
it is because that effeminacy and ———y our   have

romp-u les nœuds de cette douce et utile société que la
broken the ties that sweet useful ———y which

Science form-e entre les vivants et les illustres morts,
——— s between living and the ———ious dead,

dont elle r-anim-e les cendres pour en form-er le
of-whom she re-animate-s ashes for of them

modèle de notre conduite." *D'Aguesseau. Nécessité de*
our ———et."   ———y

la Science.

The language is further illustrated and rendered easy by a *Synopsis of the Verbs*, by which the confused mass of matter, which occupies from 50 to 60 pages in most Grammars, is here reduced to a single page, where all the regular verbs are clearly exhibited; and the toil of *months* is changed to an agreeable occupation of an HOUR!

EXTRACTS FROM THE STUDENT'S MANUAL.

PART I.

ANTHROPOS, *a man.*

ANTHROPO-PHAGI, *phago*, I eat. Cannibals or men-eaters.

Mis-anthrophy, *misco*, I hate. Hatred of mankind.

Phil-anthropy, *phileo*, I love. Love of mankind.

The-anthropos, *theos*, God. A title of our Saviour, being God and man.

ARCHE, *government,*
ARCHOS, *a chief.*

A-N-ARCHY, *a*, not, without. Want of government.

Hept-archy, *h-epta*, seven. A government under seven chiefs.

Hier-archy, *h-ieros*, holy. An ecclesiastical government.

Mon-archy, *monos*, one. A government under one chief. *Anti*-mon-archical; against government by a single person.

Olig-archy, *oligos*, few. That form of government in which the supreme power is placed in the hands of a few.

GRAPHE, *a writing, a description.*

AUTO-GRAPH, *auto*, self. The hand-writing of any person; or the original of a treatise or discourse: the word is used in opposition to copy.

Bio-grapher, *bios*, life. One who relates the actions of particular persons.

Ge-o-graphy, *ge*, the earth. Description of the surface of the earth according to its several divisions.

Litho-graphy, *lithos*, a stone. Writing upon stone.

Ortho-graphy, *orthos*, correct. That part of grammar which teaches how words should be written.

Tele-graph, *tele*, distant. An instrument that answers the end of writing, by conveying intelligence to a distance through the means of signals.

Topo-graphy, *topos*, a place. A description of particular places.

PART II.

Organ, *s.* from *organon*, an instrument. The name given to a particular musical instrument as being *the instrument*, in preference to all others. As in English we say, *I am going to* TOWN, that is, the *Town* in preference to all others, namely *London.* See BIBLE and CATHEDRAL.

Ortho-epy, *s.* from *orthos*, correct, and *epo*, I speak. Correct pronunciation.

Pagan, *s.* from *pagus*, a village. When Christianity became the established religion of the Roman empire, the Christians preferred living in towns, while unbelievers inhabited the *villages;* hence *villager, unbeliever,* and *pagan,* were synonymous terms.

EXTRACTS from *SEQUEL* to *STUDENT'S MANUAL.*

PART I.

CÆDO, *I cut, beat, kill.*
CÆSUS, *cut.*

[*Cædo* is changed into *Cido*, and *Cæsus* into *Cisus*, when compounded.]

Con-cise, con-cision, in-cision, pre-cise

Fra-tricide, (*fratis*, of a brother)

Homi-cide, (*hominis*, of a man)

Infanti-cide, (*infantis*, of an infant)

Matri-cide, (*mater*, mother)

Pari-cide, (*parens*, a parent)

Regi-cide, (*rex*, *regis*, a king)

Sui-cide, (*sui*, of himself, or, of herself)

FACIO, *I do or make.*
FACTUS, *done.*

[*Facio* is changed into *Ficio*, and *Factus* into *Fectus*, when compounded.]

FACTOR, from *factor*, one who makes or does a thing—fact, from *factum*, the thing done—facility, from *facilitas*, the ease with which a thing may be done—faculty, from *facultas*, the power of doing with ease—facetious, from *facetus*, one who has ease in saying or doing a thing —difficult, from *difficilis*, (for *disficilis*,) not easy to be done—faction, factious, from *factio*, acting, meddling.

Bene-fit, bene-ficence, bene-faction, from *benefacio*, (see BENE,) I do well —male-factor, from *malefacio*, (see MALE,) I do wrong—manu-facture, from *manufactura*, (*manu*, by the hand,) things made with the hand—satis-fy, satis-faction, from *satisfacio*, (*satis*, enough,) I do enough —of-fice, from *officium*, a place in which to do a thing

Af-fect, de-fect, ef-fect, in-fect, in-fectious, per-fect, pro-ficient, pro-ficiency, suf-fice, suf-ficient, suf-ficiency

Certi-fy, certi-ficate, (*certus*, cer-tain,)—clari-fy, (*clarus*, bright) dei-fy, (*deus*, god)

PART II.

Ab-lative, *ablatus*, (see FERO,) taken away. The ablative is the opposite to the dative, the first expressing the action of taking away, and the latter that of giving.

Ab-lution, *abluo*, (see LUO,) I wash from or away. A religious ceremony, being a sort of purification, performed by washing the body. Moses enenjoined *Ablutions*, the hea-thens adopted them, and Mahomet and his followers have continued them; thus they have been introduced among most nations.

Ab-scond, *abscondo*, (see Do,) I put together from view; figuratively, I hide myself. *To abscond*, is to retire from public view: generally used of persons in debt, or criminals eluding the law.

J. S. Hodson, Printer, 15, Cross Street, Hatton Garden.

www.ingramcontent.com/pod-product-compliance
Lightning Source LLC
Chambersburg PA
CBHW062034090426
42740CB00016B/2903